FRENCH
FOOD

AMERICAN
ACCENT

FRENCH FOOD

FOOD

AMERICAN

ACCENT

DEBRA PONZEK'S SPIRITED CUISINE

BY DEBRA PONZEK AND JOAN SCHWARTZ

CLARKSON POTTER/PUBLISHERS

NEW YORK

For my husband, Gregory, who
inspires me daily—and who encouraged me
to take the time to write this book, purely
because of how much it meant to me.

Grateful acknowledgment is made for permission to use the recipe for Bittersweet Chocolate Mousse,
adapted from Dennis Foy.

Published by Clarkson N. Potter/Publishers,
201 East 50th Street, New York, New York 10022.
Member of Crown Publishing Group.

Random House, Inc. New York, Toronto, London, Sydney, Auckland

http://www.randomhouse.com/

CLARKSON N. POTTER, POTTER, and colophon are trademarks of Clarkson N. Potter, Inc.

Printed in the United States of America

Design by Margaret Hinders

Library of Congress Cataloging-in-Publication Data is available upon request.

ISBN 0-517-70036-0

10 9 8 7 6 5 4 3 2 1

First Edition

CONTENTS

INTRODUCTION

When I was sixteen, I visited France for the first time, traveling with a friend and her family. One evening, early in our trip, we had strawberries for dinner—no entrée, no vegetables, just strawberries. Although this may seem like an odd meal, at the time it made sense to us, because these were the most beautifully ripe, juicy strawberries we had ever seen and they were all we wanted. That "meal" was a revelation to me.

On subsequent visits to France, especially to Provence, my appreciation of that kind of simple perfection grew. All throughout the region, I encountered dishes that were based on the superb local ingredients and prepared with respect for their special qualities. The onion tart I was served at a small farmhouse restaurant was extra delicious because the chef had used onions and herbs that grew in her own fields and hadn't allowed their glorious flavors to be obscured in any way. And that cook was only one of many. I could have driven down almost any country road and discovered a little mom-and-pop restaurant next to a farm where a lunch to die for could be had for very little money. Many of those meals were indebted to the cuisine of Italy, a close neighbor, in their use of such Italian staples as risotto, pasta, and polenta, which they combined with ripe vegetables and fragrant herbs. But somehow, the dishes remained unmistakably French and incomparably good.

In Provence I learned that nothing surpasses simple food, cooked really well. It's a philosophy I've taken to heart both in my professional cooking and in the foods I serve at home. I've tried to duplicate the simple perfection I so admired in Provence by using the fresh fruits, vegetables, and herbs (so much like the ones that tempted me there) from my local farmers' markets, greengroceries, and even good supermarkets. And I've incorporated some of our own products, such as cranberries or corn, to give my dishes uniquely American accents.

An American sensibility informs the food I make today in other ways as well. Rather than depending on the rich butter and cream traditional to haute cuisine, the recipes in this book derive their flavor from reduced stocks and herbs, and have just a touch of butter or cream. Although l didn't start out with the specific goal of eliminating fat, I came to see that many of the flavors central to my cooking became more intense and immediate when the fat was cut down. So while this book lays no claim to being a low-fat cookbook, you'll find that you can serve and eat these dishes without the nagging guilt so many "classical" French dishes elicit.

The techniques and recipes I've chosen for this book reflect the gradual evolution of my cooking style over the last dozen years. Training at the Culinary Institute of America and subsequent stints in professional kitchens have given me a strong foundation in classic technique. More recent experiences launching a retail store and enjoying the luxury of cooking for friends and family in my home kitchen have shown me that it is possible to turn out professional-level food in an everyday kitchen. This book is my effort to show you how to do just that and, along the way, to teach you about the process of cooking and pairing foods.

For example, in professional kitchens, most food is cooked quickly at high temperatures; it can be cooked the same way at home. This saves time and preserves flavor and juiciness—and the food looks sensational. In a restaurant, the various components that make up a dish are cooked ahead individually and assembled just before serving. What could be better for the home cook who wants to entertain in a relaxed way? Whip up the carrot oil, cook the quinoa, and set both aside for a day or more. Just before serving, sear the fish steaks and combine all the components. Then serve a sophisticated, attractive dish in a flash. Planning ahead, whenever possible, really makes the difference in a successful meal.

So does an excellent sauce, but it is one thing to reduce stock and wine all day on a huge restaurant stove until it reaches the perfect, concentrated flavor, and quite another to make a sauce in an ordinary kitchen, within a reasonable time frame. I wanted to achieve complex flavor without hours of cooking, so I began to try new methods. After much trial and error, I learned that intensely flavorful sauces could be created quickly in the pan, based on cooking juices, wine, and herbs.

And finally, I appropriated some presentation techniques from my restaurant days for home use. Placing grilled meat or seafood on a bed of grains rather than passing separate platters or dishes of each, or individually plating salads, takes only a few additional seconds in the kitchen but adds an unmistakable air of sophistication to the foods I serve. By preparing desserts in single servings, the easiest-to-prepare desserts can become the most elegant to serve, offering each person at my table an individual dessert that looks incredibly special.

Most of the recipes I have included are uncomplicated, so each component, up front for everyone to see, must be close to perfect. If there were twenty things on the plate, you could go wrong with four and no one would notice. But this isn't the case when a dish consists of fish, a vegetable, and a bright herbal broth. Preparing food this straightforward, simple, and subtle requires some courage, stripping down your cooking, throwing away the fancy sauces that can cover mistakes.

But the techniques required aren't difficult, and the results can be thrilling. Just keep these simple rules in mind:

1. Start with superior ingredients.

When my husband and I stayed at an inn located in the tiny French town of Noves, we were so impressed with the wonderful food that we went down to the kitchen very early one morning to speak to the chef. But he was nowhere to be found, and we were told, "The chef is out buying." He finally returned from his tour of the markets, carrying baskets and sacks filled with magnificent vegetables, herbs, and fruits, and the finest quality eggs, chickens, fish, and cheeses. With all these treasures, the chef told us with a smile, planning the day's menu would be easy.

Give yourself the chance to browse through the supermarkets, farmers' markets, fish stores, ethnic markets, and groceries and to be inspired by the best they have to offer. Choose the most tempting foods, the ones you would really like to eat: ripe fruits and vegetables, glistening sweet fish, plump poultry, and fresh meats. Don't pick your recipe and then try to wedge the food in; start with what's great and then pick the menu.

2. Match each component with the most appropriate cooking technique.

Choosing the food is the first part; knowing what to do with it comes next, and it's good to have some information available. How can I prepare that fish? Which herbs will enhance those vegetables? Can any of these foods be cooked ahead? This book will tell you. As you read it and cook from it, you will learn which preparation techniques bring out the best of specific foods.

Most recipes can be broken down into techniques that are uncomplicated and logical. But just because something is easy to make, don't think you shouldn't be precise about it. Simplicity doesn't exclude precision!

Learn to cook with high heat in the oven, as well as on top of the stove, to give food crispness and juiciness. Use the temperatures I give you as starting points and adjust them to fit the way your stove works. A good trick is to moderate your oven: turn it up to 475°F. to get color and crispness on a roasting chicken and turn it back down to 400°F. to cook the chicken through a little more slowly. In the oven at a lower temperature, the chicken will bake, not roast, and it will not be as crisp-skinned and juicy. Searing in very hot oil on top of the stove prevents your food from sticking to the pan; if you use nonstick pots and pans for this task, you can get away with lower heat, and the food still won't stick.

There is no absolute way to determine cooking times, because every piece of food is different. My recipes provide guidelines, but it's best to learn to rely on your judgment. Check the food often and learn the signs that indicate when it is cooked. For example, cooked in a high oven, a fillet of bass will become opaque and resistant to the touch in three to four minutes—it will be done. If you leave it in a few minutes longer, it will still look and feel that way, but its flesh will have become drier; in other words, overdone.

It is always better to undercook than overcook. Once food is done to death, it's not salvageable, but if you take it out of the oven before it's cooked through, what is the worst thing that can happen? You will just put it back in for a little while and then try it again. And don't forget to allow for carryover cooking; food always continues to cook for a few minutes after it's removed from the heat. Letting a cooked piece of meat rest before you cut it is another important technique. Perhaps it is the simplest; all you have to do is *not* cut it, and you have made the difference between the meat retaining its juices and losing them. (You can put meat back in the oven after it has rested, if you need to.)

So that you don't go beyond that instant of perfect doneness, when you think something may be ready, pull it out, touch it, and taste it. Look in your oven five times if you have to. Find that point when you can say, "Oh, this is really good, this is what it should look like!" You will soon develop an intuition about how to time your own cooking. This really will happen, but it takes time and patience.

3. MAKE SOME OR ALL COMPONENTS OF A RECIPE AHEAD OF TIME WHENEVER POSSIBLE.
At the end of each recipe you'll find make-ahead pointers that will help you to plan and cook the individual components ahead, and then assemble them just before serving, as chefs do at fine restaurants. Although preparing blanched vegetables, flavored oils, and stocks ahead may seem labor intensive, it *will* give you better meals. And when you cook a sauce early and freeze it, or pull the pasta out of the pot before it's done and reheat it later, you will end up with better results than if you had cooked everything in a frenzy at the last minute, because you will have given yourself control over each component.

4. USE YOUR JUDGMENT AND PLEASE YOUR OWN TASTE.
Seasoning correctly is one of the most important kitchen skills to master. Think about how you want a dish to look and taste; then let its balance of textures and flavors guide you. Season a dish

at each point in its preparation and then taste and reseason at the very end. Make sure you taste and season the individual components as well as the final combination, because the balance always changes. Don't pour on the salt and pepper, but use them as they are meant to be used: to bring out flavors.

Consider the measurements in a recipe merely as a jumping-off point, remembering that it's okay to stray from them. For instance, when you make a sauce, even though I give the instructions, you will determine the result. Your sauce may be just a little different from everybody else's—and even a little different each time—but it should suit your taste.

This involves tasting frequently and remembering flavors. Today you might use two shallots in a dish, tomorrow you may use three because the shallots are smaller or they aren't as full-flavored. Today you might find the perfect sweet pears for your clafouti, but the ones you buy tomorrow may need some extra sugar.

5. MAKE YOUR FOOD BEAUTIFUL.

An attractive presentation is as much a part of a dish's appeal as its flavor, but even the loveliest things don't look their best when they are crowded together. The space that is left open on a plate is just as important as the space that is filled: it frames the food and keeps the components separate. I use large, even oversize dishes for all courses; I love a first course of bright green salad on a big, white dinner plate, surrounded by lots of white.

Use dishes from different sets and fearlessly mix colors, patterns, and types of china. Experiment with pottery or ceramics. Don't feel confined to matching crockery, course after course, meal after meal. Be as experimental and bold mixing dinnerware as you have become at combining ingredients!

6. REMEMBER THAT NOTHING IS BETTER THAN SIMPLE FOOD, COOKED REALLY WELL.

At Montrachet, when we cooked a special dinner for the celebrated chef Paul Bocuse, we served prime rib, as well as pasta with some wonderful asparagus and wild mushrooms. The fussiest dishes don't taste better than that, or better than a fabulous piece of seared and roasted fish served with a drizzle of intensely flavored oil.

French Food/American Accent is a collection of the best things I have learned—and invented—since I began to cook. I've divided each chapter into sections according to cooking method or type of dish, with recipes following in approximate order of difficulty, so that you can start with a basic preparation and build toward more involved dishes. A lot of experience has gone into making these recipes work. I have cooked countless pieces of fish to get to the point where I can tell you: This is how to do it! But that doesn't mean that you must cook exactly as I do. Whether you use this cookbook or any other, the dishes you make will be your own, shaped by your unique personality and style. At all times, I encourage you to improvise.

How do you learn to improvise? Part of the answer is "practice, practice!" The more you cook, the more knowledgeable about food and sure of your skills you will become. Read the suggestions for substitutions and complementary dishes and experiment to find which please *you* most. For instance, the first time you prepare a recipe like Saddle of Lamb with Ratatouille and Basil Oil (page 218) you'll probably want to follow it to the letter. But once you understand how the bright basil flavor of the oil plays off the herbal essence of the ratatouille, and that the reduced pan sauce adds the depth and body that holds it all together, you'll understand that this is merely a suggested combination of elements, not a rigid prescription, and no doubt will come up with variations of your own. When you realize that both onion confit and ratatouille are slightly tart and slightly sweet, you'll start to see how one can substitute for the other. And you will get to know, by trying different recipes, which textures you like together and which flavors you most enjoy, so that you can make other changes as you cook.

Because this book is organized around cooking techniques, you may find the chapter breakdowns somewhat unorthodox. For instance, there is no appetizer section per se, and pastas are grouped together with grain side dishes. But it will start to make sense once you realize that any of the pasta dishes can be served as a main course or as a first course, and that an appetizer salad could easily work as a light supper. Combine two or more of the vegetable dishes with one of the grain components from a poultry recipe and you have a great meatless meal. Stocks reduce to make sauces and flavorful broths to moisten a fish fillet, and the potato galette that tops a salad shows up later in the book as a bed for seared beef. The combining and recombining of the various elements and the mastering of the techniques are the keys to understanding this book.

At first, all this may seem like a juggling act, but the more you practice, the more open you will become to inspiration. As you cook ratatouille or corn and lobster soup or seared and roasted swordfish steaks, you will find yourself learning techniques that you can apply to many other dishes. After preparing ingredients time after time, you will come to understand different foods and develop a feeling for how to bring out their fullest flavor. At that point you may not even need this book anymore—the greatest compliment that I could imagine.

A Note on Ingredients

Most of the ingredients used in my recipes are readily available from local farmers' markets, fish-mongers, butchers, and well-stocked supermarkets. Some clarifying notes on specific ingredients:

Butter: Unsalted butter is used in all recipes.

Chocolate: Always use the highest quality you can find, such as Valrona or Callebaut.

Crème fraîche: This thickened, slightly fermented cream with a tangy flavor is used for desserts, soups, and sauces; good quality prepared crème fraîche is widely available.

Olive oil: I always specify one of three varieties:

extra-virgin: Made from the first pressing of olives, without the use of any chemicals, this has the richest color, flavor, and aroma. It is best used in vinaigrettes and for herbal and spice oils.

virgin: Made from a later pressing, without the use of any chemicals, this has lighter color, flavor, and fragrance than extra-virgin. It is best used for cooking but can be used in vinaigrettes and for herbal and spice oils.

pure: Made from the remains of pressed olives, using chemicals, this has less color, flavor, and fragrance than virgin or extra-virgin oil and is best used for cooking.

Salt, kosher: Has no additives and is coarser than table salt. I prefer it in all recipes.

Techniques and Cooking Terms

While I encourage you to experiment with ingredients, some precision in preparation and cooking techniques, especially at the beginning, will ensure the best outcome. A ratatouille made with vegetables diced small will be very different from one made with coarsely chopped or large-diced ingredients. Here are definitions of some cooking terms and techniques I refer to often throughout this book.

Bake: Cook foods in an oven, so they are surrounded by dry heat. Baking is done with lower heat and for a longer time than is roasting.

Blanch and shock: Immerse food in boiling salted (1 teaspoon salt per quart) water briefly and then cool in ice water or cold water.

Boil: Cook in hot, rapidly bubbling liquid.

Braise: Cook slowly in liquid, after browning in fat.

Caramelize: Cook food, sometimes with sugar added, until its own natural sugars thicken and become golden and syrupy, as for onions. Also, to cook sugar until it melts into a golden syrup.

Chiffonade (for basil or mint): Slice in fine, thin strips. Stack 3 or 4 leaves, roll, and slice $\frac{1}{8}$ to $\frac{1}{4}$ inch thick.

Chop, coarse: Roughly cut into irregular pieces, between medium and large dice in size.

Concassée: Skinned, seeded, and diced tomatoes.

Confit: Preserves of meat, vegetables, or fruit. Meat confits are preserved in fat; lemon confits, in salt; some fruits, in sugar. Onions are sautéed with a little sugar until caramelized.

Deglaze: The process by which, after meat or poultry has been cooked, stock or other liquid is added to the pan and brought to a simmer, while the pan is stirred and brown bits of food from the bottom are scraped up into the liquid.

Dice: Cut in precise cubes of equal size. These four sizes are called for throughout the book:

brunoise: $\frac{1}{8}$ inch

small: $\frac{1}{4}$ inch

medium: $\frac{1}{2}$ inch

large: $\frac{3}{4}$ inch

Ganache: A mixture of melted chocolate and cream, used as cake filling or frosting.

Grill: Cook directly over a fire, bed of charcoal, or other heat source.

Julienne: Cut into very thin (about $\frac{1}{8}$-inch) strips.

Mince (garlic and shallots): Dice as fine as possible.

Panfry: Cook in a moderate amount of hot fat in a pan over moderate heat.

Poach: Cook in a hot liquid that is not actually bubbling (see Simmer, below).

Reduce: Boil stock, stock and wine, or cooking juices until thickened by evaporation.

Roast: Cook foods in an oven, so they are surrounded by dry heat. Roasting is done at a higher heat and in a shorter time than is baking.

Roux: A mixture of butter and flour cooked over medium heat, used to thicken soups and sauces and add a butter flavor.

Sauté: Cook quickly over high heat in a small amount of fat.

Scald: Heat liquid until small bubbles appear around the edge, just below the boiling point.

Sear: Brown food quickly to seal in its juices.

Sear and roast: Brown quickly over high heat and then finish cooking in a hot oven.

Simmer: Cook at just under boiling, with the liquid moving. Tiny bubbles will appear on the surface.

Slice: These terms are used in the recipes that follow. Use these guidelines for the best results:

paper thin: as thin as possible

thin or fine: $\frac{1}{8}$ inch

medium: $\frac{1}{4}$ inch

thick: anything larger than $\frac{1}{4}$ inch

Water bath (bain-marie): A pan of water into which a baking dish is set so that the water comes about halfway up the sides

Basic Preparation Techniques

Butter, to clarify: For 6 tablespoons clarified butter, melt 8 tablespoons butter over low heat. Skim off the foam and slowly pour or ladle off the clear butter, leaving behind the milky solids. Can be refrigerated up to two weeks. When ready to use, remelt over low heat or in the microwave.

Butter, to brown: In a small saucepan over medium-high heat, melt the butter and cook until it becomes lightly golden brown and gives off a nutty aroma. Can be refrigerated up to ten days. When ready to use, remelt over low heat or in the microwave.

Chestnuts, to shell: Cut an ✕ on the flat side or remove a thin strip of shell from the curved side. Cover with cold water in a saucepan, bring to a boil, and boil 1 minute. Remove from the heat and take out the individual chestnuts only as you are ready to shell them, leaving the others in the hot water. Using a sharp knife, peel and scrape off the shells. If some shells cannot be removed, boil them again until they soften. One pound yields about 36 chestnuts.

Clams, to clean and steam: Scrub the clams and rinse well under cold running water. In a large pot, bring about an inch of water to a boil over high heat and add the clams. Cover and steam until they open, discarding any that stay closed.

Cucumber, to dice: Peel and halve the cucumber. Cut into lengthwise strips and cut the strips into dice.

Garlic, to sweat: Garlic burns easily, so start it in warm, not hot, oil over medium heat and cook 1 minute, watching it carefully.

Half-moon slices, to cut (carrots, leeks, yellow squash, zucchini): Cut the vegetable in half lengthwise. Lay it flat-side down and rounded-side up, and slice thin.

Hard vegetables (pumpkin, winter squash), to dice: Halve and seed the vegetable and place cut-side down. Cut the halves into quarters and peel off the skin. With the quarters lying flat, cut each into slices and the slices into julienne. Then cut the julienne into dice.

Leeks, to clean: If leeks are to be used whole, slice lengthwise almost all the way to the root end, spread layers, and rinse well. If leeks are to be chopped or sliced into half-moons (see above), cut into desired size, place in a colander, and rinse well under running water.

Mussels, to clean and steam: Rinse the mussels in cold running water and pull off the beards. Cover the cleaned mussels with liquid in a large pot and bring to a boil, covered. When a few start to pop open, uncover the pot and remove them. Then keep the pot uncovered, shaking it, as the remaining mussels steam. When mussels have opened, they are cooked; discard any that do not open.

Nuts, to toast: Preheat the oven to 400°F. Place the nuts in a single layer on a baking sheet and toast until golden on both sides, 3 to 5 minutes. Or, heat 2 tablespoons oil until almost shimmering in a small skillet over medium heat, add 2 cups of nuts, and toast until golden on both sides, 1 to 2 minutes. Toasted nuts can be refrigerated up to 1 week.

Onion, to dice: Peel the onion, cut it in half, and place each half cut-side down on a cutting board. Make 2 or 3 horizontal cuts ¼ inch apart, almost but not entirely through the onion.

Then cut down in slices ¼ inch apart, entirely through the bottom. Cut down across these slices to form dice of the size desired. This way, you don't have to rechop pieces into smaller dice, so the onion retains its juices and the pieces are more uniform in size.

Onion, to sweat: Melt butter or heat oil over medium heat and cook the onions until wilted but not colored, 7 to 8 minutes. This preserves their color and releases their sweet flavor.

Pepper, to crack: On a cutting board, crush whole peppercorns with the back of a small skillet. Alternatively, use a pepper mill. Coarsely ground pepper, available at supermarkets, can be substituted, but its flavor won't be as potent.

Soft vegetables (bell peppers, cucumbers, yellow squash, zucchini), to dice: The vegetables first need to be cut into strips that will lie flat. To do this for bell peppers, cut ½ inch from each end and remove the core and seeds. For cucumbers, peel and then halve lengthwise. For yellow squash and zucchini, cut lengthwise slices about ½ inch thick all around the outside (discard the core or cook separately). Cut into strips and cut the strips into dice.

Tomatoes, to cut into concassée: First make tomato petals: Cut out the stem and cut a small cross into the skin at the other end. Plunge into boiling water to cover for 10 seconds, then immediately shock in ice water until cool. The skin will slip off easily. Cut the tomato into quarters and remove the ribs and seeds. The seeded quarters are petals, the neatest base for concassée. Cut the petals into julienne, then cut crosswise into distinct dice.

Tomatoes, to peel: Cut out the stem and cut a small cross into the skin at the other end. Plunge into boiling water to cover for 10 seconds, then immediately shock in ice water until cool. The skin will slip off easily.

CHAPTER 1

OILS, VINAIGRETTES, SAUCES, AND CONDIMENTS

Traditionally, the touchstone of French cuisine has been complicated sauces carrying many layers of subtle flavors and requiring hard labor—or, at least, a lot of patience—in the kitchen. And while these sauces are undeniably delicious, they simply don't make much sense for even dedicated home cooks. Moreover, few of us can savor a cream-laden sauce guiltlessly, as we once did. Having practiced the art of French sauce-making as a student and as a chef, I set about revising some of my favorites to make them more appealing to today's lighter tastes, and, not coincidentally, more accessible to home cooks.

The first things to go were large amounts of butter and cream. My new sauces derive their flavors from stocks and herbs and have just an occasional touch of butter or cream for embellishment. But flavor hasn't been sacrificed. You can get incredibly concentrated, intense flavor from sauces made right in the pan after meat or fish is roasted, and you don't have to work at it for hours. In the same spirit, when you cook vegetables or other foods in stock, forget about recipes! Reduce that stock down to a little bit of really flavorful liquid and use it as a simple sauce.

Flavored oils that you make in your blender with fresh herbs, fruits, and vegetables, or with pungent spices, also carry concentrated doses of taste, aroma, and bright color. They do something special for food, elevating it to the next level and expanding the landscape of each dish they meet. Use them to sauté eggplant, zucchini, potatoes, carrots, or almost any other vegetables. Brush flavored oils over late-summer vegetables before roasting. Add their sunny flavors to homespun codfish cakes (page 184) and crisp fish fillets or steaks. Mash them into steaming baked potatoes or polenta. Spoon a bit over any salad of fish, poultry, greens, or tomatoes.

Flavored oils or rich, fruity olive oils expand their range when combined with different kinds of vinegars. The resulting vinaigrettes can be tossed with crisp salad greens or drizzled over Simple Braised Lentils (page 118), Ratatouille (page 142), or Green and Yellow Squash Ribbons (page 128). Chicken, fish, or meat marinated in a vinaigrette for about a half hour before roasting or grilling become so flavorful that they won't need a sauce later. And this kind of dish doesn't require a lot of advance planning.

Suppose you've made a lemon vinaigrette for the Arugula Salade Composée on page 48 and you have some left over. Marinate the chicken breasts you're planning to cook the next night in the vinaigrette and then grill them for an effortless but delectable quick meal.

Vinaigrettes are flexible and free-form; they reflect your personal taste and style. When you put your vinaigrettes together, try to get out of the habit of measuring; keep tasting until you get exactly the balance of flavor and acidity you like.

Sauce and entrée combinations, even mine, are not sacrosanct. Most of the sauces in this book will go well with most of the main-dish recipes; they are flexible and pretty much interchangeable. As a general rule, richer sauces go best with creamy dishes (think of mashing wild mushroom sauce into polenta, page 120); fish- and shellfish-based sauces belong with fish and shellfish; sauces that are based on chicken or duck stock go best with poultry; and vinaigrettes marry well with clear, fairly sharp flavors. The more intensely flavored sauces are often better drizzled over a dish than served alongside in large portions. But these are only guidelines; try mixing and matching your sauces (many freeze well, so you can have a variety on hand to choose from) or drizzle on a bit of flavored oil in a complementary or contrasting flavor as the spirit moves you. You'll soon have a natural feeling for how these sauces and flavorings add depth and sophistication to even simple foods, and make elegant offerings truly stellar!

In addition to the listings in this chapter, you can find lamb sauce in the recipe for Saddle of Lamb with Ratatouille and Basil Oil (page 218). For an additional vinaigrette, see Red Snapper Salad with Gazpacho Vinaigrette (page 50).

OILS

When blanched herbs are combined with oil and then strained out, they produce a glistening luminous liquid. The technique below is used to create herbal infusions from virtually every green herb (the exception is rosemary, see below). Blanching ensures your herbal oils will retain a bright, vivid color. If you are short on time, you can skip the blanching and opt for a less dazzling appearance, but equally impressive flavor.

Some flavored oils do require a slightly different method. For rosemary oil and spice oils, the herb or spice is heated gently in oil, while for flavored oils made with fruit or vegetable juices, the juice is first reduced to a flavorful syrup and then combined with oil. However, all are quite quick to make, and each adds an incomparable jolt of flavor to vinaigrettes and other foods. A word of caution: To be absolutely sure that your fresh oils don't become home to harmful bacteria, make them in small batches and refrigerate them for no more than two days. It is better to make herbal oils fresh than to double the recipe and make extra for later use. A blender makes the most flavorful oils because it processes the herbs more finely than a food processor can, releasing more of the herbal essences. When you prepare herbal oils, the flavors should match, rather than compete. Robust extra-virgin olive oil has an excellent affinity for roasted garlic and black olives. Virgin olive oil, slightly lighter, combines well with fresh herbs such as basil, chives, and rosemary, as well as with curry and cumin. Mild grapeseed and canola oils are the best partners for more delicately flavored oranges, beets, and carrots.

METHOD

- Blanch fresh herbs briefly in boiling, lightly salted water.
- Shock them in a bowl of ice water and gently squeeze them dry.
- Combine with oil and blend.
- Strain the oil and discard the herbs.

BASIL OIL

This recipe illustrates the method for making a basic herbal oil. Blanching the herb reduces its volume by half and also sets its color, so this basil oil is a striking, intense green. Use this method for making cilantro oil or chive oil. Either virgin or extra-virgin olive oil will work here, but extra-virgin will lend a more pronounced flavor.

Try this as a dip for slices of fresh French or Italian bread.

SERVE WITH:

ANY SEARED AND ROASTED OR PAN-ROASTED FISH, POULTRY, OR MEAT
ROASTED COD WITH CONFIT BAYALDI (PAGE 173)
COD AND POTATO CAKES PROVENÇAL WITH RATATOUILLE (PAGE 184)
SADDLE OF LAMB WITH RATATOUILLE (PAGE 218)

If the basil is sandy, rinse it and shake dry before picking the leaves off the stems.

2 tablespoons kosher salt
1½ cups cleaned fresh basil leaves, off the stems

1 cup virgin or extra-virgin olive oil

Combine 2 quarts water and the salt in a large pot and bring to a boil over high heat. Add the basil and blanch 15 seconds, or until it is bright green and wilted; immediately plunge it into a bowl of ice water. Drain the basil, wrap it in a kitchen towel, and gently squeeze out as much water as possible. In a blender, combine the basil with the oil and blend until smooth. Strain through a cheesecloth-lined sieve, without pressing down on the solids.

MAKE-AHEAD NOTE

Basil Oil can be refrigerated up to 2 days.

CHIVE OIL

MAKES ABOUT 1 ¼ CUPS

Fresh chives, blanched and then shocked to fix their color, give this oil emerald-green hue and delicate oniony flavor. Even without blanching, chives will yield a nicely colored oil; simply place the chives and oil in a blender and process on high speed 1 minute, then strain through a chinois or fine strainer.

> **SERVE WITH:**
> **CARAMELIZED ONION TARTS (PAGE 144)**
> **CRAB CAKES (PAGE 183)**
> **COD AND POTATO CAKES PROVENÇAL WITH RATATOUILLE (PAGE 184)**
>
> **STIR A BIT INTO:**
> **RED WINE SALMON SAUCE (PAGE 36)**
> **THYME CRÈME FRÂICHE SAUCE (SEE PAGE 176)**

2 tablespoons kosher salt
3 ounces (4 bunches) chives, cut into
   1-inch pieces

1¼ cups virgin olive oil (use extra-
   virgin if you prefer a stronger
   flavor)

Combine 2 quarts water and the salt in a large pot and bring to a boil over high heat. Add the chives and blanch 15 seconds, or until they turn bright green and wilt; use a skimmer or slotted spoon to retrieve the chives, then plunge them into a bowl of ice water. Drain the chives, wrap in a kitchen towel, and gently squeeze out as much water as possible. Place in a blender with the oil and blend until smooth. Strain through a chinois or fine strainer.

MAKE-AHEAD NOTE
  The oil can be refrigerated up to 2 days.

ROSEMARY OIL

The process of making an oil from pungent, spicy rosemary differs from the usual method, in which the herbs are blanched and then pureed. Here the herbs are heated gently in oil, their flavor and aroma slowly releasing into it. A similar technique is used for making Curry Oil (page 12).

> **SERVE WITH:**
> **COD AND POTATO CAKES PROVENÇAL WITH RATATOUILLE (PAGE 184)**
> **EGGPLANT PROVENÇAL IN ROASTED TOMATOES (PAGE 136)**
> **INDIVIDUAL TIANS OF SUMMER VEGETABLES (PAGE 130),**
> **INSTEAD OF THE OLIVE OIL**

½ cup finely chopped rosemary leaves (about 4 bunches, no stems)

1 cup virgin olive oil

In a small saucepan, gently heat the rosemary and oil over low heat, until the aroma emerges, 3 to 4 minutes. Transfer to a heatproof glass or enamel container and allow to cool at room temperature for 2 hours, making sure the rosemary remains completely submerged. Cover well or pour into a jar and seal tightly and refrigerate for 2 days. Bring the oil back to room temperature and strain it through a double thickness of cheesecloth, then use immediately.

ROASTED GARLIC–BLACK OLIVE OIL

MAKES 1 CUP

This oil is pure Provence, with shiny, dark-brown olives and the irresistible aromas of roasted garlic and olive oil. The robust flavors go beautifully with lamb or fish, and will add Mediterranean notes to your salads as well. If you have previously made a batch of roasted garlic to keep on hand, this couldn't be easier to make—all it takes is a whirl in the blender. A bit of pepper perks up the oil, but no salt is needed because the olives add salt of their own.

SERVE WITH:

RAINBOW TROUT SALAD (PAGE 52)
DOUBLE-CUT LAMB CHOPS WITH CAPONATA POLENTA AND CRISPY RED ONIONS (PAGE 220)
ANY TUNA, SALMON, OR SWORDFISH DISH
MARINATED TUNA SALADE NIÇOISE (PAGE 54)
RED SNAPPER SALAD (PAGE 50), INSTEAD OF THE GAZPACHO VINAIGRETTE

½ cup pitted Niçoise olives
6 cloves Oven-Roasted Garlic
   (page 37)

¾ cup extra-virgin olive oil
Freshly ground black pepper

Combine the olives and garlic in a blender or food processor. With the motor running, slowly add the olive oil, processing until smooth. Season with pepper.

MAKE-AHEAD NOTES

☙ Roasted garlic can be refrigerated up to 2 weeks.
☙ Roasted Garlic–Black Olive Oil can be refrigerated up to 2 days.

BEET OIL

This shocking-pink oil requires an electric juicer, or purchase fresh beet juice from a health-food store or produce market. It's especially beautiful drizzled onto the same plate as Basil Oil, and the flavors spark one another beautifully.

> **SERVE WITH:**
> SAUTÉED SEA SCALLOPS WITH
> ONION CONFIT (PAGE 61)
> ROASTED SALMON WITH QUINOA
> (PAGE 156)
> GRILLED SHRIMP (SEE
> PAGE 98)
> INDIVIDUAL TIANS OF SUMMER
> VEGETABLES (PAGE 130)

1⅛ to 1¼ cups beet juice (4 medium beets, juiced)

1 cup canola oil

In a small saucepan, reduce the beet juice over medium heat to a thick syrup (2½ to 3 tablespoons), about 10 to 12 minutes. Strain through a fine strainer into a stainless-steel or glass bowl and cool. When cool, slowly whisk in the canola oil until emulsified.

MAKE-AHEAD NOTES

∽ Beet juice can be frozen.

∽ Beet Oil can be refrigerated up to 2 days.

CARROT OIL

MAKES ABOUT ½ CUP

Fresh carrot juice is reduced to a flavorful syrup, then combined with a mild oil that lets its flavor shine through. If you don't have an electric juicer, you can buy fresh carrot juice from a health-food store or produce market; frozen carrot juice is also available in some markets.

> **SERVE WITH:**
>
> ROASTED SALMON WITH QUINOA
> (PAGE 156)
> PUMPKIN RISOTTO
> (PAGE 116)
> GRILLED SHRIMP (SEE
> PAGE 98)

1 cup carrot juice (from 8 medium carrots)
¼ teaspoon kosher salt

½ cup canola or grapeseed oil
Cracked white peppercorns

In a medium saucepan, bring the carrot juice to a boil over high heat and reduce to 2 to 3 tablespoons, about 10 to 12 minutes. Strain through a fine sieve into a small bowl. Add the salt, and cool to room temperature. When cool, gradually whisk in the oil until emulsified and season with the pepper.

MAKE-AHEAD NOTES

🌿 Carrot juice can be frozen.

🌿 Carrot Oil can be refrigerated up to 2 days.

RED CURRY OIL

MAKES 1⅓ CUPS

This spicy oil has a deep rust color and an unusual flavor that is especially good with fish. Combine all the ingredients 1 day before serving. The solids will settle and you can ladle the oil from the top.

> **SERVE WITH:**
>
> GRILLED SHRIMP OR FISH
> SALAD GREENS
> SEARED SASHIMI TUNA
> (PAGE 56) INSTEAD OF
> CURRY OIL

4 ounces (1 can) Thai red curry paste	2 cups virgin olive oil

In a small saucepan, combine the ingredients and heat gently for 5 minutes over medium heat. Remove from the heat and let sit at room temperature for 3 to 4 hours, stirring occasionally; then refrigerate.

MAKE-AHEAD NOTE

Red Curry Oil can be refrigerated up to 2 days.

ORANGE OIL

MAKES ABOUT ½ CUP

The first step for flavorful Orange Oil is squeezing fresh juice, which is then reduced to a thick syrup. The reducing process simply cooks out the water and concentrates the flavor and sweetness of the fruit. The syrup is mixed with grapeseed oil, a flavorless oil that won't mask the orange taste.

> **SERVE WITH:**
>
> COLD POACHED SALMON
> (SEE PAGE 190)
> SOFTSHELL CRAB SALAD WITH
> FENNEL, RED ONION, AND
> KUMQUATS (PAGE 60)
> ANY SEARED AND ROASTED OR
> GRILLED FISH

1¼ cups fresh-squeezed orange juice (4 oranges)	Zest of 1 orange
Juice of 1 lemon	½ cup grapeseed oil

In a small saucepan, combine the orange and lemon juices and the orange zest and reduce to a syrup over high heat, about 12 to 15 minutes. Put into a small bowl and cool to room temperature. Slowly whisk in the grapeseed oil until emulsified.

MAKE-AHEAD NOTE

Refrigerate the oil up to 2 days.

CURRY OIL

This oil has a beautiful yellow color. Heating the spices before combining them with oil unlocks their aroma and flavor. Time is important in the preparation of Curry Oil. If you prepare it in the morning to use that evening, it will be too light and you won't get the full, complex flavor and aroma of the curry. For best results, make the oil 1 to 2 days before you plan to use it. You can refrigerate it an additional day. For cumin oil, substitute ground cumin for the curry powder.

SERVE WITH:

SEARED SASHIMI TUNA WITH TOMATO–GINGER FONDUE (SEE PAGE 56)

GRILLED SALMON (SEE MASTER RECIPE FOR GRILLED FISH, PAGE 178)

SAUTÉED OR GRILLED SHRIMP (SEE BROCCOLI SOUP WITH SAUTÉED SHRIMP, MUSHROOMS, AND ROASTED GARLIC, PAGE 102)

2 tablespoons Madras or other good-quality curry powder

1 cup virgin olive oil

In a small saucepan, gently heat the curry powder with a few drops of water, stirring constantly, over low heat. When the aroma emerges, remove from the heat and scrape the wet powder into a small bowl. Gradually whisk in the oil and pour into a wide-mouthed glass jar. Cool to room temperature and refrigerate overnight. The solids will settle to the bottom. Stir and refrigerate again, repeating this process for 2 days. To use, line a strainer with a double layer of cheesecloth. Ladle the oil off the top or carefully pour the oil into the strainer, leaving the solids at the bottom of the jar. The solids can be reused up to 2 additional times with fresh oil.

Vinaigrettes

Vinaigrettes are a staple of French cuisine, most familiarly served with salads. I find them versatile and useful as marinades and sauces as well, especially when made with flavored oils. Reduced to its basic elements, a vinaigrette is nothing more than a blend of acid (generally vinegar), oil, and seasonings. However, that simple formula can be varied endlessly to give different effects. After your vinaigrette is mixed, taste it carefully. If the vinegar taste is strong enough to pucker your mouth, add a few drops of oil; if there is not enough kick to the blend, try a bit more vinegar. And since a vinaigrette can stand or fall on its seasoning, don't forget the salt and pepper. Use herbs singly for a strong, defined flavor, or mix two or more. Always use fresh herbs; include dry only in combination with fresh (this is most effective when the vinaigrette is being used as a marinade). However, for freshness, add herbs only to the quantity of vinaigrette you plan to use at that moment.

An alternative is to flavor vinaigrette with herbal oils, which will retain their vibrancy better than chopped fresh herbs. Herbal oils are a wonderful way to expand your repertoire of vinaigrettes.

These vinaigrettes will keep in your refrigerator for up to three weeks. Unlike the bottled products you buy at the supermarket, your own will contain no stabilizers, so expect them to settle and separate slightly; just whisk to recombine before each use.

Method

- Whisk the vinegar with salt and pepper (and herbs or vegetables, if using) until the salt is dissolved.
- Whisk the oil in slowly until emulsified.
- Taste and add more seasonings, vinegar, or oil, if needed.

SHERRY VINAIGRETTE

*T*his recipe illustrates the fundamental method for making a balanced vinaigrette. First, salt and herbs are mixed with the vinegar. Then oil is added and the combination is mixed well. Finally, pepper is added and the vinaigrette is tasted, reseasoned, and given a few drops more of vinegar or oil, as needed.

With its delicate hint of sherry and shallots and flavoring of fresh thyme, this is the most versatile vinaigrette I make. If you haven't yet discovered sherry vinegar, this is a good introduction to its sweet flavor.

> SERVE WITH:
> **LOBSTER SALAD WITH WHITE BEANS AND FRESH THYME (PAGE 59)**
> **MARINATED TUNA SALADE NIÇOISE (PAGE 54)**
> **WARM SHRIMP SALAD WITH ARTICHOKES AND CANNELLINI BEANS (PAGE 58)**
> **WARM DUCK SALAD WITH CRANBERRIES AND WALNUTS (PAGE 64)**
>
> USE AS A MARINADE FOR:
> **SEARED AND ROASTED CHICKEN BREASTS (SEE PAGE 200)**

¼ teaspoon kosher salt, plus a little more, if needed
2 tablespoons finely chopped shallots
1 sprig fresh thyme, leaves only

¼ cup sherry vinegar, plus a little more, if needed
1 cup extra-virgin olive oil
Freshly ground black pepper

In a medium bowl, whisk the salt, shallots, and thyme with the vinegar until the salt is dissolved. Slowly whisk in the oil until emulsified. Taste. Season with pepper and a little more salt, and adjust with vinegar or oil, if needed.

MAKE-AHEAD NOTE

✍ Made without the thyme, Sherry Vinaigrette can be refrigerated up to 3 weeks. Add the thyme and whisk to recombine before using.

WILD MUSHROOM VINAIGRETTE

MAKES ¾ CUP

This vinaigrette has an earthy color and intense mushroom flavor. The recipe calls for the stems from an entire bunch of parsley; reserve the leaves for another use.

> **SERVE WITH:**
> **WARM SCALLOP SALAD WITH PARSNIPS (PAGE 62)**
> **ANY SCALLOP DISH**

½ cup plus 2 tablespoons virgin olive oil

1 pound mixed wild mushrooms (caps only), such as cremini and shiitake, sliced thin

1 sprig thyme

1 small bunch parsley stems (1 to 2 ounces)

3 cups water

Kosher salt

2 tablespoons plus 1 teaspoon balsamic vinegar

Freshly ground black pepper

In a medium skillet over high heat, heat 2 tablespoons of the oil until smoking and sauté the mushrooms until golden brown, 3 to 4 minutes.

After you strain the broth, save the mushrooms and serve over pasta or add to sauces.

Add the thyme, parsley, and water and bring to a boil. Reduce the heat to medium and simmer until the liquid is reduced by half, 20 to 30 minutes. Strain through a fine strainer, reserving the mushrooms for another use if desired. There should be about 11/2 cups of liquid.

In a clean saucepan, reduce the liquid again over medium-high heat, until 2 to 3 tablespoons remain. Strain through a fine strainer into a small bowl.

Add a pinch of salt to the liquid and whisk in the remaining ½ cup of oil until emulsified. Whisk in the vinegar. Taste and season with salt and pepper.

MAKE-AHEAD NOTE

ᐒ The vinaigrette can be refrigerated up to 3 weeks. Whisk to recombine before using.

BASIL VINAIGRETTE

Basil-flavored oil rather than fresh herbs gives this vinaigrette an emerald-green color and a subtle but unmistakable herb flavor—as well as the ultimate summer fragrance. The vinaigrette is versatile; you can hardly go wrong combining basil's peppery sweetness with any salad, vegetable, or fish.

> **SERVE WITH:**
> SALAD OF FIELD GREENS WITH LENTILS AND GOAT CHEESE (PAGE 44)
> MARINATED TUNA SALADE NIÇOISE (PAGE 54)
> ANY POACHED OR SEARED AND ROASTED FISH

¼ teaspoon kosher salt, plus a little more, if needed
¼ cup champagne vinegar, plus a little more, if needed

1 cup Basil Oil (page 5)
Freshly ground black pepper

In a medium bowl, whisk the salt with the vinegar until the salt is dissolved. Slowly whisk in the basil oil until emulsified. Taste. Season with pepper and a little more salt, if needed, and add more vinegar or oil, if needed.

MAKE-AHEAD NOTE
❧ Basil Vinaigrette can be refrigerated up to 3 weeks. Whisk to recombine before using.

MUSTARD VINAIGRETTE

MAKES ¾ CUP

This is creamy, rich, and pale yellow, with the kick of Dijon mustard. It makes an easy marinade for chicken that is to be roasted or grilled.

> **SERVE WITH:**
> ENDIVE, PEAR, AND ROQUEFORT SALAD (PAGE 43)
> MIXED GREEN SALAD

Try substituting tarragon vinegar, which also goes well with mustard.

¼ teaspoon kosher salt, plus more, if needed

2 tablespoons good-quality Dijon mustard (such as Maille)

3 tablespoons champagne vinegar

½ cup extra-virgin olive oil

Freshly ground black pepper

In a small bowl, whisk the salt and mustard with the vinegar until the salt is dissolved. Slowly whisk in the oil until emulsified. Taste. Season with pepper and a little more salt, if needed, and add more vinegar or oil, if needed.

MAKE-AHEAD NOTE

Mustard Vinaigrette can be refrigerated up to 3 weeks. Whisk to recombine before using.

BALSAMIC VINAIGRETTE

MAKES 1 ⅓ CUPS

This has deep, rich color and flavor. It makes a good marinade and also goes well with any fowl. Although fine aged balsamic vinegar is critical to the success of some recipes, any good balsamic vinegar will make a serviceable vinaigrette.

> **SERVE WITH:**
> **GRILLED QUAIL SALAD WITH PROVENÇAL VEGETABLES (PAGE 63)**
> **MIX WITH SIMPLE BRAISED LENTILS (PAGE 118)**

¼ teaspoon kosher salt, plus a little more, if needed

1 teaspoon finely chopped garlic

2 tablespoons finely chopped shallots

⅓ cup balsamic vinegar, plus extra, if needed

1 cup extra-virgin olive oil, plus extra, if needed

Freshly ground black pepper

In a small bowl, whisk the salt, garlic, and shallots with the vinegar until the salt is dissolved. Slowly whisk in the oil until emulsified. Taste. Season with pepper and a little more salt, if needed, and add more vinegar or oil, if needed.

MAKE-AHEAD NOTE

Refrigerate Balsamic Vinaigrette up to 3 weeks. Whisk to recombine before using.

LEMON VINAIGRETTE

MAKES 1 ½ CUPS

Lemon juice supplies the tart acid component to a simple, fresh-tasting vinaigrette that works well with light greens and all fish. This vinaigrette also makes a versatile marinade for chicken or fish.

SERVE WITH:
ARUGULA SALADE COMPOSÉE
(PAGE 48)
SOFTSHELL CRAB SALAD WITH
FENNEL, RED ONION, AND
KUMQUATS (PAGE 60)

Toss with your favorite greens and serve with any sautéed or seared and roasted fish.

¼ teaspoon kosher salt, plus extra, if needed
Juice of 4 medium lemons (about 1 cup)

½ cup olive oil, plus extra, if needed
Freshly ground black pepper

Depending on the tartness of the lemons, you may need a little more or less olive oil in the vinaigrette.

In a medium bowl, whisk ¼ teaspoon salt with the lemon juice until dissolved. Slowly whisk in the oil until emulsified. Taste, and season with pepper and a little more salt, if needed. Add more lemon juice if the dressing tastes too flat.

MAKE-AHEAD NOTE

Lemon Vinaigrette can be refrigerated up to 3 weeks. Whisk to recombine before using.

BEET VINAIGRETTE

MAKES A SCANT 1 ¼ CUPS

This has a fabulous red color and a sweet flavor. Try spooning a bit over seared or grilled fish. Then surround the colorful dish with a circle of bright-green Basil Oil (page 5) for additional sparkle.

SERVE WITH:
SAUTÉED SEA SCALLOPS WITH
ONION CONFIT (PAGE 61)
ANY LOBSTER, SHRIMP, OR
SALMON DISH

2½ tablespoons champagne vinegar
¼ teaspoon kosher salt, plus more, if needed

1 cup Beet Oil (page 9)
Freshly ground black pepper

In a medium bowl, mix the vinegar with salt to taste until the salt is dissolved. Slowly whisk in the beet oil until emulsified. Add pepper, then a touch more salt, if needed.

MAKE-AHEAD NOTE

❧ Beet Vinaigrette can be refrigerated up to 2 weeks. Whisk to recombine before using.

WALNUT VINAIGRETTE

MAKES ABOUT ½ CUP

This rich vinaigrette has a tempting nutty aroma. Walnut oil tends to become rancid very quickly, so buy the smallest container you can and store the unused portion in the refrigerator.

SERVE WITH:
....
WARM DUCK SALAD WITH CRANBERRIES AND WALNUTS (PAGE 64)
WARM SCALLOP SALAD WITH PARSNIPS (PAGE 62)

For hazelnut vinaigrette, substitute hazelnut oil for walnut oil.

¼ teaspoon kosher salt, plus extra, if needed
2 tablespoons champagne vinegar, plus extra, if needed

6 tablespoons walnut oil
½ teaspoon finely chopped thyme leaves
Freshly ground black pepper

In a medium bowl, whisk the salt with the vinegar until dissolved. Slowly whisk in the oil until emulsified. Whisk in the thyme. Taste, and season with pepper and a little more salt, if needed. Add more vinegar, if needed.

MAKE-AHEAD NOTE

❧ Made without the thyme, Walnut Vinaigrette can be refrigerated up to 3 weeks. Add the thyme and whisk to recombine before using.

ROSEMARY VINAIGRETTE

MAKES 1 ¼ CUPS

This vinaigrette has an assertive fresh herbal aroma.

SERVE WITH:

POACHED OR SEARED AND ROASTED FISH
ANY MEDITERRANEAN VEGETABLES

¼ teaspoon kosher salt, plus a little more, if needed

¼ cup sherry vinegar, plus a little more, if needed

1 cup Rosemary Oil (page 7)

2 tablespoons finely chopped shallots

Freshly ground black pepper

In a medium bowl, whisk the salt with the vinegar until dissolved. Slowly whisk in the rosemary oil until emulsified. Whisk in the shallots. Taste, and season with pepper and a little more salt and vinegar, if needed.

MAKE-AHEAD NOTE

❧ Rosemary Vinaigrette can be refrigerated up to 3 weeks. Whisk to recombine before using.

RED-CHILI VINAIGRETTE

MAKES 1 CUP

This has an outstanding russet color and spicy flavor. It goes especially well with fish and seafood of all kinds, highlighting their briny flavors.

SERVE WITH:

SEARED SASHIMI TUNA WITH MARINATED CUCUMBER
(PAGE 56)

¼ cup champagne vinegar

¾ cup red-chili oil

Kosher salt and freshly ground black pepper

Pinch of red-chili flakes

Place the vinegar in a small bowl and drizzle in the chili oil, whisking until incorporated. Add the salt, pepper, and chili flakes, and blend well.

MAKE-AHEAD NOTE

❧ Red-Chili Vinaigrette can be refrigerated up to 2 weeks. Whisk to recombine before using.

GINGER VINAIGRETTE

MAKES 1 CUP

This must be made 1 day before serving, to allow its light ginger flavor to ripen. Use the freshest ginger you can find; older roots will be stringy and dry. Ginger Vinaigrette is a good match for richer, steak-like fish because it cuts their oiliness.

SERVE WITH:

SESAME-CRUSTED SWORDFISH (PAGE 170) ANY SHRIMP, LOBSTER, OR SALMON DISH

¼ teaspoon kosher salt, plus a little more, if needed
¼ cup champagne vinegar, plus a little more, if needed
½ cup plus 1 tablespoon virgin olive oil

3 tablespoons sesame oil
1 tablespoon finely diced shallots
1 tablespoon grated fresh ginger
½ teaspoon cracked black pepper

Combine the salt with the vinegar in a medium bowl and whisk until dissolved. Slowly whisk in the oils until emulsified. Whisk in the shallots and ginger. Taste, and season with pepper and a little more salt, if needed. Add more vinegar, if needed, and refrigerate for at least 24 hours. Before using, strain through a fine strainer.

MAKE-AHEAD NOTE

❧ Make 1 day before serving and refrigerate up to 2 weeks. Whisk to recombine before using.

PESTO VINAIGRETTE

MAKES ⅓ CUP

*T*he *addition of Sherry Vinaigrette lightens green, garlicky pesto into a fluid sauce. One recipe makes enough to drizzle around 4 servings of any seared fish or fish salad.*

> **SERVE WITH:**
> ....
> ANY FISH SALAD
> SUBSTITUTE FOR GAZPACHO
> VINAIGRETTE IN RED SNAPPER
> SALAD (PAGE 50)

2 tablespoons Basil Pesto (page 26)   ¼ cup Sherry Vinaigrette (page 14)

In a small mixing bowl, whisk together the ingredients.

MAKE-AHEAD NOTE

Because Pesto Vinaigrette loses its color, it can be refrigerated only up to 2 days. It is best to make only what you need for a single meal.

GINGER–CITRUS VINAIGRETTE

MAKES 1 CUP

*T*his *very pale orange vinaigrette is slightly sweet, with a little kick from the ginger. Cooking the citrus juices down into a syrup gives the vinaigrette more depth of flavor.*

> **SERVE WITH:**
> ....
> ANY SEAFOOD SALAD
> ROASTED SALMON WITH QUINOA
> AND CARROT OIL (PAGE 156)

About 2 cups citrus juice, from:
    4 medium oranges
    1 medium lime
    1 medium lemon
    1 medium grapefruit

½ cup small pieces of fresh, peeled
    ginger
6 ounces canola oil

In a medium saucepan, combine all the juices and the ginger and reduce over medium heat until thick and syrupy, 10 to 12 minutes. There will be less than $\frac{1}{2}$ cup. Strain through a fine strainer into a small bowl, pushing down on the solids. Allow the syrup to cool to room temperature, then slowly whisk the oil into the syrup until incorporated.

MAKE-AHEAD NOTE

❦ Ginger–Citrus Vinaigrette can be refrigerated up to 3 weeks. Whisk to recombine before using.

CURRY VINAIGRETTE

MAKES 1 GENEROUS CUP

An *appetizing sunny color and the taste of curry combine in this appealing vinaigrette. Substituting an equal amount of cumin oil (see page 12) will make a cumin vinaigrette, good with any fish.*

SERVE WITH:
....
SEARED SASHIMI TUNA
(SEE PAGE 56)
ANY TUNA, SALMON, OR
LOBSTER DISH

$\frac{1}{4}$ teaspoon kosher salt, plus extra, if needed

2 tablespoons champagne vinegar, plus extra, if needed

1 cup Curry Oil (page 12)
Freshly ground black pepper

In a medium bowl, whisk the salt with the vinegar until the salt is dissolved. Slowly whisk in the oil until emulsified. Taste, and season with pepper and a little more salt, if needed. Add more vinegar, if needed.

MAKE-AHEAD NOTE

❦ Curry Vinaigrette can be refrigerated up to 3 weeks. Whisk to recombine before using.

PROVENÇAL VINAIGRETTE

MAKES ABOUT 1 ½ CUPS

This rosy vinaigrette is light but full-flavored. It's unusual in that the flavorings are gently simmered together with the oil and the vinegar is added later, rather than vice versa. This must be prepared at least 1 day before serving.

> **SERVE WITH:**
> ....
> **TUNA WITH GRILLED VEGETABLES (PAGE 180)** ANY VEGETABLE COMBINATION SEARED AND ROASTED TUNA OR SALMON

1 cup extra-virgin olive oil, plus a little extra, if needed
10 shallots
10 cloves garlic
2 large tomatoes, chopped
4 anchovy fillets
½ cup basil leaves
½ cup red wine vinegar, plus a little extra, if needed
Kosher salt and freshly ground pepper

In a medium saucepan, heat ¼ cup of the olive oil over medium heat until warm and add the shallots, garlic, tomatoes, anchovies, basil, and the remaining olive oil. Simmer over low heat for 30 minutes, then add the vinegar and allow to cool to room temperature. Cover and refrigerate overnight. The next day, strain through a chinois or fine strainer, pushing on the solids. Taste and add more olive oil or vinegar, if needed; season with salt and pepper.

MAKE-AHEAD NOTE

🍃 Provençal Vinaigrette can be refrigerated up to 2 weeks. Whisk to recombine before using.

LOBSTER VINAIGRETTE

MAKES 1⅔ CUPS

Because this vinaigrette is made with Lobster Stock, it is not quite as acidic as other vinaigrettes. The subtle shellfish flavor will enhance, but not overpower, delicate foods.

> **SERVE WITH:**
> ANY FISH OR SHELLFISH SALAD
> SEARED FISH FILLETS
> ROASTED WHOLE FISH
> ANY LOBSTER OR SHRIMP DISH

1½ cups Lobster Stock (page 75)
¼ teaspoon kosher salt, plus more, if needed
⅓ cup champagne vinegar, plus more, if needed

1 cup virgin olive oil
Cracked black pepper to taste

Combine with chopped fresh herbs, a drizzle of Basil Oil (page 5) or Chive Oil (page 6).

In a small saucepan, bring the lobster stock to a boil over high heat and reduce it to ⅓ cup, about 15 to 18 minutes. It will be thick and syrupy. Be careful not to let it burn. Strain through a fine strainer and cool.

In a medium bowl, whisk the salt with the vinegar until the salt is dissolved. Slowly whisk in the oil until emulsified. Add the lobster syrup and season with pepper. Taste, and add more pepper, salt, or vinegar, if needed.

MAKE-AHEAD NOTE

Lobster Stock can be refrigerated up to 1 week or frozen; lobster syrup can be refrigerated up to 1 week. The finished vinaigrette can be refrigerated up to 3 weeks. Whisk to recombine before using.

Unlike pan sauces, which are based on reductions of cooking juices or other liquids, cold sauces can be made before you cook your main course. This is a great time-saver, especially for entertaining. These sauces are uniformly fresh-tasting and quick to make.

BASIL PESTO

MAKES ABOUT ½ CUP

Crossing over from Genoa to Marseilles, herbal, garlicky Italian pesto gave its name to Soupe au Pistou (page 78), the traditional French vegetable soup redolent of garlic and fresh basil, which is also the basis of Snapper au Pistou (page 189). The sauce traditionally was pounded with a mortar and pestle, but today's version mixes up quickly in a food processor. Although the traditional use is as a room-temperature sauce for pasta, its possibilities are infinite. Add pesto to sauces for extra garlic and herb flavor. Mix a little into fresh mayonnaise and slather it on a turkey sandwich. Add a dollop to your favorite vinaigrette and use for salads or marinating. This recipe is easy to double.

Substitute coriander with a little mint for the basil.

1 cup cleaned basil leaves, packed
½ cup extra-virgin olive oil
2 tablespoons pine nuts
2 tablespoons grated Parmesan cheese

2 cloves garlic, peeled
1 teaspoon kosher salt
¼ teaspoon freshly ground black
   pepper

If your pesto seems too robust, broth or stock will lighten its flavor, texture, and density.

Place the basil, oil, nuts, cheese, garlic, salt, and pepper in the container of a food processor or blender and process to a smooth paste. Do not overprocess or the pesto will become too dark.

MAKE-AHEAD NOTE

☙ Pack the pesto into a container, brush the top lightly with oil, cover, and refrigerate up to 1 week. Pesto can also be frozen.

MAYONNAISE

If you are accustomed to bottled mayonnaise, you will find this sauce thinner and creamier, with a pleasant olive oil and egg flavor. Fresh mayonnaise is worth trying and very easy to make. Vary the taste of mayonnaise by substituting Basil Oil (page 5), Chive Oil (page 6), or Roasted Garlic–Black Olive Oil (page 8) for all or part of the olive oil. Add 2 to 3 tablespoons chopped basil or tarragon to the finished mayonnaise.

For roasted garlic mayonnaise, add 6 cloves Oven-Roasted Garlic (page 37) with the egg yolks.

2 large egg yolks
¾ cup virgin or extra-virgin olive oil, or a mixture of half each (depending on the intensity of flavor you want)

2 to 3 tablespoons water
Few drops of fresh lemon juice
Kosher salt and freshly ground black pepper

You also can prepare the mayonnaise in a mixing bowl, using a wire whisk.

In a food processor, mix the yolks until slightly pale, about 1 minute. With the processor on, slowly drizzle in the olive oil, drop by drop, until the sauce begins to emulsify. As it thickens, add a few drops of water to loosen the texture. Continue adding oil and loosening with a bit of water. Squeeze in the lemon juice to taste, and season with salt and pepper.

MAKE-AHEAD NOTE

Fresh mayonnaise can be refrigerated safely up to 2 weeks but beware of contamination; if a dirty utensil, or the like, gets into it and introduces bacteria, the mayonnaise can spoil.

MUSTARD–DILL SAUCE

MAKES A GENEROUS ½ CUP

The quality of the mustard will make or break this sauce, so be sure to choose a good-quality imported brand. Maille is one that I like. This sauce has a great affinity for salmon.

SERVE WITH:

GRAVLAX (PAGE 186)
COLD POACHED SALMON
(SEE PAGE 190)

½ cup strong Dijon mustard (such as Maille brand)
⅛ to ¼ cup honey

½ tablespoon champagne vinegar
1 tablespoon finely chopped dill fronds

In a small bowl, whisk all the ingredients together until smooth.

MAKE-AHEAD NOTE

🌿 Mustard–Dill Sauce can be refrigerated up to 1 week. It does not freeze.

SAUCES BASED ON REDUCTIONS

Although sauces can be thought of as the heart and soul of French food, the old-fashioned, complicated versions take hours to produce. Fortunately, many lend themselves to modern interpretations that are every bit as flavorful and complex as the classics. Based on the idea of maximum flavor extracted in minimum time, these use a lot of the same ingredients and techniques, but they contain less butter and the reductions on which they are based are less heavy. When sauces are kept simple, as these are, they are flexible and can be moved around from dish to dish. Work your way through the selection I've provided here; once you've mastered them all, you're well on your way to a true understanding of the possibilities of reduction-based sauces.

METHOD

🌿 Over medium-high heat, bring the cooking liquid to a boil and reduce it to a syrup.

🌿 Add stock or wine to thin the syrup and enrich the flavor.

🌿 Bring to a boil and reduce again to the desired consistency.

🌿 Correct seasonings.

CURRY SAUCE

*C*oconut milk and apple make this sauce mildly spicy and slightly sweet, but not cloying. It has a beautiful golden-yellow color and a full-bodied consistency. Cut the vegetables very small, because the sauce cooks quickly and their flavor needs to be extracted quickly. Experiment with different curry powders and pastes—such as Thai powder or paste—to vary the curry flavor and heat.

> **SERVE WITH:**
>
> BOILED LOBSTER (SEE PAGE 192) OR OVER COUSCOUS
> ANY TUNA, SALMON, BASS, OR SNAPPER DISH
> SAUTÉED SEA SCALLOPS (SEE PAGE 61)
> HERB-ROASTED HALIBUT (SEE PAGE 154)

For fish and shellfish dishes, make the sauce with Lobster Stock or shrimp stock (see page 75).

For cilantro, substitute the bulbous white portion of 1 stalk lemongrass, cut into 1-inch pieces.

2 tablespoons pure olive oil
2 stalks celery, cut into small dice
2 medium carrots, peeled and cut into small dice
4 shallots, peeled and sliced thin
1 Granny Smith apple, cored and cut into small dice
1 tablespoon good-quality curry powder (such as Madras)

1 cup Chicken Stock (page 72) or low-salt canned chicken broth
½ cup heavy cream
½ cup coconut milk
About ⅓ cup cilantro leaves or 1 teaspoon whole coriander seed (optional)
Kosher salt and freshly ground black pepper

In a medium saucepan, heat the oil over medium-high heat, until shimmering. Sauté the celery, carrots, shallots, and apple until transparent, 8 to 10 minutes, stirring often. Add the curry powder and cook 1 minute.

For a slightly richer and thicker sauce, omit the coconut milk and use all heavy cream.

Add the stock, bring to a boil, and lower the heat to medium. Simmer for 4 minutes, then add the cream, coconut milk, and optional cilantro or coriander seed. Raise the heat to high and bring to a boil, then reduce the heat to medium and simmer for 15 minutes. The sauce will thicken and reduce slightly. Strain through a fine strainer, pushing down on the solids. Taste and season with salt and pepper.

MAKE-AHEAD NOTE

☙ Curry Sauce can be refrigerated up to 3 days. It cannot be frozen. Reheat slowly over medium heat or in a microwave.

GINGER–ORANGE SAUCE WITH CANDIED GINGER

MAKES ¾ CUP

This sweet and spicy sauce is built on a deeply flavored reduction of orange juice and vegetables, lightened with stock and then electrified by pungent ginger, and served hot. Although it shares some flavors with Ginger–Citrus Vinaigrette, it is the more complex of the two sauces.

> SERVE WITH:
> ....
> PAN-ROASTED PORK LOIN
> CHOPS (PAGE 226)
> ANY PORK OR DUCK DISH

FOR THE CANDIED GINGER

4 tablespoons very thinly julienned fresh ginger

2 cups water
½ cup sugar

Combine the ginger with cold water to cover in a small pot and bring to a boil over high heat. Boil 1 minute, drain, and rinse under cold running water. Return to the pot, cover with water again, and boil for 1 minute. Drain.

Return the ginger to the pot and add the 2 cups of water and the sugar. Bring to a boil over high heat, then simmer over medium heat until the liquor is slightly syrupy and the ginger is sweetened, about 25 minutes.

FOR THE GINGER–ORANGE SAUCE

3 teaspoons pure olive oil
¼ medium onion, cut into small dice
½ medium carrot, cleaned and cut into small dice
1 stalk celery, cut into small dice
½ teaspoon black peppercorns
Scant ¼ cup thinly sliced peeled fresh ginger (about a 2-inch piece)
1 cup fresh orange juice

1 tablespoon grated orange zest
2 teaspoons honey
½ cup Chicken Stock (page 72) or low-salt canned chicken broth
½ cup Veal Stock (page 74)
2 teaspoons cold butter, cut into small pieces
4 tablespoons candied ginger (above)

In a medium saucepan over medium-high heat, heat the olive oil until shimmering. Add the onion, carrot, celery, and peppercorns and sauté until softened but not colored, about 3 minutes. Add the ginger and sauté 1 minute. Add the orange juice, orange zest, and honey, raise the heat to high, and reduce to a syrupy consistency, about 10 minutes.

Add the chicken and veal stocks and bring to a boil. Reduce the heat to medium and simmer until slightly thickened and about ¾ cup of liquid remains, 12 to 15 minutes. Strain through a fine strainer into a smaller pot and simmer 10 minutes. When ready to serve, reheat over medium heat and whisk in the butter and the candied ginger.

MAKE-AHEAD NOTES

❧ Candied Ginger can be refrigerated in its syrup up to 10 days.

❧ The completed sauce can be refrigerated up to 1 week.

❧ Without the ginger, the sauce can be frozen.

PORT WINE SAUCE

MAKES ¼ TO ⅓ CUP

*R*educe *port wine to a sweet syrup, then add the contrasting flavor of balsamic vinegar, and you have an intense, winy-rich sauce to use sparingly with meat or seafood.*

> **SERVE WITH:**
> **SNAPPER WITH POTATO GALETTE**
> **(PAGE 158)**
> **BOILED LOBSTER (SEE**
> **PAGE 192)**

2 cups port wine
1 bay leaf
¼ teaspoon black peppercorns
2 tablespoons cold butter, cut into
    small pieces

2 tablespoons balsamic vinegar
Kosher salt and freshly ground black
    pepper

For a less sweet sauce, add a touch of Veal Stock (page 74), Vegetable Stock (page 72), or low-salt canned vegetable broth, after reducing.

In a small saucepan over medium-high heat, bring the wine to a boil with the bay leaf and peppercorns and reduce by three quarters. It should have a syrupy consistency. Strain. Mix in the butter bit by bit, add the vinegar, and season with salt and pepper.

MAKE-AHEAD NOTE

❧ Port Wine Sauce can be refrigerated up to 5 days; it can be frozen up to 1 month.

SPICED PLUM SAUCE

MAKES 3 CUPS

*T*his dark red-brown sauce is a little spicy from the pepper and a little sweet from the spices, but its flavor is fruity and light. It's a lively compliment for simply pan-roasted meats. Instead of stock, red wine and port provide the liquid.

SERVE WITH:
ROASTED DUCK (PAGE 210)
**TENDERLOIN OF PORK
(PAGE 216)**
**PAN-ROASTED VEAL OR PORK
CHOPS (SEE PAGES 224, 226)**

Substitute pears, apples, or a combination of the two for the plums.

6 medium plums (any kind), pitted
   and cut into small dice
1½ cups red wine
1½ cups port
1 cinnamon stick
¼ teaspoon ground allspice
1 bay leaf

¼ teaspoon cracked black pepper
1 tablespoon red wine vinegar
1 strip (about ½ inch) lemon peel,
   thinly julienned
2 tablespoons cold butter, cut into
   small pieces

In a medium saucepan over medium-high heat, combine all the ingredients except the vinegar, lemon peel, and butter and bring to a boil. Reduce the heat to medium and simmer 15 minutes. Strain, reserving the plums and bay leaf and discarding the cinnamon stick. There should be about 1½ cups liquid.

Return the liquid to the pan along with the bay leaf and any accumulated syrup from the plums. Add the vinegar and lemon peel. Reduce over medium-high heat until thick and syrupy, 5 to 6 minutes; there should be about 1 cup.

Whisk in the butter and add the reserved plums, simmering briefly until they are hot. Remove the bay leaf before serving.

MAKE-AHEAD NOTE

℞ The sauce can be refrigerated up to 3 days.

CARAMELIZED PEAR SAUCE

MAKES 2 CUPS

*S*tock, brandy, and wine accent the pear flavor in this savory golden-brown sauce. Despite its fruit base, it is not overly sweet. Its flavor is similar to that of the Spiced Plum Sauce (page 32), but with the added richness of Duck Stock, and it makes a delicious accompaniment to roasted meats.

SERVE WITH:
ROASTED DUCK (PAGE 210)
SIMPLE ROASTED CHICKEN
(PAGE 204)
TENDERLOIN OF PORK
(PAGE 216)
PAN-ROASTED VEAL CHOPS
(PAGE 224)
PAN-ROASTED PORK LOIN
CHOPS (PAGE 226)

This is great to make and refrigerate at your leisure, before you do the roast, since it doesn't require any pan juices. But because it is so quick, you can put it together at the last minute, while the meat is resting before being carved.

For pears, substitute plums, apples, or figs.

For pear brandy, substitute a complimentary or matching fruit brandy.

2 tablespoons cold butter
4 medium to large Bosc or Bartlett
    pears, peeled, cored, and cut into
    ½-inch slices
1 tablespoon brown sugar
5 tablespoons pear brandy (such as
    Poire William)

½ cup red wine
1¼ cups Duck Stock (page 73),
    Chicken Stock (page 72), Vegetable
    Stock (page 72), or low-salt canned
    broth
Few drops of fresh lemon juice

In a large (preferably nonstick) skillet over high heat, melt 1 tablespoon of the butter, add the pears, and sprinkle with the brown sugar. Cook, turning occasionally, until golden brown and caramelized, 2 to 3 minutes. Deglaze with 4 tablespoons of the brandy and cook a few seconds more, scraping the bottom of the pan with a wooden spoon.

Add the wine, bring to a boil, and boil 1 minute. Add the stock, reduce the heat to medium-high, and simmer until just slightly thickened. Swirl in the remaining tablespoon of butter until incorporated. Mix in the remaining 1 tablespoon brandy and the lemon juice. Serve hot.

MAKE-AHEAD NOTE

❧ Caramelized Pear Sauce can be refrigerated up to 4 days.

ROASTED GARLIC–ALMOND BUTTER

MAKES ABOUT 1 CUP

SERVE WITH:

SOFTSHELL CRABS
(SEE PAGE 60)
SEARED SCALLOPS
(SEE PAGE 90)

Roasted garlic and toasted almonds make this sauce an especially delicious complement to shellfish. It is prepared like the classic French beurre blanc, except that stock, rather than vinegar, is used for the reduction. The amount of butter determines the thickness of the sauce. As you add butter, the sauce cools down, so to make sure it stays warm during the preparation, keep it over a low flame. Conversely, if you add the minimum amount of butter, the sauce won't cool down much. Be careful that it does not boil.

Toast the almonds in one layer on a baking sheet in a 350°F. oven until light golden, 3 to 5 minutes.

1 cup Chicken Stock (page 72) or low-salt canned chicken broth

2 to 3 tablespoons finely diced shallots

4 to 5 tablespoons cold butter

A few drops of lemon juice

1 to 2 teaspoons chopped dill, tarragon, or chervil, or a mixture of these (optional)

Kosher salt and freshly ground black pepper

4 to 5 cloves roasted garlic, mashed

2 to 3 tablespoons tomato concassée (see page xiii)

3 tablespoons thinly sliced toasted almonds

2 tablespoons coarsely chopped parsley

In a small saucepan over medium-high heat, combine the stock and shallots, bring to a boil, and reduce until slightly syrupy. Whisk in the butter, lemon juice, and optional herbs. Taste and season with salt and pepper.

Add the remaining ingredients and heat through.

MAKE-AHEAD NOTE

❧ This sauce cannot be done ahead. Prepare it just before serving.

RED WINE CHICKEN SAUCE

MAKES 1 ½ TO 1 ¾ CUPS

Based on a reduction of seared chicken bones, stock, red wine, and vegetables, this sauce is on the light side, with the flavors of marjoram and sage and an appealing herbal aroma. It is important to have the skillet very hot when you sear the chicken bones, so they don't steam instead of sear. Don't be intimidated by the loud crackle when they hit the pan.

SERVE WITH:

ANY POULTRY
PAN-ROASTED VEAL CHOPS
(PAGE 224)
BAKED RAINBOW TROUT WITH
LEEKS AND THYME (PAGE 174)

Substitute Veal Stock (page 74) for a richer, more full-bodied sauce.

Substitute herbs according to availability or your taste.

You can get chicken bones from the butcher, or if you bone breasts and thighs yourself, keep the bones in the freezer until you have enough. If there is a little meat attached, so much the better for the sauce.

Add some mushroom stems, to enhance the flavor.

2 tablespoons pure olive oil
Bones from one 2- to 3-pound
  chicken, chopped into 3-inch
  pieces (a small amount of meat
  will be left on the bones)
2 stalks celery, cut into small dice
1 medium carrot, cut into small dice
1 large head garlic, halved crosswise

4 cups Chicken Stock (page 72) or
  low-salt canned chicken broth
3 sprigs sage, plus 1 small sprig
3 sprigs marjoram
2 cups red table wine
Kosher salt and freshly ground black
  pepper

In a large, high-sided skillet, heat the oil over high heat until smoking. Add the chicken bones and sear until golden brown, about 5 minutes.

Add the celery, carrot, and garlic and sauté for 5 minutes. Add the stock and deglaze, scraping up the browned particles from the bottom of the pan. Add the wine, 3 sprigs of sage, and marjoram, bring to a boil, and simmer about 40 minutes, stirring occasionally to break up the bones and loosen their meat, which will add flavor to the sauce.

Strain through a coarse strainer into a small saucepan. Add the remaining sprig of sage and simmer about 20 minutes, skimming any grease from the surface. Strain again, this time through a fine strainer. Season with salt and pepper to taste.

MAKE-AHEAD NOTE

❧ Red Wine Chicken Sauce can be refrigerated up to 5 days or frozen up to 1 month.

RED WINE SALMON SAUCE

MAKES ABOUT ¾ CUP

Deep burgundy red and thick enough to lightly coat a spoon, this sauce has a complex, interesting flavor. Take the time to make a big batch of red wine sauce and freeze it in small containers. Veal Stock or a mixture of half chicken, half veal will give the sauce more body.

> **SERVE WITH:**
>
> **SALMON WITH LENTILS**
> **(PAGE 160)**
> **LOBSTER (SEE PAGE 192)**
> **ALMOST ANY**
> **STRONG-FLAVORED FISH**

1 tablespoon butter
5 large shallots, thinly sliced or diced
2 cloves garlic, thinly sliced
1 cup leek greens, cut into ¼-inch slices
1 cup celery, cut into medium dice
2 sprigs fresh thyme
1 pound salmon or other fish bones, cut into 2- to 3-inch pieces (the fishmonger can do this)

3 cups Chicken Stock (page 72), low-salt canned chicken broth, or Veal Stock (page 74)
2½ cups full-bodied red wine (such as Rhône, Pinot Noir, or Burgundy)
Kosher salt and freshly ground black pepper

In a large saucepan or high-sided pan, melt the butter over medium heat. Add the shallots, garlic, leeks, celery, and thyme and sauté for 2 minutes. Arrange the fish bones on top of the vegetables in an even layer, cover, and reduce the heat to medium. Cook until the bones become opaque, 5 to 6 minutes.

Raise the heat to high, add the stock and wine, and bring to a boil. Reduce the heat slightly and simmer until 1½ cups of liquid remain, about 30 minutes. Strain through a fine strainer, pushing down on the solids.

For delicate fish, lighten the sauce with a little Basil Oil (page 5).

Pour the strained liquid into a clean saucepan and reduce over medium-high heat until slightly syrupy, 10 to 12 minutes. Strain through a chinois or fine strainer. Taste and season. It will taste strong and salty and probably will need pepper only.

MAKE-AHEAD NOTE

Red Wine Salmon Sauce can be refrigerated up to 5 days and frozen up to 1 month.

These three creations add their own special stamp to any foods they combine with. They are easy to do ahead and in fact in some cases actually require advance preparation, so make up a batch of mellow roasted garlic or smooth, soothing crème fraîche when you have a bit of free time and use them throughout the week to add savory depth to all the foods you cook.

OVEN-ROASTED GARLIC

MAKES 2 HEADS

When a head of garlic is roasted this way, the cloves lose their sharpness and become soft, subtle, and creamy. They add an aromatic kick to all sorts of foods and give flavor and dimension to mashed or sautéed potatoes and any sautéed vegetables. And try Oven-Roasted Garlic spread on crusty French bread.

Store the garlic in the refrigerator, either well wrapped in plastic or in a small bowl, covered with oil.

USE IN:

RAINBOW TROUT SALAD WITH KALAMATA OLIVES, TOMATOES, AND LEMON CONFIT (PAGE 52) ROASTED GARLIC–BLACK OLIVE OIL (PAGE 8) BROCCOLI SOUP WITH SAUTÉED SHRIMP, MUSHROOMS, AND ROASTED GARLIC (PAGE 102)

2 heads garlic, unpeeled	2 tablespoons pure olive oil

Preheat the oven to 400°F. Cut off the top third of each garlic head to expose the cloves. Sprinkle each garlic head with 1 tablespoon olive oil and wrap in aluminum foil. Place on a baking sheet and roast until soft, about 40 minutes. Squeeze the garlic cloves out of their skins to serve.

MAKE-AHEAD NOTE

Oven-Roasted Garlic can be refrigerated up to 2 weeks.

LEMON CONFIT

*T*hese *pungent salt-preserved lemons add a Mediterranean flavor to salads or vegetable dishes. Note that only the preserved lemon peel is used; the flesh is discarded.*

> **USE IN:**
> ....
> **ARUGULA SALADE COMPOSÉE**
> **(PAGE 48)**
> **RAINBOW TROUT SALAD WITH KALAMATA OLIVES, TOMATOES, AND LEMON CONFIT (PAGE 52)**
> **ROASTED FENNEL, TOMATOES, AND OLIVES (SEE PAGE 222)**

4 lemons, halved crosswise   4 to 6 cups kosher salt

Use any wet salt you pour off for making gravlax (see page 186).

At least 2 weeks and up to 1 month before you will use the confit, select a jar large enough to accommodate the lemons. Cover the bottom of the jar with a 1-inch layer of salt and add the lemons, separating them with a 1-inch layer of salt and covering the top with a 1-inch layer of salt. Cover and refrigerate. If the salt becomes wet, pour it out and replace it with fresh.

After 2 weeks, remove lemons from the salt, rinse, and peel with a sharp paring knife. Use the skin only, discarding the flesh. In a small saucepan, cover the lemon peel with cold water, bring to a boil over high heat, and boil 30 seconds. Drain and rinse in cold water. Cut into desired size.

MAKE-AHEAD NOTE

The only way this can be done is ahead! Lemon Confit keeps for up to a month, so it is a good idea to have some in your refrigerator. Even after you remove a lemon from its salt, it will keep in the refrigerator up to 6 days.

CRÈME FRAÎCHE

MAKES 3 CUPS

This slightly fermented heavy cream is used in France for desserts. It adds a tart-sweet note to soups and sauces, and can be whipped and flavored just like heavy cream but has a more full-bodied, tangy taste. It stores quite well, so do make the full amount.

> **SERVE WITH:**
>
> **PUMPKIN AND YAM SOUP (SEE PAGE 86)**
> **SWEET-POTATO VICHYSSOISE (PAGE 87)**
>
> **SWEETEN TO GARNISH:**
>
> **PEAR CLAFOUTI (PAGE 236)**
> **MAPLE-CINNAMON BREAD PUDDING, INSTEAD OF VANILLA CREAM (PAGE 242)**

3 cups heavy cream
  (not ultrapasteurized)

2 tablespoons buttermilk

At least 2½ days before you will be serving the crème fraîche, combine the cream and buttermilk in a large bowl. Stir well and cover tightly. Let stand at room temperature for 36 hours, or until slightly thickened, then refrigerate at least another 24 hours and up to 10 days before serving. It will continue to thicken in the refrigerator.

MAKE-AHEAD NOTE

❧ Crème Fraîche must be made at least 60 hours in advance; it can be stored in the refrigerator for a week once it is fully fermented.

CHAPTER 2

SALADS AND

FIRST COURSES

Salads were my happy introduction to professional cooking, and I still love them. No other dish can match a salad for versatility; using almost any salad as a base, you can add vegetables, meat, or seafood to build terrific appetizers and even main courses. Toss some greens together. Then sauté a few scallops—you don't have to do anything else to them—and add them to the bowl. All of a sudden, you have an effortless first course. For lunch or summer dinner, try a combination of scallops, some diced raw vegetables for crispness, and a complementary vinaigrette and you have a complete meal, and a pretty one, too.

A salad served as a main course can be as simple as mixed greens surrounded by sautéed shrimp, or it can jump off from there to anything that suits your mood. Add some grilled red onions and blanched, sautéed, or raw vegetables—shredded sautéed parsnips, for instance. Dress the dish with ginger–citrus or walnut or pesto vinaigrette. Or toss together some grilled shrimp, crisp greens, white beans, lentils, and Roasted Garlic–Black Olive Oil (page 8). You don't need a recipe for salads like these, just interesting ingredients and imagination.

I love the way the heat of a piece of seared fish or fowl warms up greens; with each bite, you get a cool mouthful of salad greens along with something warm, a bit of chewy food along with a bit of crisp. The different textures make the food more exciting. In all these salads, the fish or fowl is light enough so it won't weigh down the greens, and the flavors are compatible: seared tuna with marinated cucumbers; trout with olives and tomatoes; shrimp with artichokes; duck with cranberries.

Of course, you can serve salads from your favorite bowls, but I like them best tossed with dressing and then shown off on large dinner plates, with plenty of space around the colorful ingredients. Use white or plain plates, not something with a busy design, or the salad will just get lost. Don't be afraid to use plates of a different pattern from the ones that will appear for the main course; salads lend themselves to a casual attitude.

Make sure the greens for your salad are absolutely clean and dry—a salad spinner is a big help— and that they are torn, not cut. I prefer a variety, such as green and red leaf lettuce, watercress, and arugula, or mesclun mix, but feel free to use your favorites. A mixture of different colors, flavors, textures, and looks is most interesting, including some that are peppery or spicy, some with spiky or big leaves, and some with small and tender leaves. The size of the leaves determines how much dressing you will use: great big leaves, roughly torn, will need more dressing, but smaller leaves are easier to coat—and also easier to overdress. Start with a small amount of dressing and taste, adding more if you need it.

ENDIVE, PEAR, AND ROQUEFORT SALAD

MAKES 4 SERVINGS

The slight bitterness of endive cuts the richness of the cheese and nuts in this light-colored salad. This combination of ingredients is classic French, and the salad is so easy to prepare, with no washing of greens required.

Buy firm endives and refrigerate them wrapped in paper towels and plastic (exposure to light can make them bitter).

3 large endives (about 1 pound), thinly sliced on the diagonal
¾ cup coarsely chopped walnuts, toasted
3 ounces Roquefort cheese, crumbled

2 Bosc or Anjou pears, peeled and cut into medium dice
¼ cup Mustard Vinaigrette (page 16)

Place the endives, walnuts, cheese, and pears in a medium bowl and toss to combine. Add the vinaigrette and toss to lightly coat the ingredients. Divide among 4 chilled plates.

MAKE-AHEAD NOTES

⌇ The Mustard Vinaigrette can be refrigerated up to 3 weeks; whisk to recombine before using.

⌇ The toasted walnuts can be refrigerated up to 1 week.

⌇ The diced pears can be sprinkled with lemon juice and refrigerated up to 1 day.

SALAD OF FIELD GREENS WITH LENTILS AND GOAT CHEESE

MAKES 4 SERVINGS

ORDER OF PREPARATION
- Marinate the cheese.
- Prepare the Sherry Vinaigrette.
- Cook the lentils.
- Heat the cheese.
- Assemble the salads.

*H*earty *ingredients like lentils and cheese need not be overpowering, if they are offered in small amounts and in the right proportion to greens. Marinated cheese is a Provençal touch, made with both fresh and dry herbs; note that it should be made well in advance. The fresh herbs impart emphatic flavor, and the dry herbs distribute themselves throughout the marinade and cling to the cheese even after it has been drained.*

FOR THE MARINATED GOAT CHEESE

1 cup extra-virgin olive oil
1 teaspoon crushed black pepper
1 teaspoon finely chopped fresh thyme
½ teaspoon dry thyme
1 teaspoon finely chopped fresh savory

½ teaspoon dry savory
1 teaspoon finely chopped fresh marjoram
½ teaspoon dry marjoram
4 (1-ounce) goat cheese rounds

In a small bowl, combine the olive oil and seasonings. Place the cheese rounds in a small pan, cover with the herbed oil, and refrigerate at least 2 days.

FOR THE LENTILS

½ cup imported green lentils
3 cups cold water
Kosher salt
1 bay leaf

1 tablespoon Sherry Vinaigrette (page 14)
¼ cup finely diced red onion
1 tablespoon minced chives

Place the lentils in a medium saucepan and add the water, a pinch of salt, and the bay leaf. Bring to a boil over high heat, reduce the heat to medium, and simmer until tender, 25 to 30 minutes.

Drain the lentils, removing the bay leaf, and while still warm, toss lightly with the vinaigrette. Add the onion and chives and combine.

TO SERVE

4 cups loosely packed mixed field greens

½ cup Sherry Vinaigrette (page 14)
4 tablespoons finely chopped chives

Toss the greens with just enough vinaigrette to moisten and divide among 4 plates. Arrange about 3 heaping tablespoons of lentils around the greens. Place the warm goat cheese over the greens and garnish with the chives.

꙾ The Sherry Vinaigrette can be refrigerated up to 3 weeks; whisk to recombine before using.

ANCHOÏADE WITH FRESH VEGETABLES

MAKES 3 CUPS, OR 8 TO 10 SERVINGS

ORDER OF PREPARATION
- Prepare the anchoïade.
- Cut the vegetables.

This is the easiest salad imaginable: masses of crisp, colorful, fresh vegetables served along with a Provençal anchovy–garlic paste, for dipping. Anchoïade paste has the consistency of mayonnaise and a gentle, not overpowering, flavor of anchovies.

This is a casual predinner nibble that goes well with drinks. Serve the vegetables in an interesting basket or crock and let your guests help themselves.

FOR THE ANCHOÏADE

2 (4-ounce) cans anchovy fillets, drained	3 teaspoons fresh thyme leaves
2 cups virgin olive oil	1½ tablespoons Dijon mustard
3 cloves garlic	3 tablespoons white wine vinegar
	Freshly ground white pepper

Combine all the ingredients in a blender or food processor and blend until smooth.

TO SERVE

Anchoïade is delicious with all sorts of fresh vegetables. Feel free to make substitutions.

Yellow and red cherry tomatoes	Julienne strips of fennel
Radishes	Julienne strips of cucumbers
White mushrooms, caps only	Julienne strips of red and green bell
Niçoise olives	pepper

Place the anchoïade in small crocks or shallow bowls and surround with the fresh vegetables. The amounts and proportions are up to you.

MAKE-AHEAD NOTES

꙾ The anchoïade can be refrigerated up to 1 week.

꙾ The cut vegetables can be covered and refrigerated up to 2 days.

POTATO GALETTES WITH OVEN-DRIED TOMATOES, GOAT CHEESE, AND GREENS

MAKES 4 APPETIZER SERVINGS

ORDER OF PREPARATION

- Prepare the Sherry Vinaigrette.
- Prepare the clarified butter.
- Roast the tomatoes.
- While the tomatoes are roasting, prepare the galettes.
- Combine the galettes, cheese, and tomatoes and bake.
- Toss the greens with the Sherry Vinaigrette.

*A*ll the flavors complement one another in this great summer appetizer of crisp, golden potato cakes layered with cheese, fresh herbs, and slowly roasted tomatoes. Serve the galettes over or beside your favorite greens.

The components all can be done ahead and combined just before serving. Oven-dried tomatoes will be best in the summer, when tomatoes are really ripe and at their best. You may vary the herbs you sprinkle on them; try tarragon, chervil, dill, parsley, or cilantro.

> **TRY POTATO GALETTES TOPPED WITH:**
>
> GRILLED VEGETABLES (SEE TUNA WITH GRILLED VEGETABLES AND PROVENÇAL VINAIGRETTE, PAGE 180)
> CONFIT BAYALDI (PAGE 138)
> RATATOUILLE (PAGE 142)
> BITS OF GOAT CHEESE

FOR THE OVEN-DRIED TOMATOES

4 medium-size ripe tomatoes, sliced ¼ inch thick	1 tablespoon combined finely chopped fresh savory, thyme, and parsley
2 tablespoons extra-virgin olive oil	

Preheat the oven to 225°F. and line a baking sheet with parchment paper. Arrange the tomato slices in a single layer on the paper, drizzle lightly with the olive oil, and sprinkle with the herbs. Roast 2 hours. They will shrink and darken slightly and be drier in appearance, but they will remain somewhat firm and moist.

FOR THE POTATO GALETTES

2 large Idaho potatoes, peeled	6 to 8 teaspoons clarified butter (page xiv)

To slice potatoes easily, first cut an even lengthwise slice off the bottom, so the potato can stand firmly on a cutting board.

Using a mandoline if possible, cut each potato into ⅛-inch slices; there should be about 32 in all. Brush a small nonstick skillet with about 1 teaspoon of clarified butter. Place over medium heat until hot, then arrange about 8 potato slices in the center, overlapping slightly to form a pancake. Cook until golden brown, 2 to 3 minutes on each side. Repeat with the remaining potato slices. Drain on paper towels. You may use a larger skillet and cook 2 or 3 galettes at a time.

TO SERVE

½ log good-quality goat cheese (about 6 ounces), cut into ¼-inch rounds
Kosher salt and freshly ground black pepper

4 cups mesclun leaves, or other greens
½ cup Sherry Vinaigrette (page 14)

Preheat the oven to 200° F. Place the galettes on a baking sheet and top each with a slice of cheese and some dried tomatoes. Season with salt and pepper. Place in the oven until warmed through and the cheese has softened, 3 to 4 minutes.

In a bowl, toss the mesclun with the sherry vinaigrette.

Arrange each galette on an individual serving plate and top with the mesclun.

MAKE-AHEAD NOTES

ɔ. The Sherry Vinaigrette can be refrigerated up to 3 weeks; whisk to recombine before using.

ɔ. The clarified butter can be refrigerated up to 2 weeks.

ɔ. The roasted tomatoes can be refrigerated up to 2 days.

ɔ. The galettes can be wrapped tightly in plastic and kept at room temperature several hours, or in the refrigerator up to 1 day.

To vary potato galettes:
ɔ sprinkle whole leaves of sage or tarragon between the layers
ɔ serve as a base for seared and roasted fish or meat (see page 158)

ARUGULA SALADE COMPOSÉE

MAKES 6 APPETIZER OR 4 LUNCHEON SERVINGS

ORDER OF PREPARATION

- Prepare the Lemon Vinaigrette.
- Cut, blanch, and shock the vegetables.
- Toss the vegetables with the Lemon Vinaigrette.

If you don't want to use both asparagus and beans, use a double quantity of either one. Or add some zucchini or shredded carrots. The amounts and vegetables are very flexible.

*T*his salad combines vegetables with salad greens, for a crunchy mix of fresh tastes and crisp textures. Delicate asparagus and haricots verts, along with heartier raw vegetables, are garnished with sharp-flavored cheese and black pepper and tossed with a refreshing, lemony dressing. Serve it as a dinner appetizer or a luncheon main course.

Slice the raw vegetables as thin as possible, so they will be easy to eat. A mandoline does the best job, but you may slice them by hand. The cheese also may be sliced thin on a mandoline or by hand.

12 thin asparagus spears, peeled if they are woody at the base
Kosher salt
1 to 1¼ cups haricots verts or slender green beans
2 bunches of arugula (about 4 cups of leaves with 1 inch of stem)
1 large bulb fennel, with any discolored outer pieces removed, cored and very thinly sliced
¼ medium head red cabbage, cored and very thinly sliced
3 tablespoons blanched and julienne Lemon Confit (page 38), or 2 tablespoons julienne fresh lemon zest
½ cup Lemon Vinaigrette (page 18)
4 ounces Pecorino Romano or Parmesan cheese, very thinly sliced
Coarsely ground black pepper

Blanch the asparagus in a large pot of boiling salted water until bright green and still crisp, 3 to 4 minutes, and shock in a bowl of ice water. Remove it by grasping the stems, rather than the tips, with tongs.

Repeat the blanching, shocking, and draining for the haricots verts, using a colander to drain.

In a medium bowl, toss the asparagus, haricots verts, arugula, fennel, and cabbage with the lemon confit and enough lemon vinaigrette to dress lightly. Season to taste with salt.

To serve, divide the salad among chilled plates and top with the sliced cheese. Grind a little coarse black pepper over each salad.

For a main-course salad, top each serving with a portion of sautéed or grilled fish or chicken.

MAKE-AHEAD NOTES

✎ The Lemon Vinaigrette can be refrigerated up to 3 weeks; whisk to recombine before using.

✎ The blanched and shocked vegetables can be refrigerated up to 1 day.

These salads can be served alongside your main course, or indeed as a main course themselves, but I like them best as light, easy first courses. Adding some fish, shellfish, or poultry to greens will give you a dish that is lighter than most appetizers, but full of contrasting flavors and textures. And it will provide an easy transition to your next course, whether it is fish, poultry, meat, or vegetables.

CRAB SALAD WITH GINGER–CITRUS VINAIGRETTE

MAKES 6 APPETIZER SERVINGS

ORDER OF PREPARATION

- Prepare the Ginger–Citrus Vinaigrette.
- Prepare the crabmeat salad; slice the avocado.

Ripe mangoes and papayas should be soft but not mushy when you buy them. In this salad they are cut into small dice, for a tumble of tropical orange and gold beside slices of delicate green avocado and glistening, sweet crab. Try this as an appetizer or lunch salad, but don't serve huge portions—the crab is very rich.

1 pound lump crabmeat, picked over and shredded

½ ripe mango, peeled, cut away from the pit, and cut into small dice

½ ripe papaya, peeled, seeded, and cut into small dice

½ medium red onion, peeled and cut into small dice

3 scallions, white and green parts, cut on the bias into ⅛-inch slices

6 mint leaves, cut into thin strips

1 teaspoon cracked black pepper

Kosher salt to taste

About ¾ cup Ginger–Citrus Vinaigrette (page 22)

1 ripe, firm avocado, thinly sliced

In a medium bowl, combine all the ingredients except the vinaigrette and avocado. Gently toss the crab mixture with the vinaigrette to moisten.

For an elegant look, mold each serving of crabmeat in a 3- or 4-inch ring mold.

Divide the avocado slices among 6 plates, arranging them in a small fan, and sprinkle with pepper and salt. Arrange a mound of crabmeat salad alongside the avocado.

MAKE-AHEAD NOTES

The Ginger–Citrus Vinaigrette can be refrigerated up to 3 weeks; whisk to recombine before using.

The diced fruits, onion, and scallions can be refrigerated up to 1 day.

RED SNAPPER SALAD WITH GAZPACHO VINAIGRETTE

MAKES 6 APPETIZER OR 3 LUNCHEON SERVINGS

ORDER OF PREPARATION

- Prepare the Sherry Vinaigrette.
- Dice the vegetables and prepare the gazpacho vinaigrette.
- Sear and roast the snapper.

Each plate of this beautiful summer salad is filled with bright colors and fresh flavors. This excellent all-purpose gazpacho vinaigrette will enhance any cold or hot fish or cold chicken. It is made with a base of Sherry Vinaigrette, to which the colorful vegetables of a gazpacho—bell pepper, cucumber, tomato, and onion—are added. Neat, uniformly diced vegetables are the secret of the vinaigrette's beautiful appearance. The smaller you cut the vegetables, the prettier the dish will be.

FOR THE GAZPACHO VINAIGRETTE

½ small red bell pepper, cut into brunoise (⅓ to ½ cup)

½ small yellow bell pepper, cut into brunoise (⅓ to ½ cup)

1 medium-size ripe tomato, cut into brunoise (⅓ to ½ cup)

½ small cucumber, peeled (not seeded) and cut into brunoise (about ¾ cup)

½ small red onion, cut into brunoise (about ½ cup)

1 tablespoon chopped dill (no stems)

½ cup Sherry Vinaigrette (page 14)

Kosher salt and freshly ground black pepper

In a large bowl, combine all the diced vegetables and toss gently with the chopped dill. Add the sherry vinaigrette and season with salt and pepper.

FOR THE RED SNAPPER

3 (8-ounce) red snapper fillets, halved

Kosher salt and freshly ground black pepper

2 tablespoons vegetable oil

1 teaspoon butter

Preheat the oven to 400° F. Season the fillets to taste with salt and pepper. In a medium ovenproof skillet over medium-high heat, heat the oil until very hot and sear the fish, flesh-side down, until golden brown. Place the pan in the oven for 3 to 4 minutes, remove from the oven, and add the butter to the pan. Return to high heat on the stove top, turn the fillets, and cook until medium-rare, about 1 minute. Drain on paper towels.

*Substitute Basil
Vinaigrette (page 16) for
Sherry Vinaigrette, as a
base for the gazpacho
vinaigrette.*

6 cups mesclun or mixed salad greens

6 tablespoons Sherry Vinaigrette
(page 14)

Toss the salad greens with just enough sherry vinaigrette to moisten and
divide among 6 plates, placing the greens off center. Place 1 red snapper fillet alongside each serving of greens. (Or, center the greens and place the fish
on top.) Spoon 3 tablespoons of the gazpacho vinaigrette over or around each
serving of fish. Serve immediately.

MAKE-AHEAD NOTES

☙ The Sherry Vinaigrette can be refrigerated up to 3 weeks; whisk to
recombine before using.

☙ The gazpacho vinaigrette can be refrigerated up to 3 days; whisk to
recombine before serving.

RAINBOW TROUT SALAD WITH KALAMATA OLIVES, TOMATOES, AND LEMON CONFIT

MAKES 4 APPETIZER OR 2 MAIN-COURSE SERVINGS

ORDER OF PREPARATION

- Roast the garlic.
- Prepare the Roasted Garlic–Black Olive Oil.
- Prepare the Sherry Vinaigrette.
- Stuff and roast the trout.

*W*arm roasted trout stuffed with garlic and thyme sits right on top of this salad—it is not cut up and lost among the other ingredients. The Mediterranean flavors of garlic, Kalamata olives, preserved lemon, and tomatoes are echoed in the Roasted Garlic–Black Olive Oil.

This is my favorite kind of salad, in which the juices from roasted or seared fish (or meat or poultry) add their warmth and flavor to greens.

FOR THE TROUT

Substitute rosemary or tarragon for thyme; baby coho salmon for trout.

2 rainbow trout, 8 to 10 ounces each, boned (your fishmonger can do this)

Kosher salt and freshly ground black pepper

4 cloves Oven-Roasted Garlic (page 37)

2 sprigs thyme

Preheat the oven to 375°F.

When you remove the thyme sprig from the trout after roasting, let some leaves remain in the cavity to flavor each serving.

Season the inside of each fish with salt and pepper and stuff with 2 roasted garlic cloves and 1 sprig of thyme. Place the fish on a lightly oiled baking sheet and roast until medium-rare, 12 to 13 minutes. Cut off the head and tail, remove the thyme sprigs, and halve the fish crosswise.

FOR THE SALAD

4 cups field greens, or a mix of green and red leaf lettuce and arugula

20 Kalamata or Niçoise olives, pitted

12 red pear or cherry tomatoes, halved

2 tablespoons julienne Lemon Confit (page 38) or fresh lemon zest

4 to 6 tablespoons Sherry Vinaigrette (page 14)

In a large bowl, combine the salad greens, olives, tomatoes, and lemon confit and toss with the vinaigrette.

About ½ cup Roasted Garlic–Black
Olive Oil (page 8)

Divide the salad greens among 4 plates. Place half a trout over each portion
and surround with a drizzle of roasted garlic–black olive oil.

MAKE-AHEAD NOTES

❧ The Oven-Roasted Garlic can be refrigerated up to 2 weeks.

❧ The Sherry Vinaigrette can be refrigerated up to 3 weeks; whisk to
recombine before using.

❧ The Roasted Garlic–Black Olive Oil can be refrigerated up to 2 days.

❧ The stuffed trout can be refrigerated up to 8 hours before roasting.

MARINATED TUNA SALADE NIÇOISE

MAKES 4 SERVINGS

**ORDER OF
PREPARATION**

- Marinate the tuna.
- Roast the garlic.
- Cook the potatoes and
  the haricots verts.
- While the vegetables
  are cooking, prepare the
  Sherry Vinaigrette and
  the Roasted Garlic–
  Black Olive Oil.
- Sear the tuna.

*N*ew potatoes and blanched haricots verts tossed in Sherry Vinaigrette provide the foundation for another vegetable salad, my version of salade Niçoise. Rather than the usual canned tuna, it is made with marinated fresh tuna that has been quickly seared and is rare and juicy beneath its golden-brown crust. The fish is sliced thin, then drizzled with pungent Roasted Garlic–Black Olive Oil. The salad is full of sunny Mediterranean flavors and the aroma of garlic and olives.

If you prefer a salade Niçoise with greens, toss 4 cups mesclun or lettuce and about 4 tablespoons of vinaigrette with the haricots verts.

FOR THE MARINATED TUNA

⅔ cup virgin olive oil

2 sprigs fresh rosemary

2 sprigs fresh thyme

2 sprigs fresh savory

2 tablespoons cracked fennel seed

Freshly ground black pepper

1 pound tuna loin

Kosher salt

Combine the olive oil, herbs, fennel seed, and pepper to taste and spread over the tuna. Cover and refrigerate without turning for 8 hours or overnight.

When ready to cook, remove the tuna from the oil, leaving some seasonings on its surface. Sprinkle with salt and pepper. In a large skillet over high heat, sear the tuna on all sides, 2 to 3 minutes, until cooked rare.

FOR THE VEGETABLES

12 new potatoes

⅓ cup Sherry Vinaigrette (page 14)

12 haricots verts or slender green beans

Place the potatoes in a medium saucepan with cold salted water and bring to a boil over high heat. Reduce the heat to medium and simmer until tender, about 15 minutes. Drain and cut into quarters. While still warm, toss with ¼ cup of the sherry vinaigrette. Taste and reseason, if necessary.

Half-fill a medium saucepan with salted water, bring to a boil over high heat, and blanch the haricots verts until tender, 2 to 3 minutes. Immediately plunge into ice water and drain in a colander for 5 minutes. Toss the beans with the remaining sherry vinaigrette, and check the seasoning.

8 tablespoons Roasted Garlic–Black
Olive Oil (page 8)

Sprigs of fresh thyme, tarragon, or
chives (optional)

Divide the potatoes and haricots verts among 4 serving plates, arranging them in the center. Slice the tuna ¼ inch thick and fan the slices around the vegetables. Drizzle the tuna with the roasted garlic–black olive oil. Garnish with the herbs, if desired.

MAKE-AHEAD NOTES

⁌ The tuna in its marinade can be refrigerated 8 hours or overnight.

⁌ The roasted garlic can be refrigerated up to 2 weeks.

⁌ The cooked potatoes can be refrigerated up to 2 days.

⁌ The cooked haricots verts can be refrigerated up to 1 day.

⁌ The Sherry Vinaigrette can be refrigerated up to 3 weeks; whisk to recombine before using.

⁌ The Roasted Garlic–Black Olive Oil can be refrigerated up to 2 days.

SEARED SASHIMI TUNA TWO WAYS

ORDER OF PREPARATION

- Prepare the vinaigrette or Curry Oil.
- Marinate the cucumber or make the fondue.
- Sear the tuna and refrigerate.
- Slice the tuna and garnish with chosen accompaniments.

*I*n both versions of this appetizer, the salad is really a backdrop for rich tuna, providing texture to the dish. In one version, thin slices of seared tuna surround a sweet and tart fondue of ripe tomatoes, pungent ginger, and sharp cilantro. Curry Oil adds its complex flavor and aroma. In the other variation, marinated cucumbers surround the tuna slices, and with each mouthful, you get their sweet-and-sour coolness along with the spice and chewiness of the tuna. Red-Chili Vinaigrette adds dimension and flavor, but it is used sparingly because the cucumbers give sufficient moisture to the dish.

Either way, the tuna may be served as an hors d'oeuvre on a piece of toast or a cracker.

FOR THE TUNA

Sashimi-quality tuna is the freshest you can buy, with a deep red color. Buy a block of tuna, rather than a steak. A 3-inch-thick rectangle will be thick enough to stay raw inside when seared.

1 teaspoon kosher salt
1 teaspoon crushed cumin seed
1 teaspoon crushed fennel seed
¼ teaspoon red-chili flakes

1 teaspoon coarsely ground or cracked black pepper
½-pound chunk of sashimi-quality tuna, cut into 3 by 3-inch portions
Few drops of vegetable oil

In a small bowl, combine the salt, cumin seed, fennel seed, chili flakes, and pepper. Coat the tuna well on each side with the mixture.

Heat a skillet or sauté pan over high heat until very hot. Heat the oil until it is smoking and sear the tuna 15 seconds on each side.

Place the tuna on a plate and refrigerate until firm, about 10 minutes or up to 3 hours.

FOR THE TOMATO–GINGER FONDUE

2 tablespoons butter
6 ripe tomatoes, cored and cut into medium dice
3 tablespoons finely grated fresh ginger

2 tablespoons sugar
2 tablespoons balsamic vinegar
Kosher salt and freshly ground black pepper to taste
2 tablespoons chopped fresh cilantro

In a shallow pan over medium heat, melt the butter and add the tomatoes, ginger, and sugar. Simmer until the tomatoes are stewed and softened, about 30 minutes. Add the vinegar and cook 2 more minutes. Remove from the heat, drain off the liquid (there should be very little left, if any), and season with salt and pepper. Allow to cool at room temperature, add the chopped cilantro, and refrigerate until chilled (not super-cold).

FOR THE MARINATED CUCUMBER

If you don't have a mandoline, cut the cucumber crosswise into thirds before slicing thin.

½ cup champagne vinegar
3 to 4 tablespoons sugar

1 long, thin, seedless cucumber, peeled, sliced very thin lengthwise on a mandoline or with a sharp knife

In a small saucepan over low heat, combine the vinegar and sugar and heat gently, stirring occasionally, until the sugar is dissolved. Remove from the heat and allow to cool to room temperature. Pour the cooled mixture over the cucumber slices and marinate at room temperature for 30 minutes. Drain the cucumber and reserve.

TO SERVE

4 tablespoons Curry Oil (page 12)   *or*   4 tablespoons Red-Chili Vinaigrette (page 20)

Slice each piece of tuna about ⅛ inch thick, using a very sharp knife or an electric knife. Place 2 tablespoons tomato–ginger fondue on each plate and surround with 3 or 4 slices of tuna and a drizzle of the curry oil. Alternatively, make mounds of cucumber slices on 4 chilled plates and surround them with 3 or 4 slices of tuna. Drizzle the red-chili vinaigrette around the tuna.

MAKE-AHEAD NOTES

ᐳ The Red-Chili Vinaigrette can be refrigerated up to 2 weeks.
ᐳ The cucumber in its marinade can be refrigerated up to 1 day.
ᐳ The Curry Oil can be refrigerated up to 2 days.
ᐳ The tomato–ginger fondue can be refrigerated up to 3 days.
ᐳ The seared tuna can be refrigerated up to 3 hours.

ᐳ Use a super-hot pan when you sear the spice-coated tuna—it can't be too hot!
ᐳ Cut the seared fish into 4 pieces before you slice it.
ᐳ Slice with an electric knife or a very sharp regular knife.

WARM SHRIMP SALAD WITH ARTICHOKES AND CANNELLINI BEANS

ORDER OF PREPARATION

- Prepare the Sherry Vinaigrette.
- Sauté the shrimp and the artichokes.
- Toss the greens with the vinaigrette.

For Sherry Vinaigrette, substitute 4 tablespoons Lobster Vinaigrette (page 25) combined with 2 tablespoons Sherry Vinaigrette.

H*ere is a delicious, quick first-course or luncheon salad for those times when you can't start a meal from scratch. It combines seafood with vegetables and offers a good combination of textures and colors.*

Obviously, I prefer to use fresh ingredients 99 percent of the time, but this salad is a departure in that it uses canned artichoke hearts and white beans. There are some good products on the market, so choose the best quality you can find.

4 teaspoons extra-virgin olive oil, plus 1 to 2 tablespoons, if needed

12 medium or large shrimp, peeled and deveined

Salt and freshly ground black pepper

6 canned artichoke hearts, cut in eighths

2 cups drained canned cannellini beans

1 teaspoon finely chopped fresh thyme leaves

About ½ cup Sherry Vinaigrette (page 14)

4 cups loosely packed mesclun greens (about ½ pound), or other salad greens

In a large skillet, heat 2 teaspoons of the oil over high heat. Season the shrimp with salt and pepper and sear 2 minutes on each side. Remove from the pan and reserve.

In the same pan, heat the remaining oil until shimmering, adding more, if needed. Sauté the artichoke hearts until light golden brown, about 1 minute. Add the beans and thyme and toss to heat through. Add 6 table-spoons of the sherry vinaigrette and the shrimp and toss to heat through. Remove the pan from the heat.

Toss the mesclun with the remaining sherry vinaigrette (or just enough to coat lightly).

To serve, divide the mesclun among 4 plates or shallow bowls and place a few spoonfuls of the artichoke–shrimp mixture in the center of the greens.

MAKE-AHEAD NOTE

❧ The Sherry Vinaigrette can be refrigerated up to 3 weeks; whisk to recombine before using.

LOBSTER SALAD WITH
WHITE BEANS AND FRESH THYME

MAKES 6 APPETIZER OR LUNCHEON SERVINGS

ORDER OF
PREPARATION

- Boil the lobsters and refrigerate.
- Cook the beans.
- While the beans are cooking, prepare the Sherry Vinaigrette.
- Toss the greens with the dressing.

I *love the textural combination of starchy beans with chewy lobster or shrimp, as well as the way these beans absorb flavor from their marination in Sherry Vinaigrette. Pink lobster, white beans, and bright salad greens make this a beautiful dish.*

Nothing is as elegant as lobster, so I recommend serving this as an appetizer for a special dinner party. For 3 cups lobster meat, you will need about 6 pounds of boiled lobster (see page 192). Or buy whole lobsters or tail, claw, or knuckle meat already cooked. If you can't find really good tomatoes, leave them out. But shop around, because good Florida tomatoes are available even in the winter.

Substitute 18 cooked jumbo shrimp, shelled and left whole, for the lobster.

For Sherry Vinaigrette, substitute Lobster Vinaigrette (page 25).

1½ cups dried Great Northern beans
½ cup plus 2 tablespoons Sherry Vinaigrette (page 14)
10 sprigs thyme, leaves only, roughly chopped
2 medium-size ripe tomatoes, peeled and seeded, cut into small dice

½ red onion, cut into small dice
Kosher salt and cracked black pepper
3 cups mesclun or mixed greens
3 cups cooked lobster meat, cut into ½-inch pieces

Place the beans in a medium saucepan, with cold water to cover, and bring to a boil over medium-high heat. Reduce the heat to medium and simmer until tender, about 45 minutes. Drain well. In a mixing bowl, combine the beans with ¼ cup of the vinaigrette and the thyme, tomatoes, and onion. Cool to room temperature. Season to taste with salt and pepper.

In a large bowl, toss the mesclun with ¼ cup of the vinaigrette.

Place about ½ cup of the white bean salad on each of 6 plates. Arrange the greens and lobster meat in 3 small alternating mounds around them. Drizzle with the remaining vinaigrette.

MAKE-AHEAD NOTES

The cooked lobster meat can be refrigerated up to 12 hours.

The cooked beans can be refrigerated up to 1 day.

The Sherry Vinaigrette can be refrigerated up to 3 weeks; whisk to recombine before using.

SOFTSHELL CRAB SALAD WITH FENNEL, RED ONION, AND KUMQUATS

MAKES 4 LUNCHEON SERVINGS

ORDER OF PREPARATION

- Prepare the Lemon Vinaigrette.
- Prepare the Orange Oil.
- Blanch the fennel, toss with the vinaigrette, and refrigerate.
- Roast the crabs.

*Y*ou don't see many recipes for kumquat, a tiny member of the citrus family, but here is a good one, an improvisation on the classic French combination of fennel and orange. The salad combines the textures of barely crisp fennel, raw onions, and juicy kumquats into a bed for sweet, buttery crab. It will taste best if it is served chilled, not super-cold.

Roasting is an unusual way to prepare softshell crab; sautéing is most common. But I find that removing the top shell and baking just until the meat turns white and opaque preserves the crab's delicate flavor. Plus, this is the easy way to do it.

FOR THE FENNEL

If you cannot find kumquats, substitute fresh orange segments from 1 to 2 oranges, cut in ¼-inch pieces.

2 to 3 bulbs fennel, halved and cored, greens reserved

1 medium-size red onion, thinly sliced

8 kumquats, thinly sliced

2 to 4 tablespoons Lemon Vinaigrette (page 18)

Slice the fennel ⅛ inch thick and place in a pot of boiling salted water over high heat. Cook until tender, 3 to 4 minutes, and drain. Cool under cold running water and drain well. In a large bowl, toss the fennel with the onion slices, kumquats, and enough vinaigrette to moisten well. Refrigerate for 4 hours or overnight.

FOR THE SOFTSHELL CRABS

Buy very fresh, lively, medium-size softshell crabs and have the fish-monger clean them.

4 medium softshell crabs, cleaned

2 tablespoons butter, melted

Kosher salt and freshly ground black pepper

Preheat the oven to 400°F. Lift and remove the top shell flap from each crab, exposing the meat. Place the crabs on a baking sheet, brush with melted butter, and season with salt and pepper. Place in the oven just until the crabmeat becomes opaque, 2 to 3 minutes.

TO SERVE

Few drops of lemon juice, if needed

½ cup Orange Oil (page 11)

Retoss the salad, taste, and add a bit of lemon juice, if necessary. Divide among 4 plates, place 1 crab over each portion, and drizzle with the orange oil. Garnish with the fennel greens.

MAKE-AHEAD NOTES

☙ The Lemon Vinaigrette can be refrigerated up to 3 weeks; whisk to recombine before using.

☙ The Orange Oil can be refrigerated up to 2 days.

☙ The blanched fennel can be refrigerated overnight.

SAUTÉED SEA SCALLOPS WITH ONION CONFIT AND BEET OIL

MAKES 6 APPETIZER SERVINGS

ORDER OF PREPARATION

- Prepare the onion confit.
- Prepare the beet and chive oils.
- Sear the scallops.

Substitute Basil Oil (page 5) for Chive Oil.

This dish shows what you can do with those delicious bits of leftovers that may be sitting in your refrigerator. I first made it when I wanted to combine some ingredients I already had: onion confit left over from Caramelized Onion Tarts, and some beet and chive oils. Everything but the scallops had been done ahead.

In combining several equally rich ingredients here, I disregard my usual preference for contrasts, and somehow it all works. But keep the portions small.

6 large sea scallops, tendon removed	About ½ cup Beet Oil (page 9)
Salt and freshly ground black pepper	About ½ cup Chive Oil (page 6)
2 tablespoons pure olive oil	Chopped chives, for garnish
3 cups onion confit (see page 145)	

Season the scallops with salt and pepper. In a medium saucepan, heat the oil over high heat until shimmering and sauté the scallops until golden brown.

Meanwhile, warm the onion confit over medium heat until heated through.

To serve, place 2 tablespoons of onion confit on a plate and top with 1 scallop. Surround with a drizzle of beet oil and a drizzle of chive oil. Sprinkle with chopped chives.

MAKE-AHEAD NOTES

☙ The onion confit can be refrigerated up to 3 days.

☙ The beet and chive oils can be refrigerated up to 2 days.

WARM SCALLOP SALAD WITH PARSNIPS AND WILD MUSHROOM VINAIGRETTE

MAKES 4 APPETIZER SERVINGS

ORDER OF
PREPARATION
- Prepare both vinaigrettes.
- Cook the parsnips; cook the scallops.
- Assemble the salads.

*T*his salad is packed with exciting flavors and textures. At its center is a pile of crisp greens mixed with sweet parsnips that have been sautéed in butter and then quickly cooked in stock. Seared, juicy scallops surround the greens and mushroom-infused vinaigrette is drizzled around everything. Serve it all on big white plates.

FOR THE PARSNIPS

4 parsnips, peeled

2 tablespoons butter

¼ cup Vegetable Stock (page 72) or low-salt canned vegetable broth

Salt and freshly ground black pepper

Vegetables cut into thin strips cook quickly and retain their flavor and juiciness.

With a vegetable peeler or mandoline, cut the parsnips into thin strips.

In a medium skillet, melt the butter over medium-high heat until it bubbles, and sauté the parsnips 1 minute. Add the stock, season with salt and pepper, and cook until tender, 3 to 4 minutes. Reserve, keeping warm.

FOR THE SCALLOPS

Substitute shrimp for scallops.

12 large sea scallops

Salt and freshly ground black pepper

2 tablespoons virgin olive oil

Season the scallops with salt and pepper. In a large skillet over high heat, heat the oil until smoking and sear the scallops until golden brown and medium rare, about 1 to 2 minutes on each side. Remove from the pan.

TO SERVE

Substitute your favorite greens, torn into small pieces, for mesclun.

4 cups mesclun greens

¼ cup Sherry Vinaigrette (page 14)

About ½ cup Wild Mushroom Vinaigrette (page 15)

In a salad bowl, toss the mesclun with the sherry vinaigrette. Add the warm parsnip strips and toss. Arrange on 4 salad plates and surround with 3 scallops. Drizzle with the wild mushroom vinaigrette.

MAKE-AHEAD NOTES

The sherry and wild mushroom vinaigrettes can be refrigerated up to 3 weeks; whisk to recombine before using.

GRILLED QUAIL SALAD WITH PROVENÇAL VEGETABLES AND BALSAMIC VINAIGRETTE

MAKES 4 APPETIZER SERVINGS

Thin slices of crusty, smoky quail are the draw here. This is my favorite kind of salad, in which the greens get extra flavor and wilt slightly from the juices of the grilled birds. If you haven't made quail before, this easy recipe is a good introduction.

ORDER OF PREPARATION

- Prepare the vinaigrette.
- Marinate the quail.
- Prepare the vegetables.
- Grill the quail.

FOR THE QUAIL

Boned quail are available at butcher shops and specialty groceries.

4 boned quail	1 cup Balsamic Vinaigrette (page 17)

Separate the quail legs from the breasts. Arrange the pieces in a single layer in a bowl and drizzle with the vinaigrette. Cover and refrigerate for 12 hours.

When ready to grill, prepare a charcoal fire and let it burn down to ashes, or preheat a broiler. Grill or broil the quail legs and breasts until medium rare, about 3 minutes on each side. Slice each breast crosswise into 3 pieces.

FOR THE PROVENÇAL VEGETABLES

3 tablespoons virgin olive oil	1 medium zucchini, finely diced
1 medium red bell pepper, finely diced	1 medium yellow squash, finely diced

In a large skillet, heat the oil over medium-high heat until shimmering. Add the pepper, zucchini, and squash and sauté until tender, 3 to 4 minutes.

TO SERVE

1 cup greens of your choice	About ½ cup Balsamic Vinaigrette

When ready to serve, toss the greens with ¼ cup of the vinaigrette and the Provençal vegetables. Divide among 4 plates, arrange 1 quail breast and 2 legs around the greens, and drizzle with additional vinaigrette.

MAKE-AHEAD NOTES

❧ The Balsamic Vinaigrette can be refrigerated up to 3 weeks; whisk to recombine before using.

❧ The quail in its marinade should be refrigerated for 12 hours.

❧ The Provençal vegetables can be refrigerated up to 2 days.

WARM DUCK SALAD WITH CRANBERRIES AND WALNUTS

MAKES 4 SERVINGS

ORDER OF PREPARATION

- Braise the duck legs.
- Prepare the Walnut Vinaigrette.
- Combine the vinaigrette, cranberries, walnuts, and duck.

When duck is braised in stock, the meat is as moist and tender as classic duck confit (for which duck is cooked entirely in fat), but it is far less greasy. No oil is needed for searing because the duck skin has its own fat, which will be rendered into the stock as it simmers.

> **SERVED BRAISED DUCK WITH:**
>
> **ONION CONFIT (SEE PAGE 144)**

This recipe calls for duck legs, which you may have left over after preparing Seared and Roasted Duck Breasts with Green Peppercorn Sauce (page 202). They are paired with crunchy toasted walnuts, sweet and tart chewy dried cranberries, and crisp greens. Walnut Vinaigrette echoes the walnut flavor.

FOR THE BRAISED DUCK LEGS

For Chicken Stock, substitute Duck Stock (page 73), or a combination of duck and chicken stocks.

4 duck legs (from two 5-pound ducks)	1 cinnamon stick
Kosher salt and freshly ground black pepper	½ teaspoon whole allspice berries
	½ teaspoon whole black peppercorns
5 cups Chicken Stock (page 72) or low-salt canned chicken broth	2 bay leaves
	6 sprigs thyme

Preheat the oven to 400° F. Season the duck legs well with salt and pepper.

Over medium-high heat, heat a medium skillet until smoking and sear the legs, skin-side down, until golden, 1 to 2 minutes. Turn and sear the flesh side 1 minute.

Place the legs skin-side up in a pot large enough to hold them snugly and add the stock, spices, and herbs. Bring to a boil over high heat and then place in the oven for 1 hour. Reduce the oven to 375° F., turn the legs, and cook 30 minutes longer. Remove from the oven and cool in the cooking liquid.

If you cook the duck legs in advance, refrigerate on the bone to retain more of their juices.

Remove the duck legs when cool and discard the cooking liquid, which will be fatty. Discard the duck skin and pull the meat from the bones (it will come off very easily) and shred it.

TO SERVE

For Walnut Vinaigrette, substitute Sherry Vinaigrette (page 14).

For walnuts, substitute pine nuts.

4 cups mixed greens
½ cup Walnut Vinaigrette (page 19)
4 tablespoons dried cranberries

4 tablespoons coarsely chopped toasted walnuts
Kosher salt and freshly ground black pepper

Toss the greens with the vinaigrette, cranberries, walnuts, and duck. Season lightly with salt and pepper, toss, and divide among 4 serving plates.

MAKE-AHEAD NOTES

❧ The braised duck legs, with the meat kept on the bone, can be refrigerated up to 3 days; reheat in a little stock over medium heat.

❧ The Walnut Vinaigrette can be refrigerated up to 10 days; whisk to recombine before serving.

CHAPTER 3

SOUPS AND STOCKS

Soup always lifts my spirits. One of my earliest memories is of my mother bringing me a steaming bowl of cream of celery soup (still one of my favorites) as I lay in bed recovering from a childhood illness. It could have been lunchtime, or maybe I was sleeping off a fever, but that savory aroma awoke and cheered me. Soup means nurturing, and isn't that what cooking is all about?

Anybody can make an okay soup—just follow the recipe, and in less than an hour, it will be done and on the table. But if you take care to monitor the flavor after each step, constantly reevaluating the texture and balance of ingredients, your soup can be *great.*

Seasoning is crucial. While a dish with several components can conceal seasoning mistakes, there is no place to hide errors or misjudgment in a pot of soup. Season your soup well and then taste it critically. Even if it seems fine, push it just a little bit further. Take out half a cup, add some salt and pepper to it, and taste. If it makes you say "wonderful!" you can proceed with the rest of the batch.

The same approach works with texture. If you're making a pureed soup, note how you can vary the coarseness of the soup to create a completely different effect. Strain one ladleful through a medium strainer, then strain another through a fine strainer and see which is more pleasing to your palate. If your soup is a little on the thin side to begin with, don't strain it at all or use a medium strainer to preserve some body. If it is really thick and you want to thin it without diluting the flavor with additional stock or cream, then the fine strainer is better. You might even do half each way, and combine them.

Notice how a soup changes as it waits before being served. Vegetable purees will thicken if they sit for one or two days and may require some additional stock; soups that are perfectly seasoned when hot can taste bland after they have been chilled. Each time you prepare a soup recipe, you will become more familiar with its special qualities and better able to improvise. You may want to substitute vegetables, herbs, or garnishes, or add more stock than the recipe calls for. You have the freedom to experiment.

Give some thought to how much body you want your soup to have. Chunky vegetable soups like pistou and Garbure are hearty and need no thickening, and soups made with starchy vegetables such as yams and split peas thicken themselves. But when I create pureed soups with asparagus or broccoli, I add some cream to give body and silky texture, as well as to make the flavors a little more subtle and rich. Since only a cup or less is divided among four to eight servings of soup, it's a forgivable indulgence.

Of course before you can make a perfect soup or consommé, you must begin with a really flavorful, well-rounded stock. The best stocks are made by cooking poultry, fish, or meat bones, shellfish shells and bodies, or vegetables in water with aromatic vegetables and then straining out the solids. For brown stocks, the bones and vegetables are first roasted, to give the stock deeper color and taste. A weak stock will give you a weak result, so don't cut corners on this step. My stocks are made without any salt, allowing you to add them to your dishes and then season the final product with total control. If you do find it necessary to substitute canned broth for homemade, make sure it is low-salt broth.

Garnishes

You'll note that most of the soups in this chapter feature a substantial garnish of some kind to add the final level of flavor and introduce a textural counterpoint. It may be a small mound of diced blanched vegetables, cooked shellfish, or some sautéed mushrooms; any of these will dress up a bowl of soup. In addition to making soup more visually interesting, garnishes like these add needed texture to a creamy puree—that's why croutons are so appetizing with a dense pea soup. I often place the garnishes in the bowl first and ladle the soup around them, but when I have a nice seared garnish, such as scallops, I prefer to drop it in just before serving so that it doesn't get too coated by the soup. Creamy garnishes, such as crème fraîche, are best floated on top of each serving. Have your garnishes at room temperature, so they don't cool the soup. If spoilage is a concern, as with lobster or crabmeat, keep them refrigerated until 30 minutes before serving time. The garnish is the showpiece of your soup, so take care with its appearance, but you don't need a lot; a piece of vegetable cut into a few thin slices or pretty shapes will do. And don't use anything so strong that it will overpower the soup's main ingredient.

Soups are naturals to prepare ahead because they keep well in the refrigerator, to be reheated when you are ready to serve. Before serving hot soups, it is a good idea to heat the bowls in a 200° F. oven for 5 minutes. For cold soups, chill the bowls in the refrigerator or freezer at least an hour, or even overnight.

All the soups in this chapter cook in under an hour, but they don't cook in fifteen minutes. Too long a cooking time produces a dull-looking soup; yet if it's not cooked long enough, the soup might look good and bright, but it will lack depth of flavor. As in any recipe, your goal should be to balance flavor and appearance.

STOCK

Stocks give body and flavor to soups and make good foundations for delicious sauces. They are an invaluable ingredient of pan sauces, which are made from only cooking juices, seasonings, and stocks. I think they work best when not salted, allowing you to season your sauces and soups more precisely, without any added salt from the stock.

For quick-cooking stocks (duck, chicken, fish), cut vegetables small so they give up their flavors quickly. For longer-cooking stocks (veal, beef, lamb), cut vegetables larger, because their flavors will be extracted over time. Be generous with vegetables, and add extras, such as mushroom stems or parsnips, if you like. But don't include vegetables with very strong flavors, such as bell peppers or broccoli—I don't even use those in vegetable stock.

It is important to skim stocks as they cook, to remove grease and impurities. If you don't, these unwelcome ingredients will cook back into the stock.

METHOD

- Cut ingredients into dice. If making a brown stock, brown the bones in a 450°F. oven about 45 minutes.
- Combine the prepared ingredients with liquid and simmer, skimming as needed, for about 2 hours.
- Strain and cool.

Stocks can be refrigerated up to one week, but no longer. After three days, bring to a boil. Then boil, skim, and cool every two days. If not using immediately, freeze in small containers, so you can defrost just enough for each use.

FISH STOCK

MAKES 1 QUART

Cut all the vegetables into small dice, because this stock cooks quickly. Don't allow it to cook longer than specified below; if cooked too long, it develops an overly fishy taste. I often mix Fish Stock with an equal amount of Chicken Stock for poaching fish (see Poached Salmon with Lemon Butter Sauce, page 190), as I find fish stock alone is a little too strong.

3 pounds fish bones from lean white
    fish (snapper, bass, or flounder)
2 tablespoons butter
1 leek, cleaned and cut into 1-inch
    pieces, both white and green parts
1 medium onion, cut into small dice
4 stalks celery, cut into small dice

½ head garlic, unpeeled, halved
    crosswise
1 small bunch thyme
1 small bunch parsley, stems only
1 teaspoon black peppercorns
2 cups white wine
4 cups water

Place the fish bones in a large bowl and rinse under cold running water until the water in the bowl is clear. Drain well.

In a large pot over medium heat, melt the butter. Add the leek, onion, celery, and garlic, and sauté until softened but not browned, 5 to 6 minutes. Add the thyme, parsley, peppercorns, and bones, cover, and cook over low heat for 10 minutes.

Remove the cover and add the wine and water. Raise the heat to high and bring to a boil; reduce the heat to medium and simmer 40 minutes, skimming occasionally. Strain through a fine strainer, pushing down on the solids to extract all the liquid.

Cool to room temperature, then refrigerate up to 1 week. After 3 days, bring to a boil. Then boil, skim, and cool every 2 days; or freeze.

VEGETABLE STOCK

MAKES ABOUT 1½ QUARTS

When you are making a completely vegetarian dish, this is the stock of choice, with a pronounced vegetable and herb flavor. It is a good substitute for chicken or fish stock in other recipes, as well.

3 celery stalks, cut into ½-inch slices

1 clove garlic, unpeeled, halved crosswise

1 medium onion, cut into medium dice

10 ounces domestic mushrooms (about 24), quartered

1 small bunch parsley, stems and leaves

1 small bunch thyme, stems and leaves

1 small bunch tarragon, stems and leaves

1 bay leaf

1 teaspoon black peppercorns

3 parsnips, ends removed but not peeled, cut into medium dice

3 carrots, cut into medium dice

Place all the ingredients in a large pot or stockpot and cover with 3 to 4 quarts of cold water. Bring to a boil over high heat, then reduce the heat to medium and simmer for 2 hours, or until a good vegetable flavor is achieved. Strain through a fine strainer, pushing down on the solids to extract all the liquid. Cool to room temperature and refrigerate or freeze.

CHICKEN STOCK

MAKES 2 QUARTS

This is essential for use in soups, sauces, and grain, meat, fish, and poultry dishes, and is very easy to make. When you prepare whole chicken, cut off and freeze the wing tips, backs, and necks for stock; likewise, freeze the carcass when you remove breasts and legs from a whole bird.

3 pounds chicken parts, including backs and necks, rinsed well in cold running water

3 stalks celery, cut into medium dice

1 clove garlic, halved

2 carrots, cut into medium dice

1 bay leaf

1 teaspoon black peppercorns

3 quarts water

Place all the ingredients in a stockpot or large pot over high heat and bring to a boil, skimming the top. Reduce the heat to medium and simmer 2 to 2½ hours, skimming occasionally, until a good chicken flavor is achieved.

Strain through a fine strainer, pushing down on the solids to extract all the liquid, and skim any grease off the top. Cool to room temperature, then refrigerate until the fat solidifies, and lift it off the soup. Refrigerate up to 1 week. After 3 days, bring to a boil. Then boil, skim, and cool every 2 days; or freeze.

DUCK STOCK

MAKES 3¼ CUPS

A base of chicken stock simmered with duck bones, neck, and gizzard makes a double-strength stock with a strong, full flavor that's perfect for pan sauces. When you make roasted duck (see page 210), freeze the necks and gizzards for stock, and freeze the carcass after you have removed the breasts and legs for other recipes.

1 teaspoon pure olive oil
Bones, neck, and gizzard from one
    5- to 6-pound duck
½ medium onion, cut into small dice
2 stalks celery, cut into small dice
2 medium carrots, scraped and cut
    into small dice

1 bay leaf
½ teaspoon black peppercorns
1 cup red wine
2 cups Chicken Stock (page 72) or
    low-salt canned chicken broth
2 cups water

In a large pot, heat the olive oil over medium-high heat until smoking and sear the duck bones until golden brown. Add the onion, celery, and carrots and sauté 2 to 3 minutes. Add the bay leaf, peppercorns, wine, stock, and water and bring to a boil.

Reduce the heat to medium and simmer for 45 minutes, stirring occasionally and skimming. Strain, cool to room temperature, then refrigerate until the fat solidifies and lift it off the soup. Refrigerate up to 1 week. After 3 days, bring to a boil. Then boil, skim, and cool every 2 days; or freeze.

VEAL STOCK

MAKES 2 QUARTS

Veal Stock is a deep brown color, with more body than chicken stock. It is wonderful for flavoring rich sauces like the one accompanying seared and roasted duck breasts (see page 202), lending a special complexity and depth. For a brown stock like this one, the bones are browned in the oven before they are cooked in liquid.

For lamb or beef stock, substitute lamb or beef bones.

8 pounds veal bones
2 medium onions, cut into medium dice
4 medium carrots, cut into medium dice
4 stalks celery, cut into medium dice
1 head garlic, halved crosswise
½ cup tomato paste
1 bay leaf
1 teaspoon black peppercorns

Preheat the oven to 450° F.

Arrange the bones in 1 layer in a large roasting pan or 2 smaller pans and roast 45 minutes. Add the remaining ingredients and roast, turning every 10 minutes or so, until the bones and vegetables are golden brown, another 30 to 45 minutes.

With a large spoon or tongs, transfer the bones and vegetables to a stockpot. Pour off any fat from the roasting pan, add 2 to 3 cups water to the pan, and scrape up browned particles from the bottom.

Pour the liquid into the stockpot over the bones and vegetables and add water as needed to cover them by 3 inches. Bring to a boil over high heat; then reduce the heat to medium and simmer 4 to 5 hours, skimming frequently. When done, the stock will have full flavor and color.

Strain through a fine sieve into a large pot and reduce over high heat until 2 quarts remain. Cool to room temperature, then refrigerate until the fat solidifies, and lift it off the soup. Refrigerate up to 1 week. After 3 days, bring to a boil. Then boil, skim, and cool every 2 days; or freeze.

LOBSTER STOCK

MAKES ABOUT 6 QUARTS

Lobster stock is one of the more time-consuming stocks in my repertoire, but it makes an incomparably rich, delicious base for elegant soups and sauces such as Lobster Consommé (page 76) and Lobster Vinaigrette (page 25). Collect and freeze raw lobster bodies until you have enough to make stock; fishmongers and restaurants are good sources. You'll be surprised how many uses you'll find for this most luxurious of stocks once you have it on hand.

For shrimp stock, substitute 5 to 6 cups of shrimp shells for the lobster bodies; collect and freeze the shells each time you cook shrimp.

1 tablespoon vegetable oil
4 or 5 lobster bodies, split (available from a fishmonger)
2 stalks celery, cut into small dice
1 medium carrot, cut into small dice
1 medium onion, cut into small dice

2 medium tomatoes, cut into small dice
2 sprigs tarragon
2 sprigs dill
1 bunch cilantro
6 quarts Chicken Stock (page 72) or low-salt canned chicken broth

In a large shallow pan, heat the oil over medium-high heat until it is fragrant and shimmering. Add the lobster shells and sauté until they are golden brown. Add the celery, carrot, and onion and sauté 1 minute.

Keep everything in the shallow pan if it can accommodate the stock, or transfer the browned vegetables and shells and any particles from the bottom of the pan to a large pot or stockpot. Add the tomatoes, herbs, and chicken stock, stirring well.

Reduce the heat to medium and simmer 15 minutes. Strain through a chinois or fine strainer. Cool to room temperature, then refrigerate up to 1 week. After 3 days, bring to a boil. Then boil, skim, and cool every 2 days; or freeze.

CONSOMMÉ

Consommé is stock that has been fortified and clarified. To turn stock into consommé, simmer it with finely chopped vegetables and some egg whites, fish, or beef, to absorb its impurities. (I bend the rules and clarify all my consommés with beef, which adds the richest flavor and color.) As the protein and vegetables cook, they rise to the top and form a floating "raft." When the raft is removed the impurities go with it, leaving only the pure consommé.

Consommé always starts with double-strength stock. You can reduce any stock, such as chicken or duck stock, by half and clarify it using the method below.

As the stock boils:

- adjust the heat so you don't get a rapid boil that breaks up the raft
- bring the stock up to a slight boil
- pull it off the stove for a few seconds, then return it to the heat
- if necessary, poke a hole through the side or top of the raft so the stock can bubble through

LOBSTER CONSOMMÉ

MAKES 4 TO 6 SERVINGS

ORDER OF PREPARATION

- Prepare and clarify the consommé.
- Chill and degrease the consommé.
- Reheat the consommé and prepare the garnish.

This consommé is clear and very rich, with a deep amber color and sweet lobster taste. Since it takes some time and effort, it is a good idea to make 1 large batch and freeze it in small portions. It freezes well and is a good thing to have on hand to serve as an elegant first course, and to use in sauce or vinaigrette.

To make an excellent sauce for 4 to 6 portions of fish, reduce ³/₄ cup of Lobster Consommé by half over medium-high heat. Remove from the heat and whisk in 3 teaspoons of cold butter.

4 quarts Lobster Stock (page 75)

3 egg whites

1 pound lean ground beef

1 medium carrot, peeled, finely ground in a food processor

1 medium leek, white part only, finely ground in a food processor

1 medium onion, peeled, finely ground in a food processor

2 sprigs tarragon, minced

2 sprigs dill, minced

2 sprigs cilantro, minced

6 ounces tomato juice

1 teaspoon kosher salt

½ teaspoon freshly ground white pepper

In a large pot, bring the stock to a boil over medium-high heat. Continue to cook until reduced by half, 50 minutes to 1 hour. Cool to room temperature and then refrigerate until cold.

Combine all the ingredients except the lobster stock in a large, heavy pot and whisk well. Slowly pour in the stock while whisking. Place the pot over low heat and do not disturb. The solids will slowly rise to the top and become firm, forming a raft that clarifies the stock. Allow the stock to simmer about 30 minutes without coming to a boil.

Line a chinois or fine strainer with a double thickness of cheesecloth and place it over a large bowl. Gently ladle the consommé into the strainer (it may be necessary to create a hole in the raft to reach the liquid). Discard the raft.

Taste and reseason, if necessary. Allow the consommé to cool to room temperature and refrigerate it for several hours or even overnight to allow all the fat to congeal. The next day, restrain through cheesecloth to remove any congealed fat. Refrigerate up to 1 week. After 3 days, bring to a boil. Then boil, skim, and cool every 2 days; or freeze.

TO SERVE

About ½ cup sautéed wild mushrooms, thin-sliced raw vegetables, or cooked lobster

Over medium-high heat, reheat the consommé. Ladle into warm bowls and garnish.

Soupe au Pistou and Garbure are classic French examples of chunky vegetable soups. Because they are loaded with diced vegetables, they don't require any thickening or garnish. Pistou is the more versatile of the two: you can add any fish or shellfish, such as snapper or lobster, and let the soup act as a sparkling, vegetable-rich sauce. If you want a more careful presentation, skim out the vegetables, arrange them in the bowl, and ladle the broth around them. The more rustic Garbure is simply served as it comes from the pot.

SOUPE AU PISTOU

MAKES 8 SERVINGS

ORDER OF PREPARATION

- Soak the beans overnight, if desired.
- Dice and blanch the vegetables.
- Prepare the soup.
- While the soup is simmering, prepare the pesto.

*B*eans, squash, tomatoes, carrots, and leeks, uniformly diced and bathed in glistening stock, give this soup appealing color and flavor. The vegetables, which comprise about two thirds of the soup, will be cooked through, but will retain their bright color and fresh taste. A heaping tablespoon of garlicky, green pesto stirred into each bowl just before serving provides extra flavor.

Pistou doesn't require a lot of technique. Dicing the vegetables is the most time-consuming part of the recipe, but the most important because it ensures a beautiful dish. Once the vegetables are ready to go in the pot, the cooking is simple and quick.

FOR THE SOUP

2 tablespoons olive oil

1 tablespoon finely chopped garlic (about 4 cloves)

½ cup dried white beans, soaked overnight and drained

1½ quarts Chicken Stock (page 72) or low-salt canned chicken broth

¼ cup fresh fava, lima, or string beans, blanched and cooled

1 cup zucchini, cut into small dice (3 medium zucchini)

1 cup yellow squash, cut into small dice (3 medium squash)

½ cup skinned and seeded tomato, cut into small dice (1 medium-size tomato)

½ cup peeled carrot, cut into small dice (1 medium carrot)

½ cup leek, white part only, cut into thin half-moon slices (2 medium leeks)

Kosher salt and freshly ground black pepper

In a medium pot, heat the olive oil over medium-high heat until just warm. Add the garlic and sauté for 1 minute, taking care that it does not burn. Add the presoaked white beans and stock, reduce the heat to medium, and cook until the beans are tender, 20 to 30 minutes. Add the remaining vegetables and cook until tender, about 6 minutes. Season to taste with salt and pepper.

TO SERVE

½ cup Basil Pesto (page 26), at room
temperature

Add 1 tablespoon of pesto to each serving of soup and stir. Serve in a warm bowl.

MAKE-AHEAD NOTES

❧ The beans can be soaked overnight.

❧ The vegetables can be diced and blanched up to 48 hours in advance.

❧ The pesto can be made up to a week ahead of time; brush the top lightly with oil, cover, and refrigerate or freeze.

❧ The soup itself can be refrigerated up to 3 days or frozen for about 1 month; reheat over medium heat.

VARIATION

For a more elegant and substantial presentation, add 2 cups seared bay scallops or shrimp (see page 90) or cooked lobster meat (see page 192); skim the vegetables from the pistou onto the center of a plate and arrange the lobster meat around them. Then add the pesto to the broth and spoon that over the lobster. Or just put lobster in a bowl and ladle the pistou over it.

GARBURE

*T*hick with potatoes and beans and flavored with sausage and smoked ham, this is a satisfying, hearty soup. It is a meal in itself and can be served with just some bread and salad, or served in small portions as an appetizer.

It will be about two-thirds vegetables and one-third liquid, but you may add more stock if you want to—there are no rigid rules about the proper balance. You can vary the amounts of vegetables or omit those you are less partial to.

Soak the beans or not and they will cook well either way— they will just take a little longer without soaking. However, if you prepare the other vegetables ahead for cooking (see below), it is easy to soak the beans ahead, as well.

For kielbasa, substitute turkey sausage.

2 tablespoons olive oil

2 teaspoons minced garlic (about 4 cloves)

2½ quarts Chicken Stock (page 72) or low-salt canned chicken broth

⅔ cup dried white beans

½ cup thin half-moon slices of carrots (2 medium carrots)

½ cup medium-diced potato (1 small potato)

¼ cup thin half-moon slices of leek, white part only (1 medium leek)

⅓ cup thin half-moon slices of kielbasa (about ¼ pound)

⅓ cup medium-diced smoked ham (from a ½-inch-thick slice)

⅔ cup medium-diced Savoy cabbage

Kosher salt and freshly ground black pepper

In a large soup pot over medium-high heat, heat the oil until just warmed. Add the garlic and sauté until softened, taking care that it does not burn. Reduce the heat to medium, add the chicken stock and beans, and simmer until the beans are tender, 20 to 30 minutes. Add the carrots and potato and cook until tender, about 10 minutes. Add the leeks, kielbasa, ham, and cabbage. Simmer 10 minutes and season to taste. Serve in a warm bowl.

MAKE-AHEAD NOTES

- The beans can be soaked overnight.
- The vegetables can be sliced and refrigerated up to 48 hours in advance.
- The finished soup may be cooled to room temperature and refrigerated up to 3 days; reheat over medium heat.

SPLIT PEA SOUP

ORDER OF
PREPARATION
• Prepare the soup.
• While the soup sim-
  mers, fry the croutons
  and make the garnish.

*R*ich *with sweet root vegetables, thick, and deep green, this is a stick-to-your-ribs soup. For real old-fashioned flavor, replace the bacon with a ham hock (ask your butcher to cut it in chunks) and sauté, then add the diced vegetables. After cooking, cut off any meat that remains on the ham hock and add it to the strained soup.*

1 teaspoon vegetable oil	1 teaspoon whole black peppercorns
4 slices bacon, cut into ½-inch pieces	1½ cups green split peas
2 medium onions, cut into small dice	5 to 5½ cups Chicken Stock (page 72)
2 medium carrots, peeled and cut into	or low-salt canned chicken broth
small dice	Kosher salt and freshly ground black
3 stalks celery, cut into small dice	pepper
1 bay leaf	

In a medium to large saucepan over medium-high heat, heat the oil until shimmering. Add the bacon and sauté 1 minute. Add the diced vegetables, bay leaf, and peppercorns and sauté until the onions are transparent, 5 to 8 minutes. Add the peas and stock, raise the heat to high, and bring to a boil. Reduce the heat to medium and simmer until the peas are tender, about 1 hour. Remove the bay leaf and puree the soup in a blender. Strain through a medium-mesh strainer and season with salt and pepper.

TO SERVE

2 tablespoons butter	¼ cup smoked ham, cut into small
3 slices good-quality white bread or	dice
brioche, cut into 1-inch dice	

In a medium skillet over medium heat, melt the butter and sauté the bread, shaking the pan frequently, until browned on all sides. Divide the ham and croutons among 8 warm bowls and ladle the hot soup over them.

MAKE-AHEAD NOTES

ᴥ Cool the soup to room temperature and refrigerate up to 3 days or freeze; reheat over medium heat.

ᴥ The croutons can be fried and stored at room temperature in an airtight container for up to 3 days.

Soups made from vegetables cooked in stock until very tender and then pureed are soothing and satisfying, and each has its own particular flavor and personality. Those made from starchy vegetables such as legumes, root vegetables, or winter squash have a substantial and pleasing texture even without the addition of cream. Some thicken naturally on their own, while others may require pureeing and straining to ensure a smooth quality.

Sweet cream or its tart cousin, crème fraîche, add smoothness and rich flavor to soups made with vegetables such as yams, sweet potatoes, and white potatoes, and gives pureed vegetables, such as broccoli or asparagus, silkiness and body. A moderate amount—a cup or less—is enough for 6 to 8 servings of soup. These are updated, more healthful versions of the traditional French veloutés, soups enriched with egg yolks as well as cream. The primary flavors here come from the vegetables, balanced by light stocks.

METHOD

- ❧ Simmer the vegetables until tender.
- ❧ Puree in a blender (it makes a much smoother soup than a food processor does). Or use a hand-held blender to puree the soup in the pot.
- ❧ Strain the soup to achieve the desired texture.
- ❧ If using cream, add before or after pureeing, depending on the recipe.

CREAMLESS BUTTERNUT SQUASH SOUP WITH PAN-ROASTED CHESTNUTS

MAKES 6 SERVINGS

ORDER OF PREPARATION

- Roast the squash.
- Prepare the soup.
- While the soup cooks, blanch and toast the chestnuts.

*W*hen homemade soup is as easy as this, it doesn't pay to buy soup in cans! This perfect fall soup is smooth, with a beautiful orange color and a crunchy garnish of buttery chestnuts. Roasting brings out the slightly sweet flavor of butternut squash, which is enhanced by the nutmeg-like mace and sweet sautéed onions.

Because butternut squash is delicately flavored, this soup needs to be well seasoned. Depending on your stock, you may need to adjust the amount of salt and pepper up or down, so taste carefully.

For Chicken Stock, substitute Vegetable Stock (page 72) or low-salt canned vegetable broth.

1 medium butternut squash, halved and seeded

2 tablespoons butter

2 medium onions, thinly sliced

$\frac{1}{2}$ teaspoon ground mace

5$\frac{1}{2}$ cups Chicken Stock (page 72) or low-salt canned chicken broth

Kosher salt and freshly ground black pepper

Preheat the oven to 400° F.

Place the squash cut-side up on a baking sheet and bake until fork tender, about 50 minutes. Scoop out the pulp; there should be about 4 cups.

In a medium saucepan, melt the butter over low to medium heat. Add the onions, and cook until light golden brown, about 10 minutes. Add the squash, mace, and stock, raise the heat to high, and bring to a boil. Reduce the heat to medium and simmer until the squash is tender. Puree in a blender or in the pot, using a hand-held blender. Strain through a medium to coarse strainer. Taste and season with salt and pepper.

TO SERVE

12 chestnuts

1$\frac{1}{2}$ tablespoons butter

Cut a small $\times$ on the flat side of each chestnut. Place in a medium saucepan over high heat, cover with cold water, and bring to a boil. Blanch the nuts until softened a bit, 3$\frac{1}{2}$ to 4 minutes; if they feel very hard, boil 1 to 2 minutes more. Remove 2 or 3 from the water and peel off the shell, using a sharp knife or your fingers. Repeat with the remaining nuts.

In a small skillet over medium heat, melt the butter and cook the chestnuts until golden. Remove to paper towels and when cooled, chop into small pieces.

Divide the hot soup among 6 warm bowls and garnish each with 1 to 2 tablespoons of chopped chestnuts.

MAKE-AHEAD NOTES

∞ Slice the squash and onions and refrigerate up to 1 day in advance.

∞ Roast the squash and refrigerate up to 2 days in advance.

∞ Cool the soup to room temperature and refrigerate up to 3 days or freeze; reheat over medium heat.

∞ Prepare the chestnut garnish and refrigerate up to 2 days in advance.

SPICED SQUASH SOUP
WITH CARAMELIZED APPLES

MAKES 6 SERVINGS

**ORDER OF
PREPARATION**
- Prepare the soup.
- While the soup is sim-
  mering, toast the
  pumpkin seeds.
- Prepare the
  caramelized apples.

*I*n Indian restaurants, you often find pumpkin and squash cooked with curry and turmeric—the combination that inspired this unique soup. It is a sharp rust-orange color, with an apple garnish reminiscent of the apples that are served to cool hot curries. These aren't classic French flavors, but they offer another way to treat a time-honored combination of vegetables.

Squash pairs well with many different flavors because it doesn't have a strong flavor of its own. It can be cooked in stock, as in this recipe, or roasted to enhance its mild taste, as in the recipe that follows.

FOR THE SOUP

2 tablespoons butter	1 teaspoon good-quality curry powder
1 medium onion, cut into medium dice	(such as Madras)
2 medium carrots, scraped and cut into medium dice	½ teaspoon ground turmeric
	1½ pounds butternut or buttercup squash, peeled, seeded, and cut into 1- to 2-inch dice
1 stalk celery, cut into medium dice	6 cups Chicken Stock (page 72) or
1 clove garlic, thinly sliced	low-salt canned chicken broth
1 bay leaf	

In a medium saucepan, melt the butter over medium heat and add the onion, carrots, celery, and garlic. Sauté until the onion is transparent, 5 to 8 minutes. Add the bay leaf, curry powder, and turmeric and sauté 30 seconds. Add the diced squash and chicken stock, raise the heat to high, and bring to a boil. Reduce the heat to medium and simmer until the squash is very tender, about 20 minutes.

FOR THE APPLES

To dice apples, peel and cut off the 4 sides around the core; then cut each side into small dice.

2 teaspoons butter	2 teaspoons light brown sugar
2 medium Granny Smith apples, peeled, cored, and diced small	

In a medium sauté pan over medium heat, heat the butter until it begins to bubble. Add the apples, sprinkle with the brown sugar, and sauté until the apples soften and caramelize, 1 to 2 minutes. Strain through a medium to coarse strainer and keep warm.

TO SERVE

2 tablespoons pumpkin seeds
(optional)

You can substitute pur-chased toasted pumpkin seeds to save a step.

Spread the pumpkin seeds in one layer on a lightly oiled or oil-sprayed baking sheet and put into a preheated 350° F. oven until browned on both sides, 8 to 10 minutes. Divide the diced apples among 6 warm bowls and ladle the hot soup over them. Sprinkle with toasted pumpkin seeds, if desired.

MAKE-AHEAD NOTES

 Cool the soup to room temperature, then refrigerate up to 3 days or freeze; reheat over medium heat.

 The caramelized apples can be refrigerated for up to 1 day.

PUMPKIN AND YAM SOUP
WITH SPICED CRÈME FRAÎCHE

MAKES 3 QUARTS, OR 12 SERVINGS

ORDER OF PREPARATION

- Prepare the soup.
- Prepare the spiced crème fraîche.

A*great soup for fall—almost a subtle take on pumpkin pie—this combines the deep flavor of yams with the lighter vegetable taste of pumpkin. It has a burnished orange color, and the subtle hint of cinnamon is reinforced by a spicy crème fraîche garnish.*

FOR THE SPICED CRÈME FRAÎCHE

½ cup Crème Fraîche (page 39)
⅛ teaspoon ground cloves
⅛ teaspoon ground ginger
⅛ teaspoon ground cinnamon

Combine the crème fraîche, cloves, ginger, and cinnamon in a small bowl, beat until the mixture forms stiff peaks, and reserve.

FOR THE SOUP

Make with all yams and no pumpkin or all or part butternut squash.

Delete the Crème Fraîche for a less rich soup.

1½ pounds yams (about 3 medium), peeled and cut into 1½-inch cubes
1¾ pounds peeled pumpkin, cut into 1½-inch cubes (see page xv)
8 cups Chicken Stock (page 72) or low-salt canned chicken broth, plus an extra 2 cups, if needed

¼ teaspoon ground cinnamon
¼ teaspoon grated nutmeg
1½ cups Crème Fraîche or heavy cream, heated to just below boiling
Kosher salt and freshly ground black pepper

In the pot, the stock should cover the vegetables by about 1½ inches. Yams thicken the soup (pumpkin alone wouldn't do it) and no other thickener is needed.

Place the yams and pumpkin in a large pot over medium-high heat, cover with 8 cups of the chicken stock, and bring to a boil. Reduce the heat to medium, cover, and simmer until tender, about 45 minutes.

Pour the cooked vegetables and stock into a food processor or blender and puree until it has the consistency of heavy cream. Strain through a fine strainer and return to the saucepan. Add the spices, heated crème fraîche, and additional stock if needed to thin. Season with salt and pepper and serve immediately, garnished with a dollop of spiced crème fraîche.

MAKE-AHEAD NOTES

❧ Crème Fraîche can be refrigerated up to 10 days, or substitute a good-quality purchased crème fraîche.

❧ The spiced crème fraîche can be refrigerated up to 24 hours.

❧ The soup can be refrigerated up to 3 days; do not freeze.

SWEET-POTATO VICHYSSOISE

Sweet potatoes, stock, and cream make a pale orange soup with a clear sweet-potato flavor. It has an earthy undertone of onions and leeks that is discernible but not strong enough to overwhelm the potatoes. This soup is served chilled.

After you have made this soup once or twice and have become familiar with the proportion of vegetables to stock, you will almost be able to make it without a recipe.

A hot soup will taste different after it has been chilled, and cooling the soup makes the salt and pepper less potent, so always reseason after chilling.

Light cream or half-and-half can be substituted for the heavy cream.

To make a classic vichyssoise, substitute white potatoes for sweet.

2 tablespoons butter
6 leeks, white part only, cleaned, halved lengthwise, and cut into ¼-inch half-moon slices
4 medium to large sweet potatoes, peeled and cut into medium dice
1½ quarts Chicken Stock (page 72) or low-salt canned chicken broth, plus an extra ½ cup, if needed

1 cup heavy cream
Kosher salt and freshly ground black pepper
Minced chives, for garnish

In a medium saucepan, melt the butter over low to medium heat. Add the leeks and sweat until soft and wilted but not colored, about 12 minutes. Add the sweet potatoes and stock and bring the mixture to a boil over high heat.

Lower the heat to medium and simmer until the sweet potatoes are tender, 20 to 25 minutes. Add the cream, raise the heat to medium-high, and bring to a boil. Reduce the heat slightly and simmer 2 minutes, skimming if necessary.

Pour into a blender, or keep in the pot and use a hand-held blender, and blend well. Strain through a medium or coarse strainer. Add the extra stock if the soup seems too thick. Taste and season with salt and pepper. Cool to room temperature, then refrigerate until well chilled.

Before serving, reseason and garnish with minced chives. Serve chilled.

MAKE-AHEAD NOTE

The soup can be refrigerated up to 3 days; do not freeze.

POTATO AND LEEK SOUP WITH WILD MUSHROOMS

MAKES 8 SERVINGS

ORDER OF PREPARATION
- Prepare the wild mushroom garnish.
- Prepare the soup.

Hints of other flavors elevate the classic vichyssoise combination of potatoes, leeks, and cream in this pale white soup. Mushrooms enrich the flavor even further and are echoed by a bit of mushroom in the garnish. The soup contains just enough bacon to add a slightly smoky dimension. Pureeing and adding some cream give it a rich texture.

The soup also is delicious served chilled, without the mushroom garnish. Remember to taste and reseason when it is cold—you may add some salt and pepper.

FOR THE WILD MUSHROOM GARNISH

Kosher salt

3 leeks, green part only, cleaned and cut on the diagonal into ¼-inch slices

1 tablespoon butter

12 wild mushroom caps (such as shiitake or chanterelles), halved if they are large (reserve the stems for the soup)

Freshly ground black pepper

Fill a medium saucepan three-quarters full of water, add 2 teaspoons salt, and bring to a boil over high heat. Blanch the leeks until tender, about 30 seconds. Cool in a bowl of ice water and drain.

In a medium sauté pan over medium-high heat, melt the butter. When it begins to bubble, add the mushroom caps and sauté until tender. Season with salt and pepper, add the drained leek greens, and toss to heat through. Drain.

FOR THE POTATO AND LEEK SOUP

For cream, substitute light cream or half-and-half.

For bacon, substitute 2 to 3 tablespoons butter.

3 strips bacon, cut into 1-inch pieces

1 tablespoon butter

4 to 6 leeks, white part only, cleaned, halved lengthwise, and cut into ¼-inch half-moon slices

Stems of 12 wild mushrooms

4 medium Idaho potatoes, peeled and cut into medium dice

1½ quarts Chicken Stock (page 72) or low-salt canned chicken broth, plus an extra ½ cup, if needed

1 cup heavy cream

Kosher salt and freshly ground black pepper

Place a large soup pot over medium-high heat until hot, about 2 minutes. Add the bacon and render until golden brown, about 2 minutes. Reduce the heat to low, add the butter, and melt.

Raise the heat to medium, add the leeks and mushroom stems, and sweat until softened but not colored, about 8 minutes. Raise the heat to high, bring to a boil, and add the potatoes and stock.

Reduce the heat to medium and simmer until the potatoes are tender, about 20 minutes. Add the heavy cream, raise the heat to high, and bring to a boil. Reduce the heat slightly and simmer 2 minutes, skimming if necessary. In a blender or in the pot using a hand-held blender, puree well and season with salt and pepper, then strain through a coarse strainer. If the soup is too thick at this point, bring the extra stock to a boil and add it.

TO SERVE

Place a spoonful of the mushroom garnish in the bottom of a large soup plate. Ladle the hot soup over the garnish and serve hot.

MAKE-AHEAD NOTES

∞ The mushrooms can be refrigerated up to 2 days.

∞ The soup can be cooled to room temperature, then refrigerated up to 3 days and reheated over medium heat; do not freeze.

CELERY ROOT SOUP
WITH SEARED BAY SCALLOPS

MAKES 6 TO 8 SERVINGS

ORDER OF PREPARATION

- Prepare the soup.
- When the soup is almost done, sauté the scallops.

*C*elery root soup is creamy white, with a few darker specks of celery root. The celery root and seeds give it a true celery taste and aroma. Scallops seared to a glistening golden brown are a good textural contrast and have a mildly briny flavor that doesn't dominate the delicate soup.

This root vegetable soup thickens naturally and is then pureed. It should be slightly thinner than heavy cream; thin it with additional stock if necessary. A small amount of cream per serving is an optional addition that enhances the flavor and consistency.

FOR THE SOUP

Place peeled and diced celery root in a bowl of cold water until ready to use, to prevent discoloration.

2 tablespoons butter

3 medium onions, thinly sliced (2 to 2¼ cups firmly packed)

1 teaspoon celery seed

3 medium celery roots (3½ to 4 pounds total), peeled and cut into ½-inch dice

1½ quarts Chicken Stock (page 72) or low-salt canned chicken broth

1 cup heavy cream (optional)

Kosher salt and freshly ground black pepper

In a medium pot, melt the butter over medium-high heat and add the onions and celery seed. Sauté until the onion has softened but not colored, 8 to 10 minutes, and add the celery roots. Reduce the heat to medium, add the chicken stock, and simmer until the celery roots are tender, about 30 minutes. Add the optional cream and simmer an additional 10 minutes.

Pour the soup into a blender and puree. Strain through a medium strainer and season to taste with salt and pepper. If serving immediately, keep warm over very low heat. If serving later, cool to room temperature and refrigerate.

FOR THE SEARED SCALLOPS

1 tablespoon olive oil

1 pound bay scallops

Kosher salt and freshly ground black pepper

The scallops will not brown if they touch in the pan; do in 2 batches, if necessary.

In a large skillet over medium-high heat, heat the oil until very hot but not smoking. Season the scallops with salt and pepper and sauté, shaking the pan frequently, until colored, about 1 minute.

TO SERVE

2 to 3 teaspoons chopped parsley

For the garnish, substitute 1/2 cup diced blanched celery root or 1/2 cup diced seared shrimp.

Pour the soup into warm bowls. Garnish the soup with the scallops and sprinkle with the chopped parsley.

MAKE-AHEAD NOTES

The soup can be refrigerated up to 3 days; reheat over medium heat. Do not freeze if cream has been added.

The scallops can be sautéed a few minutes ahead; keep warm.

To make croutons, cut 3 slices good-quality white bread or brioche into 1/2-inch dice. In a medium skillet over medium heat, melt 2 tablespoons butter and sauté the bread, shaking the pan frequently, until browned on all sides.

ASPARAGUS SOUP WITH MORELS

MAKES 8 SERVINGS

ORDER OF PREPARATION
- Blanch the asparagus tips.
- Make and puree the soup.
- While the soup is simmering, prepare the morel garnish.

This soup has an attractive pale green color and a fresh asparagus flavor. Both are clear and true because the asparagus is cooked in 2 separate batches: first, a small portion is cooked thoroughly to flavor the stock. Then the remaining asparagus is simmered with cream for just a few minutes, so its green color is preserved. A garnish of earthy morels complements the asparagus taste.

The soup is thickened with small amounts of flour and heavy cream, giving it the consistency of half-and-half.

For asparagus, you can substitute broccoli.

Kosher salt
3 bunches (about 25 stalks each) medium-size asparagus, top 1½ inches cut off (to yield 2½ cups asparagus tips) and stems cut into 1-inch slices
2 tablespoons butter
3 medium onions, sliced thin

3 tablespoons flour
1 sprig thyme
6 cups Chicken Stock (page 72) or low-salt canned chicken broth, plus an extra ½ cup, if needed
½ cup heavy cream
Freshly ground black pepper

In a medium saucepan filled halfway with boiling salted water, blanch the asparagus tips for 1 minute and shock in a bowl of ice water. Halve lengthwise and reserve for garnish. Process the asparagus stems in a food processor until shredded, or cut them into ⅛-inch slices.

In a medium pot over medium heat, melt the butter and sauté the onions until translucent, 5 to 8 minutes. Add ¼ cup of the processed asparagus stems and the flour and cook for 2 minutes, stirring constantly until the flour and vegetables cling together. Raise the heat to medium-high, add the thyme and stock, and bring to a boil, making sure to stir around the bottom of the pot so the vegetables don't stick. Reduce the heat to medium and simmer 15 minutes, skimming, if necessary. Add the remaining shredded or chopped asparagus and the cream and cook 10 to 12 minutes. Taste for doneness: If there is a crunch to those little bits, you need to cook it a couple of minutes more.

Remove the sprig of thyme, pour the soup into a blender in small batches, and puree. The blended soup should have the consistency of half-and-half; thin with the reserved hot chicken stock, if necessary. Strain through a medium strainer and season with salt and pepper.

TO SERVE

For morels, substitute chanterelles or any other flavorful wild mushrooms.

2 tablespoons butter
12 medium or 6 large morels, halved
   lengthwise, tips trimmed if they
   are discolored

Kosher salt and freshly ground black
   pepper

In a small skillet, melt the butter over medium-high heat. Add the morels and sauté until tender, about 5 minutes. Add the reserved asparagus tips and toss until warm. Taste, and season with salt and pepper. Ladle the soup into 8 warm soup bowls and drop the morels and asparagus into the hot soup. Serve immediately.

MAKE-AHEAD NOTES

🍃 The soup can be refrigerated for up to 3 days; reheat over medium heat. Do not freeze.

🍃 The blanched asparagus tips can be refrigerated for up to 3 days.

🍃 The morel garnish can be refrigerated up to 1 day; reheat in a little stock and butter over medium-low heat.

TOMATO SOUP WITH CRÈME FRAÎCHE AND BASIL

MAKES 4 TO 6 SERVINGS

ORDER OF PREPARATION

- Prepare the soup.
- Whip the Crème Fraîche for the garnish.

*M*ake *this soup with the best red, ripe tomatoes you can find—wait for summer, if you have to. The soup has a pale orange color and a rich tomato flavor, with the delicate fragrance and taste of thyme and a harmonizing basil garnish. It is thickened with cream and a little flour, then pureed. It should be somewhat peppery, so add as much pepper as you like.*

2 tablespoons butter
2 medium onions, thinly sliced
1 sprig thyme
1 teaspoon coarsely ground or cracked black pepper
3 tablespoons flour

4 cups Chicken Stock (page 72) or low-salt canned chicken broth, plus 1 cup more, if needed
6 medium-size ripe tomatoes, cut into medium dice
1 cup heavy cream
Kosher salt

In a medium saucepan, melt the butter over low to medium heat. Add the onions and sauté until softened but not colored, 5 to 8 minutes. Add the thyme, black pepper, and flour and cook 2 minutes, stirring constantly.

Raise the heat to high, add the chicken stock, stir well, and bring to a boil. Reduce the heat to medium, add the tomatoes, and simmer, skimming, 30 minutes. Add the heavy cream and simmer another 10 minutes.

The consistency should be slightly thinner than heavy cream; thin it with additional stock, if necessary.

Remove the sprig of thyme, puree the soup in a blender, and strain through a medium strainer. Taste and season with salt and pepper. If serving immediately, keep warm over very low heat. If serving later, allow to cool to room temperature and refrigerate.

TO SERVE

For the garnish, substitute blanched corn kernels or diced, blanched tomatoes, carrots, or peas.

½ cup Crème Fraîche (page 39)
Kosher salt and freshly ground black pepper

4 or 5 large basil leaves, cut in chiffonade

In a small, cold bowl, whip the crème fraîche until it forms stiff peaks and season with salt and pepper. Ladle the soup into warm bowls, garnish each serving with 1 teaspoon whipped crème fraîche, and sprinkle with the basil.

MAKE-AHEAD NOTES

🍂 The Crème Fraîche must be made 60 hours in advance, and can be refrigerated up to 1 week.

🍂 Prepare the soup up to 3 days ahead, and reheat over medium heat; do not freeze.

FRESH PEA SOUP WITH PEARL ONIONS AND CUMIN

MAKES 6 TO 8 SERVINGS

ORDER OF PREPARATION

- Prepare and puree the soup.
- Prepare the onions and keep warm.

A bowl *of this smooth, pale mint-green soup, garnished simply with tiny caramelized onions and finished with a little cream, is beautiful and fragrant. Onions and peas are a classic flavor combination; add some spicy cumin, for an unusual alliance that works very well.*

For purest flavor, I prefer fresh peas to frozen, although sometimes I compromise and combine the two. If you must use some frozen peas in a recipe, they should comprise no more than half the total, and possibly only one quarter.

FOR THE ONIONS

Kosher salt

24 pearl onions, peeled

1 tablespoon butter

1 teaspoon sugar

Freshly ground black pepper

Fill a medium saucepan three-quarters full of water, add 2 teaspoons salt, and bring to a boil over high heat. Add the onions and blanch 1 minute. Remove, drain, and rinse under cold running water. Cut into quarters.

In a medium skillet, heat the butter over medium heat until melted and bubbling. Add the onions and sugar and cook, shaking the pan, until the onions are evenly brown and caramelized, about 8 to 10 minutes. Season lightly with salt and pepper and drain on paper towels.

FOR THE SOUP

2 tablespoons butter

3 medium onions, thinly sliced

2 teaspoons ground cumin, plus a little more, if needed

3 cups fresh peas (from 3 pounds of peas in the pod)

1½ quarts Chicken Stock (page 72) or low-salt canned chicken broth

1 cup heavy cream

Kosher salt and freshly ground black pepper

In a medium saucepan, melt the butter over medium heat. Add the onions and cumin and sweat until the onions are transparent, about 5 minutes.

Add the peas, stock, and cream. Raise the heat to high and boil the soup until the peas are just cooked and tender, 2 to 3 minutes. Blend well in a blender or in the pot, using a hand-held blender, and strain through a coarse strainer. Season with salt and pepper and add more cumin, if necessary.

TO SERVE

For the garnish, substitute blanched fresh peas.

Place the caramelized onions in bowls and ladle the hot soup over, or ladle the soup into bowls and drop the caramelized onions in.

MAKE-AHEAD NOTES

ॐ The soup can be refrigerated up to 3 days and reheated over medium heat, but will be at its best if served the same day. Do not freeze.

ॐ The onion garnish can be refrigerated up to 3 days; reheat gently or microwave to remelt the butter.

CHILLED CUCUMBER SOUP WITH GRILLED SHRIMP AND CAVIAR

MAKES 8 SERVINGS

ORDER OF PREPARATION

- Marinate the shrimp.
- Prepare the soup.
- Grill the shrimp.
- Whip the Crème Fraîche.

*M*int-green and flecked with bits of fresh dill, this creamy, silky soup has a mellow cucumber flavor and an underlying accent of dill. The saltiness of the caviar garnish plays off against these fresh, green flavors, and the entire combination makes a great summer soup. The garnish of grilled shrimp can be room temperature, cold, or hot. As with all cold soups, season when hot and reseason after chilling.

Use unwaxed cucumbers, available at farmers' markets and some greengrocers. If unavailable, substitute European or seedless "gourmet" cucumbers.

FOR THE SHRIMP

6 ounces olive oil	16 large shrimp or prawns, shelled,
Zest of 3 lemons, in strips	deveined, and butterflied
4 tablespoons finely chopped shallots (about 6 shallots)	Kosher salt and freshly ground black pepper
6 tablespoons minced fresh dill fronds	

At least 4 or up to 8 hours before serving, combine the olive oil, lemon zest, shallots, and dill and pour over the shrimp in a shallow container. Cover and refrigerate.

If you are going to grill the shrimp, prepare a wood or charcoal fire and let it burn down to ashes. Just before serving, remove the shrimp from the marinade, season with salt and pepper, and grill until medium rare, about 1 minute on each side. Or heat a heavy skillet over high heat until very hot and sear the shrimp 1 minute on each side. Let the shrimp cool slightly at room temperature and cut into large dice.

FOR THE SOUP

Substitute Vegetable Stock (page 72) for the Chicken Stock, Crème Fraîche (page 39) for the heavy cream.

3 tablespoons unsalted butter	6 cups Chicken Stock (page 72) or
2 medium onions, sliced thin	low-salt canned chicken broth
3 tablespoons flour	$\frac{3}{4}$ cup heavy cream
5 medium cucumbers, peeled (skins reserved) and sliced $\frac{1}{4}$ to $\frac{1}{2}$ inch thick	Kosher salt and freshly ground black pepper
	$\frac{3}{4}$ cup dill fronds, or to taste

Melt the butter in a large, heavy saucepan over medium heat and cook the onions until transparent, 5 to 8 minutes. Add the flour, stirring constantly, and cook 1 minute. Add the cucumber slices and chicken stock, raise the heat to high, and bring to a boil, skimming as needed. Reduce to medium-high and cook 30 to 45 minutes. Add the cream, simmer 5 minutes, and season with salt and pepper. Add the cucumber peels and dill and simmer 2 minutes.

Puree the soup in a blender. Pass through a medium strainer and refrigerate until thoroughly chilled. When the soup is cold, taste and reseason.

TO SERVE

Substitute smoked salmon for the shrimp and caviar garnish.

½ cup Crème Fraîche (page 39), optional

4 tablespoons salmon caviar
Dill sprigs

With a wire whisk, whip the crème fraîche until it forms stiff peaks. Divide the soup among 8 chilled bowls and garnish each with 2 diced shrimp and a small dollop of the optional crème fraîche, topped with a teaspoon of the caviar and a sprig of dill.

MAKE-AHEAD NOTES

๛ You can prepare the Crème Fraîche 2½ days or up to 1 week in advance.

๛ The shrimp can be marinated for up to 8 hours before cooking, and can be grilled 1 day in advance and refrigerated; return to room temperature.

๛ The soup can be refrigerated up to 3 days; do not freeze.

To cool the soup quickly:

๛ pour into a container;

๛ fill the sink with ice and water and immerse the soup, stirring occasionally.

MUSSEL AND SAFFRON SOUP WITH CRABMEAT

MAKES 6 SERVINGS

*T*he mussel cooking liquid gives an extra layer of flavor to this aromatic and intensely flavored soup. A medium strainer leaves it with a slightly textured consistency—the minuscule mussel bits that go through the mesh are just enough to give it body. The finished soup will have the thickness of half-and-half and a luscious golden color.

2 pounds cultivated mussels, scrubbed and debearded	3 tablespoons butter
	3 medium onions, thinly sliced
3¼ cups Chicken Stock (page 72) or low-salt canned chicken broth	1½ teaspoons saffron threads
	2 tablespoons flour
1¼ cups white wine	1 cup heavy cream

Place the mussels, chicken stock, and white wine in a large skillet. Cover and steam over medium-high heat, shaking the pan occasionally, until most of the mussels have opened, 5 to 6 minutes in all; discard any that do not open. Remove the mussels from the shells, reserving 12 small or 6 large mussels for the garnish. Strain the liquid through a fine sieve and reserve.

In a medium saucepan over medium-high heat, melt the butter and sauté the onions until softened but not colored, 5 to 8 minutes. Add the saffron and sauté 1 minute. Add the flour and cook 1 minute, stirring constantly.

Reduce the heat to medium, add the mussels and the cooking liquid, and simmer about 15 minutes. This will fully incorporate the flour and cook off the alcohol. Add the cream and bring to a boil, then simmer 10 minutes. Process in a blender until smooth and strain though a medium strainer.

TO SERVE

For garnish variations, omit the crabmeat and garnish only with reserved mussels, or puree all the mussels and garnish only with crabmeat.

½ cup lump crabmeat, picked over

Ladle the hot soup into warmed bowls and garnish with the crabmeat and reserved mussels. Serve hot.

MAKE-AHEAD NOTE

❧ The soup and mussel garnish can be refrigerated separately up to 3 days; reheat over medium heat. Do not freeze.

CORN–LOBSTER SOUP

MAKES 8 SERVINGS

*T*his is a summer soup I return to again and again. It's a perfect combination of 2 winners—fresh corn and lobster. Making Lobster Stock involves a little extra work, but the delicious result is definitely worth it.

Both the lobsters and the corn contribute sweetness to this pale yellow soup, which is silky and slightly spicy, with little flecks of red lobster meat. Starch released from the corn kernels acts as a natural thickener, giving it the texture of heavy cream.

Kernels from 12 ears sweet corn	1 sprig tarragon
2 tablespoons butter	1 cup heavy cream
1½ quarts Lobster Stock (page 75), plus 2 cups more, if needed	Kosher salt
	Pinch of cayenne

To remove kernels, hold an ear of corn vertically on a cutting board and move a sharp knife down the ear, cutting toward the board.

Place ¼ cup corn kernels in a small saucepan, cover with cold water, and bring to a boil. Blanch 30 seconds, drain, and run under cold water. Reserve.

Melt the butter in a medium saucepan over medium heat and sauté the remaining kernels 1 minute. Add the lobster stock and tarragon, raise the heat to high, and bring to a boil. Reduce the heat to medium and simmer for 20 minutes. Add the cream and simmer 10 more minutes.

Pour the soup into a blender in 2 batches, and process each batch for 2 minutes, until very well blended. Strain through a coarse strainer. Season with salt and cayenne—it should be just a bit spicy.

TO SERVE

For the garnish, substitute cooked shrimp; ladle each serving of hot soup over 1 or 2 fresh shucked oysters.

½ cup cooked lobster meat (see page 192), chopped fine	Chopped chives

Divide the lobster meat and reserved corn kernels among 8 warm bowls and ladle the hot soup over it. Sprinkle with the chopped chives.

MAKE-AHEAD NOTES

The soup can be refrigerated up to 3 days; reheat over medium heat. Do not freeze.

You can cook the lobster, remove the meat from the shells, wrap in plastic, and refrigerate up to 12 hours; or purchase cooked lobster meat.

BROCCOLI SOUP WITH SAUTÉED SHRIMP, MUSHROOMS, AND ROASTED GARLIC

MAKES 8 SERVINGS

ORDER OF PREPARATION

- Prepare the soup.
- Cook the mushrooms.
- Just before serving, cook the shrimp.

For Chicken Stock, substitute half Chicken, half Lobster Stock (page 75).

As in the Asparagus Soup with Morels, here the broccoli is cooked in 2 batches to extract maximum flavor, yet preserve its lively brightness. Chinese cuisine inspired the combination of broccoli, garlic, shrimp, and mushrooms.

2 tablespoons butter
2 medium onions, sliced thin
1 pound broccoli, sliced thin
10 cloves Oven-Roasted Garlic (page 37)

3½ cups Chicken Stock (page 72) or low-salt canned chicken broth
1 cup heavy cream or half-and-half
Kosher salt and freshly ground black pepper

In a large skillet, melt the butter over medium heat and sauté the onions until transparent, 5 to 8 minutes. Add half the broccoli and the roasted garlic and sauté until soft, 8 to 10 minutes. Add the stock and bring to a boil. Reduce the heat and simmer gently for 10 minutes.

Add the remaining broccoli and the cream. Bring to a boil and cook until the newly added broccoli is tender, about 10 minutes. Puree in a blender and strain through a coarse strainer. Season with salt and pepper and keep hot.

FOR THE SHRIMP AND MUSHROOMS

Instead of sautéing the shrimp and mushrooms, grill the mushroom caps until golden and the shrimp until medium rare, 1 to 2 minutes each side.

1 tablespoon pure olive oil
12 ounces shiitakes, caps only

12 large shrimp, deveined, butterflied, and tail left on

Preheat the oven to 200° F. In a large skillet, heat the olive oil over medium-high heat until shimmering. Add the mushroom caps and sauté until soft, about 6 minutes. Remove from the skillet. Add the shrimp to the skillet and sauté until medium-rare, 1 to 2 minutes each side. Keep warm in the oven.

TO SERVE

Put the mushrooms and shrimp in 8 warm bowls and ladle the soup over.

MAKE-AHEAD NOTES

Refrigerate the soup up to 3 days and reheat slowly; do not freeze.

Refrigerate the mushrooms up to 1 day. Reheat in a little stock and butter over medium-low heat.

CHAPTER 4

PASTA, GRAINS, AND LEGUMES

While most often associated with Italy, pasta is widely served in Provence, where it is thought of as more rustic than sophisticated. Although it isn't classically French, pasta fits my style of cooking perfectly, and when I want to prepare something hearty without meat or fish, it is my alternative. Of course, any of these pasta entrées can be served as a first course, as well. Pasta dishes allow me to go overboard with vegetables and herbs, my favorite ingredients; my pasta dishes often are fifty-fifty pasta and vegetables, offering some of the chunky, delicious ingredients in every mouthful. These dishes are substantial and chewy, and when you have almost finished eating, you won't find yourself down to a mound of bare pasta, with all the good stuff gone.

Surprising as it may seem, pasta is a natural for do-ahead preparation (see the method, page 106). This is more of a labor saver than a time-saver; with guests waiting for dinner, you won't have to worry about pouring a large pot of boiling water and pasta into a colander and giving yourself a steambath in the process. And you will control the quality—the pasta won't be gummy and overdone at a moment when it's too late to start over. Preparing pasta this way helps you remember to season each element as you cook it, and then reseason the whole, before serving—which is crucial for any dish, not just pasta.

Risotto also is good vehicle for vegetables. Pumpkin, wild mushrooms, zucchini, asparagus, broccoli, and corn are some of the defining flavors in risottos that have equal parts of vegetables and rice. These chunky dishes are light enough so they won't leave you feeling overstuffed, yet each is a meal in itself. Use Arborio rice, a short-grain, starchy variety that will cook to the proper al dente texture, soft and creamy on the outside and firm at the center. Risotto takes some time at the stove, but the results are worth it, and once you master the technique, you can put together your own favorite combinations.

Polenta is another warming and satisfying grain dish, one that I am especially partial to. It cooks in just a few minutes and couldn't be easier to prepare—forget those images of grandma stirring a pot for hours. It holds heat well, so it can wait in a warm spot for an hour after it is done. Combine it with a variety of garnishes and herbs or serve it unadorned. I prefer polenta that is creamy and fluid, not dense and solid, as a bed for seared swordfish (see page 168) or lamb chops or rack of lamb (see page 220). When you are not in the mood for pasta, polenta is an excellent alternative.

And that is only the tip of the iceberg. So many intriguing grains, rices, and legumes are available—so many flavors and textures to experiment with. And I always have a virtuous feeling when I serve them. They are healthful alternatives to the same old things, yet they are so easy—all can be cooked simply in stock and water. The distinctive taste of quinoa may be unfamiliar (try Roasted Salmon with Quinoa and Carrot Oil, page 156), but couscous makes itself welcome from the first. You may make them as a side dish or bed for roasted or seared meat the first time, but soon you'll see the enormous potential grains have as appetizer courses or the focal point of a meatless meal.

For other pasta, grain, and legume recipes, see also:

- Coq au Riesling with Spaetzle (page 214)
- Pan-Roasted Squab with Wild Mushroom Risotto (page 212)
- Double-Cut Lamb Chops with Caponata Polenta and Crispy Red Onions (page 220)
- Salmon with Lentils and Red Wine Salmon Sauce (page 160)
- Warm Shrimp Salad with Artichokes and Cannellini Beans (page 58)
- Lobster Salad with White Beans and Fresh Thyme (page 59)
- Bass with Flageolets, Pancetta, and Thyme, in Red Wine Salmon Sauce (page 162)

PASTA

Matching appropriate sizes and shapes is the key to winning pasta-and-vegetable mixes; when vegetable cuts are compatible with the pasta they accompany, the whole dish works smoothly. Diced tomatoes nestle companionably into the cups of orecchiette (one of my favorite shapes), as do peas and small chunks of lobster. Thin strips of zucchini and yellow squash cooked in stock and butter (see page 128) make an inspired combination with pappardelle or fettuccine. On the other hand, slippery little peas will roll off slick strands of fettuccine and make every bite a challenge.

It should go without saying that overcooked pasta is unacceptable pasta; use the cook-ahead method below if you won't be able to monitor its progress carefully.

COOK-AHEAD METHOD

- Cook pasta in boiling salted water until two-thirds done (check often).
- Remove from the pot and drain.
- Rinse in cold water until completely cooled, then drain well.
- Toss with a little olive oil to keep the pasta from sticking.
- Cover with plastic wrap and refrigerate up to two days.
- Reheat with the sauce over high heat in a skillet or saucepan.

ORECCHIETTE BRUSCHETTA

MAKES 4 SERVINGS

ORDER OF PREPARATION

- Prepare the tomato mixture and marinate.
- Cook the pasta.
- Combine the pasta with the tomato mixture and cheese.

Bruschetta—*the rustic grilled bread rubbed with oil and garlic and topped with tomatoes—was the inspiration for this summer pasta. Here, chewy orecchiette pasta stands in for the bread, supporting a juicy mixture of ripe, fresh tomatoes, the best olive oil, aromatic garlic, and a touch of vinegar. The dish is almost an even mix of pasta and chunky tomatoes. Make it when your tomatoes are so bursting with flavor that you just hate to cook them into a sauce.*

This dish is a perfect illustration of how garnishes and sauces need to be matched with appropriate pasta shapes. If you served this chunky topping with a long pasta like linguine, you would be fiddling madly to combine them on your fork. With orecchiette, "little ears," you get it all—tomatoes and pasta—in one swoop.

FOR THE TOMATOES

Meaty ripe tomatoes are a must, and if you use 2 or more varieties, the dish will be even better.

3 cups large-diced ripe tomatoes, preferably a combination of yellow and red, cherry beefsteak, or plum tomatoes

6 cloves Oven-Roasted Garlic (page 37), smashed

4 tablespoons extra-virgin olive oil

1 tablespoon plus 1 teaspoon balsamic vinegar

Freshly ground black pepper

1 tablespoon roughly chopped mixed fresh herbs (such as tarragon, savory, thyme, and basil)

One to three hours before serving, place the tomatoes, garlic, oil, vinegar, pepper, and herbs in a small bowl. Mix gently and set aside at room temperature for 1 hour, or refrigerate up to 3 hours.

FOR THE PASTA

For the orecchiette, substitute penne, ziti, small shells, or cavatelli.

Kosher salt

1 tablespoon vegetable oil

6 ounces orecchiette

Bring a large pot of salted water to a boil. Add the vegetable oil, then add the pasta and cook until al dente, about 10 minutes. Drain and rinse in cold water. Drain again.

TO SERVE

Kosher salt and freshly ground black pepper

8 tablespoons grated Pecorino Romano cheese (optional)

In a large skillet, heat the tomato mixture over medium heat until hot. Add the pasta and toss to heat through. Taste and season with salt and pepper.

Divide the pasta among 4 bowls and sprinkle with the cheese, if desired. Serve immediately.

MAKE-AHEAD NOTES

ॐ The tomato mixture can marinate in the refrigerator up to 3 hours; bring to room temperature before serving.

ॐ The pasta can be partially cooked and refrigerated up to 2 days; reheat in boiling water.

ORECCHIETTE WITH ARTICHOKES, TOMATO, AND CHORIZO

MAKES 4 LUNCHEON OR 6 APPETIZER SERVINGS

ORDER OF PREPARATION

- Cook and slice the artichokes.
- Cook the pasta.
- While the pasta cooks, combine sauce ingredients.
- Toss the vegetables and pasta together.

This satisfying dish is chunky with tomatoes and artichokes; it is vegetables with pasta, not the other way around. The garden-fresh vegetable flavors are accented by the smokiness of the sausage. Use the best, ripest tomatoes you can find for this dish—despite the heartiness of the other ingredients, the tomato flavor will be foremost. This is practically a meal in itself. Just serve with loaf of bread, and you're set!

Here is another example of a good match between the pasta shape and the garnish, with each forkful providing the diner with a bit of everything good.

FOR THE SAUCE

For chorizo, substitute kielbasa or Portuguese linguiça.

4 medium to large artichokes

Kosher salt

Juice of 3 lemons

4 ounces chorizo sausage

4 tablespoons plus a few drops extra-virgin olive oil

2 cloves garlic, minced

2 medium-size ripe tomatoes, cored, seeded, and cut into medium dice

¼ cup Chicken Stock (page 72), Vegetable Stock (page 72), or low-salt canned broth

Cut off the stem and the top quarter of each artichoke. Snap off the tough outer leaves, leaving only the pale green leaves surrounding the heart. Place the artichokes in a large pot with lightly salted water to cover. Add the lemon juice and bring to a boil over high heat. Reduce the heat to medium and simmer until fork tender, 20 to 25 minutes. Drain and set aside at room temperature to cool. Remove the leaves and reserve; spoon out the choke and discard, and cut each heart into ¼-inch slices.

Cut the chorizo in half lengthwise, then crosswise into ¼-inch slices.

In a large skillet, heat the olive oil over medium heat until shimmering. Add the garlic and sauté until softened but not colored, about 1 minute. Add the artichoke hearts, tomatoes, and chorizo and sauté 1 minute. Add the chicken stock, and keep warm.

For orecchiette, substitute penne, ziti, small shells, or cavatelli.

Kosher salt
1 tablespoon vegetable oil

6 ounces orecchiette

Bring a large pot of salted water to a boil. Add the vegetable oil, then add the pasta and cook over high heat until al dente, about 10 minutes. Drain and rinse quickly in cold water. Drain again.

TO SERVE

1 teaspoon medium-finely chopped
   thyme leaves
2 teaspoons medium-finely chopped
   parsley leaves

Kosher salt and freshly ground black
   pepper

Add the vegetable sauce to the cooked pasta and toss to heat through. Add the thyme and parsley and season with salt and pepper.

MAKE-AHEAD NOTES

∾ The artichokes can be cooked up to a day in advance and refrigerated.

∾ The chorizo and tomatoes can be prepared and refrigerated up to 1 day.

∾ The pasta can be cooked up to 48 hours ahead and refrigerated (see page 106); bring to room temperature before proceeding with recipe.

PASTA WITH WILD MUSHROOMS

MAKES 4 SERVINGS

ORDER OF PREPARATION

- Prepare the mushroom cream.
- Cook the pasta.
- Combine the mushroom sauce and pasta.

*T*his is a simple dish, but when every component is right, it is unbeatable. The base of the sauce is mushroom cream, heavy cream that has been steeped with sautéed vegetables and mushroom trimmings. When combined with luxurious wild mushrooms, it adds far more complexity than plain cream would. Tripolini is a tiny pasta that combines perfectly with a smooth, creamy mushroom sauce. The sauce should be almost completely absorbed by the pasta—you don't want a soupy dish—and the pasta must be cooked al dente. Even a wonderful sauce made with the most expensive mushrooms in the world will be ruined if the pasta is overcooked.

> **USE WILD MUSHROOM SAUCE IN:**
> ....
> **PENNETTE WITH MUSHROOM CREAM, LOBSTER, AND ASPARAGUS (PAGE 112)**

FOR THE PASTA

For tripolini, substitute cavatelli or tortellini.

Kosher salt
2 to 3 tablespoons olive oil

2 cups tripolini

Bring a large pot of salted water to a boil. Add the olive oil, then add the pasta and cook until al dente, about 10 minutes. Drain and rinse in cold water. Drain again.

FOR THE MUSHROOM CREAM

8 to 10 ounces wild mushroom stems or domestic mushrooms, or a combination of both, cleaned
2 tablespoons olive oil
2 stalks celery, cut into small dice
1 medium carrot, peeled and cut into small dice

8 shallots, cut into small dice
Chicken Stock (page 72) or low-salt canned chicken broth to cover (about 1 cup)
1½ cups heavy cream
Kosher salt and freshly ground black pepper

Grind the mushrooms or stems in a food processor until finely chopped but not pulverized, or mince by hand.

In a medium saucepan over medium heat, heat the olive oil until just smoking. Add the celery, carrot, and shallots and sauté until softened but not colored, 3 to 4 minutes. Add the minced mushroom stems and chicken stock to cover, bring to a simmer, and cook 10 minutes.

Add the heavy cream, return to a simmer, and cook until slightly thickened, about 20 minutes, stirring occasionally. Strain through a fine strainer, discarding the solids, and season with salt and pepper.

TO SERVE

About 1⅓ cups thinly sliced wild mushrooms (shiitake, cremini, chanterelles)

4 tablespoons truffle juice or truffle oil (available at specialty food shops), optional

Kosher salt and freshly ground black pepper

Minced parsley or chives, for garnish

Spoon the sauce into a large skillet and add the sliced mushrooms and optional truffle juice. Over medium-high heat, bring the sauce to a boil and let it reduce by about one third; it should be thick enough to coat the pasta.

Add the cooked pasta, stir well, and reseason, if necessary. Garnish with parsley or chives.

MAKE-AHEAD NOTES

✆ Slice the carrot, celery, and shallots and refrigerate up to 2 days.

✆ Grind the mushroom stems and slice the mushrooms and refrigerate up to 1 day.

✆ The mushroom cream can be reduced partway and refrigerated up to 3 days. Before serving, bring to a boil and finish reducing.

✆ The pasta can be undercooked, tossed with a little oil, and refrigerated for 2 days. Rewarm in the sauce or in hot water.

PENNETTE WITH MUSHROOM CREAM, LOBSTER, AND ASPARAGUS

MAKES 4 TO 6 APPETIZER SERVINGS

ORDER OF PREPARATION

- Cook the lobster.
- While the lobsters boil, cook the asparagus and the pasta.
- Prepare the mushroom cream.
- Combine with the pasta, asparagus, and lobster.

*V*ersatile mushroom cream can be dressed up even further with the addition of complementary ingredients. Compare the refinement of this dish to the simple earthiness of Pasta with Wild Mushrooms (page 110) to see just how adaptable that rich sauce can be in different guises. Here, crisp asparagus and chunks of lobster make the simple sauce richer and give the dish a variety of textures. Delicate snow peas would also be an attractive and delicious foil for the mushroom cream and the lobster meat. Pennette, a more diminutive version of sturdy penne pasta, suits the elegance of the sauce.

FOR THE ASPARAGUS

Kosher salt	16 to 20 stalks asparagus

In a large pot of boiling salted water over high heat, blanch the asparagus until bright green and still crisp, 3 to 4 minutes, and shock in a bowl of ice water. Remove it by grasping the stems, rather than the tips. Cut off the tips about 3 inches from the top and halve lengthwise. Thinly slice the remaining stems.

FOR THE PASTA

For pennette, substitute penne, small tortellini, or cavatelli.

Kosher salt	Virgin olive oil, for drizzling
2½ cups pennette	

In a large pot of boiling salted water over high heat, cook the pasta until al dente, about 10 minutes. Drain and rinse in cold running water. Lightly drizzle with olive oil.

TO SERVE

Each pound of live lobster will yield ⅓ to ½ cup cooked meat. Cooked lobster meat from the fish store will work in this recipe.

About 2 cups mushroom cream (see page 110)	2 tablespoons finely chopped chives
1½ to 2 cups cooked lobster meat (see page 192), cut into medium dice	Kosher salt and freshly ground black pepper
2 tablespoons truffle juice (available at specialty groceries), optional	

In a medium skillet or sauté pan, bring the mushroom cream to a boil over medium-high heat; reduce the heat to medium and simmer until it reduces slightly. Add the cooked pennette and toss until heated through. Add the asparagus and lobster and heat through. Add the optional truffle juice and chopped chives. Taste and season with salt and pepper, if necessary.

Divide among 4 to 6 bowls.

MAKE-AHEAD NOTES

෨ The lobsters can be cooked and the meat removed from the shells and refrigerated for 12 hours.

෨ The mushroom cream, partially reduced, can be refrigerated for 3 days. Before serving, bring to a boil and finish reducing.

෨ The pasta can be undercooked, tossed with a little oil, and refrigerated for up to 2 days. Rewarm in the sauce or in hot water.

SPRING VEGETABLE RISOTTO

MAKES 5 CUPS (4 APPETIZER OR 2 MAIN-COURSE SERVINGS)

I *love rich risottos but after a few bites, I'm full. This dish, however, has an equal mix of veggies and rice and is lighter than the typical risotto—I often go back for seconds. The rice is creamy, with a slight bite at the center, and the vegetables are crisp and fresh-tasting.*

Although the proportion of rice and vegetables is unusual, the method of preparation is the same as for other risottos.

Kosher salt

Kernels from 1 ear sweet corn

¼ cup fresh peas or frozen peas, thawed

4 cups Vegetable Stock (page 72) or low-salt canned vegetable broth

2 tablespoons butter, plus 1 tablespoon (optional)

1 cup Arborio rice

½ cup thinly sliced shiitake mushroom caps

½ cup broccoli florets

1 medium yellow squash, in small dice (use just the outside, cutting through the squash about ½ inch all around)

20 asparagus tips, halved lengthwise (about 2 inches long)

10 snow peas, cut in ¼-inch julienne

2 scallions, thinly sliced on the diagonal

4 radicchio leaves, cut in ¼-inch julienne

4 to 5 tablespoons freshly grated Parmesan cheese (optional)

¼ cup heavy cream or half-and-half (optional)

2 to 3 tablespoons finely chopped mixed herbs (such as thyme, tarragon, and parsley)

Freshly ground black pepper

Fill a 2-quart saucepan three-quarters full of water, adding 1½ teaspoons of salt, and bring to a boil over high heat. Blanch the corn 1 minute, drain, refresh under cold water, and drain again. Repeat for the peas.

In a small or medium saucepan over high heat, bring the stock to a boil. Reduce the heat to low and keep the stock hot.

In a medium saucepan, melt the 2 tablespoons of butter over medium heat. Add the rice and sauté for 1 minute. Add ¼ cup of the stock, and cook, stirring, until it is absorbed. Continue adding stock, about ¼ cup at a time, waiting until it is absorbed before adding more, and stirring often. After 1½ cups of stock have been incorporated (about 5 minutes), add the mushrooms, broccoli, and squash. Raise the heat slightly and cook, continuing to add stock, another 5 to 6 minutes. Add the asparagus, snow peas, scallions, and corn and continue cooking and adding stock for another 5 minutes. Add the peas and radicchio and any remaining stock. Add the Parmesan cheese, the cream, and the additional tablespoon of butter, if using. Stir in the herbs and season with salt and pepper.

MAKE-AHEAD NOTES

☙ Slice the vegetables and refrigerate up to 1 day.

☙ Blanch and shock the corn and peas and refrigerate up to 1 day.

PUMPKIN RISOTTO

MAKES 6 SERVINGS

This risotto has almost equal amounts of vegetables and rice, and the vegetables are cooked in the stock along with the rice, so that all their flavor goes right into the dish.

Pumpkin by itself doesn't have a lot of flavor, but rather than enhance it by adding spices, I combine carrot juice with the stock. This adds sweeter taste, as well as some subtle color.

SERVE WITH:

SEARED AND ROASTED CHICKEN
OR DUCK BREASTS
(SEE PAGES 200, 202)
PAN-ROASTED SQUAB
(SEE PAGE 212)
DOUBLE-CUT LAMB CHOPS,
INSTEAD OF CAPONATA POLENTA
(SEE PAGE 220)
PAN-ROASTED VEAL CHOPS
(SEE PAGE 224)

FOR THE RISOTTO

For the pumpkin, substitute an equal amount of butternut squash (it will have a slightly stronger flavor).

4 tablespoons unsalted butter (no substitutes)

2 cups diced pumpkin (see page xv; sugar pumpkins are best)

¾ cup celery, cut into small dice

½ cup onion, cut into small dice

½ cup carrot, cut into small dice

1¼ cups Arborio rice

2¼ cups Chicken Stock (page 72) or low-salt canned chicken broth, plus ½ cup extra, if needed, heated to a simmer

2¼ cups fresh carrot juice, plus ½ cup extra, if needed, warmed

In a medium saucepan, melt the butter over medium heat. Add the pumpkin, celery, onion, and carrot and sauté until softened but not colored, about 4 minutes. Add the rice and sauté 1 minute. Add the stock to the rice ¼ cup at a time, not adding more until the previous addition has been absorbed. Add the carrot juice the same way. When all the liquid has been absorbed, the risotto should be al dente; add more liquid if necessary and cook until the grains are tender, with slightly hard centers, and the sauce is creamy.

TO SERVE

4 tablespoons grated Parmesan cheese

2 tablespoons minced fresh parsley

Kosher salt and freshly ground black pepper

¼ teaspoon grated nutmeg

Stir in the Parmesan cheese and parsley and season with salt, pepper, and nutmeg. Serve immediately.

MAKE-AHEAD NOTES

Juice the carrots and refrigerate up to 1 day ahead of time.

Dice the vegetables (or do ahead and refrigerate up to 2 days).

CURRIED COUSCOUS

MAKES 3 CUPS

Although it resembles a grain, couscous is a semolina product that does not need cooking; rather, it is combined with boiling liquid, which it absorbs in a few minutes. It is light and fluffy, with a mild flavor. Curry gives it spice and character.

> SERVE WITH:
>
> HALIBUT WITH TOMATO-CUMIN BROTH (PAGE 152)
> ROASTED SALMON WITH QUINOA AND CARROT OIL (PAGE 156), IN PLACE OF THE QUINOA

2½ cups Chicken Stock (page 72), Vegetable Stock (page 72), or low-salt canned broth
½ teaspoon kosher salt
1 tablespoon butter

1 small onion, cut into fine dice
1 teaspoon good-quality curry powder (such as Madras)
1 cup couscous
Freshly ground black pepper

In a small saucepan, combine the stock and salt and bring to a boil over high heat. Remove from the heat and set aside, covered.

In a medium saucepan, melt the butter over medium heat. Add the onion and sauté until soft, 1 to 2 minutes. Add the curry powder and sauté 30 seconds. Add the couscous and stir to coat. Add the hot stock, remove from the heat, and let sit 6 to 8 minutes, until absorbed by the couscous. Stir and season with salt and pepper, if needed.

MAKE-AHEAD NOTE

Curried Couscous can be refrigerated up to 3 days.

I'm still discovering grains that excite and intrigue me, and I urge you to incorporate more of them into your menus. Grains as well as cooked legumes, such as lentils, make a chewy or creamy bed for seared and roasted fish and for meat and poultry, and they make the perfect center of a vegetarian meal. Beyond that, grains offer interesting textures, a variety of flavors, ease of cooking, and high nutrition and fiber content, all good reasons to try some of the dishes that follow (and those that accompany many of the fish and meat recipes), however you choose to serve them.

SIMPLE BRAISED LENTILS

MAKES 1 1/2 CUPS, OR 4 SERVINGS

This simple-to-make, delicious dish also is nutritious, low in fat, and rich in protein. French lentils are my favorite— they don't break up in cooking, and their flavor is superior to that of the domestic lentils. Stock, a little butter, and seasonings are the only added ingredients, so nothing overpowers their earthy flavor.

SERVE WITH:

PAN-ROASTED PORK LOIN CHOPS AND GINGER–ORANGE SAUCE WITH CANDIED GINGER (PAGE 226) SEARED AND ROASTED DUCK BREASTS (SEE PAGE 202) PAN-ROASTED SQUAB (PAGE 212), IN PLACE OF THE WILD MUSHROOM RISOTTO

3/4 cup French green lentils
2 1/2 cups Vegetable Stock (page 72), Chicken Stock (page 72), or low-salt canned broth

1/2 teaspoon kosher salt
1 bay leaf
1 tablespoon butter
Freshly ground black pepper

In a medium saucepan, combine the lentils, stock, salt, and bay leaf and bring to a boil over high heat. Reduce the heat to medium and simmer until the liquid is absorbed and the lentils are tender, about 35 minutes. Stir in the butter and season with salt and pepper.

MAKE-AHEAD NOTE

🍂 Cooked lentils can be refrigerated up to 3 days.

WILD RICE WITH PINE NUTS

MAKES 4 SERVINGS

ORDER OF PREPARATION

- Cook the wild rice.
- While the rice is cooking, sauté the pine nuts and the leeks and scallions.

*W*ild rice has a nut-like flavor; the sautéed pine nuts emphasize this and add a bit more crunch. The combination is delicious with any chicken or duck dish.

Wild rice is not really rice, but is a member of the grass family. It takes a little longer to cook than regular rice, but be careful not to overcook, or you will have a mushy dish.

> **SERVE WITH:**
>
> SALMON WITH RED WINE SALMON SAUCE, INSTEAD OF LENTILS (SEE PAGE 160)
> SEARED AND ROASTED CHICKEN OR DUCK BREASTS (SEE PAGES 200, 202)
> SIMPLE ROASTED CHICKEN OR ROASTED DUCK (PAGES 204, 210)

FOR THE RICE

½ cup wild rice
2½ cups water

¼ teaspoon salt

Place the rice, water, and salt in a large saucepan and bring to a boil over high heat. Reduce the heat to medium-low and simmer until the rice is tender, 45 to 55 minutes. Drain.

TO SERVE

1 tablespoon butter or walnut oil
2 heaping tablespoons pine nuts
¼ cup finely diced leeks, white part only
¼ cup finely diced scallions, white part only

1 to 2 tablespoons Chicken Stock (page 72), Vegetable Stock (page 72), low-salt canned broth, or water (optional)
Kosher salt and freshly ground black pepper

In a medium sauté pan over medium heat, melt the butter (or heat the oil until shimmering) and sauté the pine nuts 1 minute. Add the leeks and scallions and sauté 1 minute, until softened slightly. Add the rice and heat through. Add stock, if needed, to moisten. Season to taste with salt and pepper.

POLENTA WITH WILD MUSHROOMS

MAKES 4 SIDE DISH OR APPETIZER SERVINGS

ORDER OF PREPARATION

- Bring stock for polenta to a boil.
- Start mushrooms, add stock.
- While sauce reduces, cook polenta.

I like this soft, delicious polenta so much it's all I can do to keep from eating it in the kitchen as I make it. The addition of cream along with the broth makes it a polenta-to-die-for, soft and irresistible. This proportion of cornmeal to liquid will give you the looser, less stiff consistency that I prefer. The wild mushrooms are first sautéed and then simmered in stock, to make a richly flavored sauce that is ladled over the top of each serving.

For an elegant touch:

- *add a few drops of truffle oil or juice to the polenta along with the cream*
- *use the most exotic mushrooms you can find, such as chanterelles or morels*
- *add truffles to the mushroom mixture or shave some over the top*

> **SERVE WITH:**
> **SIMPLE ROASTED CHICKEN (PAGE 204)**
> **SADDLE OF LAMB (SEE PAGE 218)**
> **RACK OF LAMB (SEE PAGE 220)**
> **LAMB LOIN CHOPS (SEE PAGE 222)**
>
> **SERVE MUSHROOMS IN BROTH WITH:**
> **ROASTED VEAL CHOPS (SEE PAGE 224)**
> **ROASTED PORK LOIN CHOPS (SEE PAGE 226)**

FOR THE POLENTA

2 cups Chicken Stock (page 72), or Vegetable Stock (page 72), regular or low-salt canned broth, or water

½ teaspoon kosher salt

⅓ cup finely ground yellow cornmeal

¼ cup heavy cream or half-and-half

Freshly ground black pepper

In a medium saucepan, bring the stock and salt to a boil over high heat. Whisk in the cornmeal slowly, to avoid lumps. When combined, reduce the heat to medium and boil until thickened, 1 to 2 minutes. Add the cream and heat through. Season with pepper and additional salt, if needed, and keep the cornmeal warm over low heat, stirring occasionally, or in a stainless-steel bowl, covered with plastic wrap, set in a warm spot.

FOR THE MUSHROOM SAUCE

1 tablespoon extra-virgin olive oil

8 ounces medium mixed wild
mushrooms (such as shiitake,
portobello, oyster, or cremini)
diced or sliced (about 1½ cups)

1 teaspoon finely chopped thyme
leaves

1 cup Veal Stock (page 74), Chicken
Stock, Vegetable Stock, or low-salt
canned broth

2 teaspoons butter

Kosher salt and freshly ground black
pepper

In a medium skillet, heat the olive oil over high heat until shimmering. Add
the mushrooms and sauté until golden, 2 to 3 minutes. Add the thyme and
sauté for 1 minute longer. Add the stock and bring to a boil. Reduce the heat
to medium and cook at a gentle boil until slightly reduced, 3 to 4 minutes.
Swirl in the butter until incorporated. Season with salt and pepper.

TO SERVE

Divide the hot polenta among 4 warmed bowls and ladle the mushroom
broth on top.

MAKE-AHEAD NOTES

⁓ The mushrooms in broth can be refrigerated up to 3 days; reheat over
medium heat.

⁓ Prepare the polenta about an hour ahead and keep in a covered bowl on
a warm part of your stove.

ROSEMARY POLENTA

MAKES ABOUT 2 CUPS

*A*lthough polenta, the rich cornmeal porridge, is Northern Italian in origin, it is widely enjoyed in Provence. Fresh herbs add an interesting dimension—and this creamy, soft version is fragrant with fresh rosemary. It provides the underpinning for Swordfish with Rosemary Polenta, Tomatoes, and Fresh Herbs (page 168) and many other full-flavored meat and fish dishes. Polenta holds its heat well. It can be prepared up to an hour ahead of serving and placed in a covered bowl on a warm part of your stove.

SERVE INSTEAD OF PASTA OR RICE WITH:

SIMPLE ROASTED CHICKEN (PAGE 204)
SADDLE OF LAMB (SEE PAGE 218)

FOR AN ALL-VEGETABLE MEAL, SERVE WITH:

RATATOUILLE (PAGE 142)
CONFIT BAYALDI (PAGE 138)
INDIVIDUAL TIANS OF SUMMER VEGETABLES (PAGE 130)
ROASTED FENNEL, TOMATOES, AND OLIVES (SEE PAGE 222)

For rosemary, substitute fresh oregano.

For Chicken Stock, substitute Vegetable Stock (page 72) or water.

2 cups Chicken Stock (page 72) or low-salt canned chicken broth
3 tablespoons minced fresh rosemary
1 tablespoon salted butter
⅓ cup plus 1 tablespoon fine yellow cornmeal

2 tablespoons extra-virgin olive oil
¼ cup heavy cream
Kosher salt and freshly ground black pepper

In a medium saucepan, combine the stock, rosemary, and butter and bring to a boil over high heat. Slowly whisk in the cornmeal until thick and bubbly. Boil 1 to 2 minutes, whisking continuously, until smooth, thick, and soft. Whisk in the oil and cream and bring to a boil. Remove from the heat and season with salt and pepper. Keep the polenta warm over low heat, stirring occasionally, or in a stainless-steel bowl, covered with plastic wrap, set in a warm spot, until ready to serve.

CHAPTER 5

VEGETABLES

As a working chef, I learned to go into my walk-in refrigerator every day and take a careful look around. Even though I had a pretty good idea of what was in there, as I made my way among the green beans and onions, the arugula and leeks, I began to imagine wonderful combinations. At home, when I plan a meal, I choose the vegetables first and then build a main course around them. Whether that main course is chicken, meat, or fish, I try to balance all the flavors so the vegetables won't be overwhelmed.

A farmers' market, a greengrocery, a Chinatown market, or the vegetable aisle in a supermarket offers the same happy experience. I can buy cranberry, wax, or fava beans; and not only are domestic white mushrooms available, there are also creminis, shiitakes, chanterelles, and morels. And each variety offers another way to dress up or dress down a dish or to change a meal.

Growing my own vegetables is even more satisfying than shopping for them. I am part of the process from start to finish, and the peas, zucchini, and tomatoes are available when the creative spirit moves me. Nothing compares to the taste of a tomato fresh off the vine and warm from the sun.

As you read through this book, you'll see that vegetables are really central to my cuisine; I doubt I could serve a piece of fish, whip up a pot of soup, or put together a pasta dish without them. Although you will find many other vegetable combinations in the other chapters, the goal of this particular chapter is to present the most versatile of my free-standing vegetable recipes. Preparing them will help you develop a better understanding of how different vegetables can be coaxed to their fullest flavors and of how I pair them with herbs, sauces, and—of course—other vegetables.

I look forward to each season and what it promises—the inspiration of seasonal vegetables at their peak. In the summer, there will be ripe corn and pungent basil; in the spring, young stalks of asparagus and the tenderest leaves of spinach; in the winter, squash and deep green broccoli. Such winter root vegetables as sweet potato, parsnip, and celery root, when cooked until very tender and whirled in a food processor, make purees that are creamy and satisfying, with clear vegetable flavors. Don't add herbs or a lot of spices that will detract from their taste. I would rather have a puree that tastes of delicate, sweet parsnips than one overwhelmed by tarragon.

The foods I see inspire me because they are fresh and tempting, and also because they are familiar and I have learned the best methods for preparing them. I think of all the ways I can put them together and how delicious they will be roasted or sautéed or baked or grilled or pureed.

SAUCE COMBINATIONS:

~ Creamy, rich sauces without vinegar combine best with butter-enriched purees that echo their texture; for example, Red Wine Salmon Sauce with mashed potatoes.

~ Vinaigrettes are good with slightly acidic, slightly sweet vegetable combinations. Their sharpness brings out the tart notes in Ratatouille and Confit Bayaldi, heightens the quieter flavors of blanched vegetables, and gives a piquant accent to the meaty texture of roasted vegetables.

VEGETABLE COMBINATIONS:

~ With grilled vegetables: any fish or shellfish, saddle of lamb, rack of lamb, lamb loin chops, roasted veal chops

~ With sweet-potato, celery root, or parsnip puree: snapper, bass, roasted chicken, roasted duck

~ With roasted tomatoes and eggplant Provençal: roasted chicken, saddle of lamb, rack of lamb

~ With creamed spinach: roasted chicken, roasted duck

~ With Green and Yellow Squash Ribbons, or Individual Tian of Summer Vegetables: lemon–thyme chicken breasts, roasted chicken, roasted duck, rack of lamb, saddle of lamb

~ With Ratatouille, Confit Bayaldi, Caponata, roasted tomatoes and eggplant Provençal: everything!

Grilled vegetables, with their meaty texture, go with everything. Their textural opposite, purees, also are compatible with just about every dish. It always is best to avoid clashes of flavor; as with sauces, creamy flavors marry well with one another and tart flavors do the same.

Timing

When you choose vegetables, think about how long you want to spend on their preparation. You can do something fast, like Green and Yellow Squash Ribbons or Individual Tians of Summer Vegetables, for almost any meal; when you have a little extra time, you can make a slow-cooking Confit Bayaldi. Purees all take 20 minutes to an hour, depending on the vegetable's boiling time, although it's not labor-intensive time; and most potato dishes will require at least 30 minutes.

Many vegetables can be started before you prepare the main course and reheated just before serving (see the blanch and shock method, opposite). Braised or roasted vegetable combinations, such as Ratatouille, Caponata, Eggplant Provençal in Roasted Tomatoes or roasted fennel, tomatoes, and olives, can be doubled and the extra portions refrigerated and then reheated for another meal. They will taste even better the second or third day. Simply prepared vegetables can become special with the proper sauce or drizzle.

In addition to the recipes in this chapter, many of the meat and fish recipes have strong vegetable components that would stand well alone or could be recombined with other dishes of your choice. Try the vegetables in the following recipes:

Tuna with Grilled Vegetables and Provençal Vinaigrette (page 180)

Snapper with Potato Galette and Port Wine Sauce (page 158)

Herb-Roasted Halibut with a Ragout of Wild Mushrooms, Leeks, and Potatoes (page 154)

Salmon with Onion Confit, Winter Vegetables, and Red Wine Salmon Sauce (page 164)

Baked Rainbow Trout with Leeks and Thyme (page 176)

Baked Rainbow Trout with Leeks, Apples, and Walnuts (page 174)

Lamb Loin Chops with Roasted Fennel, Tomatoes, and Olives (page 222)

COOKING SIMPLE VEGETABLES

Although the classic French way is to cook vegetables thoroughly, I prefer cooking them until crisp and just done. My method is to blanch and shock—immerse them briefly in boiling water and then in ice water—and then heat them through in a mixture of half stock and half butter. This is much better than heating in butter alone, for two reasons: the stock quickly forms steam in the hot pan, warming up the vegetables fast; and you don't get too much butter with your veggies. This is a technique you can use freely—it isn't specific to any recipe.

Rather than doing all this at the same time, you can blanch and shock up to 24 hours ahead of time and reheat just before serving. This way you can concentrate on your main course. (If you like your vegetables cooked to a softer state, just increase the blanching time until they are done to your taste.)

How you reheat depends on the vegetable. Thick stalks of broccoli are hard to heat all the way through and you may have to dunk them first in hot water for about thirty seconds. But if you have thin spears of asparagus, it's easy just to toss them quickly over heat in butter and stock.

METHOD

✒ Fill a large pot with salted water (use 1 teaspoon for every quart) and bring to a boil over high heat.

✒ Add the vegetables and blanch until just tender, from 30 seconds to 4 minutes; drain.

✒ Plunge the drained vegetables into a bowl of ice water and allow to cool, or rinse under cold running water. Drain.

✒ Set a skillet large enough to accommodate the vegetables over medium-high heat. Add equal amounts of butter and stock to just cover the bottom. Bring to a simmer, add the vegetables, and cook, stirring, until heated through. Taste and season with salt and pepper.

GREEN AND YELLOW SQUASH RIBBONS

MAKES 4 SERVINGS

*T*hin-sliced vegetables require no blanching; they and the green herbs are cooked very briefly in butter and stock. This straightforward dish is an easy way to prepare vegetables at the last minute.

> FOR A PASTA ENTRÉE,
> TOSS WITH:
>
> **1 POUND COOKED PAPPARDELLE
> OR FETTUCCINE**

   A mandoline is the best tool for achieving super-thin squash ribbons that cook quickly. Although a professional mandoline is costly, good, low-priced plastic versions are available.

Substitute any of your favorite fresh herbs.

1 tablespoon butter

2 medium zucchini, trimmed, cut in ⅛-inch lengthwise slices on a mandoline or by hand

2 medium yellow squash, trimmed, cut in ⅛-inch lengthwise slices on a mandoline or by hand

½ cup Vegetable Stock (page 72), Chicken Stock (page 72), or low-salt canned broth

1 teaspoon finely chopped fresh herbs (such as tarragon, savory, chives, oregano, or any combination of these)

Kosher salt and freshly ground black pepper

In a large skillet, melt the butter over high heat. Add the zucchini and squash and the stock, cover, and cook until the zucchini is tender and wilted, 2 to 3 minutes. Sprinkle with the herbs, season with salt and pepper, and serve immediately.

MAKE-AHEAD NOTE

❧ Slice the squash and refrigerate up to 2 days.

ARTICHOKES COUNTRY-STYLE

MAKES 4 SERVINGS

In *Provence, artichokes are served* à la barigoule, *with garlic, onions, and bacon or ham, among other ingredients. My lighter, quicker version preserves the Mediterranean flavors while it allows the sweet, green taste of the vegetable to come through.*

> **SERVE WITH:**
> **SIMPLE ROASTED CHICKEN (PAGE 204)**
> **ROASTED DUCK (PAGE 210)**
> **ROASTED COD (SEE PAGE 173)**
> **GRILLED FISH STEAKS (SEE PAGE 178)**

12 baby artichokes, outer leaves removed, and ⅛ inch trimmed from both the bottom and the top
Juice of 1 lemon
3 tablespoons extra-virgin olive oil
4 slices bacon, cut into small dice
6 cloves Oven-Roasted Garlic (page 37)
1 tablespoon finely diced shallots
Kosher salt and freshly ground black pepper

Place the artichokes in a large pot and cover generously with cold water. Add the lemon juice. Bring to a boil over high heat, then reduce the heat to medium and simmer until just tender, 8 to 10 minutes. Drain and allow to cool. Halve the artichokes lengthwise.

In a medium sauté pan, heat the oil over high heat until smoking. Add the bacon and sauté until it begins to color. Add the garlic and shallots and sauté for 1 minute. Add the artichokes and sauté until light golden brown, about 2 minutes. Season with salt and pepper. Serve warm.

MAKE-AHEAD NOTES

∽ The trimmed artichokes can be placed in a bowl, covered with cold water mixed with the juice of 1 lemon, and refrigerated up to 1 day, or overnight. Cook them in this soaking water.

∽ The simmered and halved artichokes can be refrigerated up to 2 days.

∽ The finished dish can be refrigerated up to 2 days; reheat in 1 tablespoon extra-virgin olive oil over medium heat.

INDIVIDUAL TIANS OF SUMMER VEGETABLES

MAKES 4 SERVINGS

Thin slices of yellow squash, zucchini, and tomatoes are baked together in small pans or ramekins until juicy and fragrant. With their overlapping yellow and green layers, these pretty vegetable side dishes look like little flowers when you unmold them. The combination of thyme and zucchini is a good one, with light, fresh vegetable and herbal flavors. This is easy to double or triple.

SERVE WITH:

SIMPLE ROASTED CHICKEN (PAGE 204)
ROASTED DUCK (PAGE 210)
SEARED AND ROASTED CHICKEN BREASTS WITH LEMON AND THYME (PAGE 200)
ANY SEARED AND ROASTED FISH (SEE PAGE 151)

For the fresh herbs, substitute all savory, all thyme, or 1 teaspoon herbes de Provence.

For olive oil, substitute Rosemary Oil (page 7).

A tian is a shallow ramekin. Disposable 4½-inch aluminum pie tins are a good substitute.

If you have really flavorful zucchini and squash, you may omit the herbs altogether.

Extra-virgin olive oil, as needed
1 medium to large yellow squash, thinly sliced crosswise
1 medium to large zucchini, thinly sliced crosswise
Kosher salt and freshly ground black pepper

1 tablespoon finely chopped mixed thyme and savory leaves (2 to 3 sprigs each)
4 plum tomatoes, thinly sliced crosswise

Preheat the oven to 350° F. Drizzle a few drops of oil in each of four 4- to 6-ounce ramekins.

Arrange 4 or 5 slightly overlapping slices of yellow squash over the bottom of each mold. Cover with a layer of zucchini and sprinkle with a little oil, salt, pepper, and half the herbs. Add another layer of squash, seasonings, and herbs. Top with a final layer of tomatoes and sprinkle with oil, salt, and pepper. Be sure to season the squash and the final tomato layer well.

Place the molds on a baking sheet and bake until bubbly, 25 to 30 minutes. To serve, invert each tian onto a spatula, let the juices drain off, and then invert again from the spatula onto a serving dish.

MAKE-AHEAD NOTE

Prepare the tians and refrigerate up to 2 days; reheat in the molds in a 350° F. oven until hot.

WILD MUSHROOMS WITH BALSAMIC VINEGAR

MAKES 4 SERVINGS

*W*hen I prepare sautéed mushrooms to serve as a garnish, there never seem to be enough to satisfy my guests so I like to present these on their own, in generous portions. Balsamic vinegars vary from brand to brand in flavor and mellowness, and like fine wines the aged varieties generally taste the best—and cost the most.

> **SERVE WITH:**
>
> **PAN-ROASTED VEAL CHOPS WITH CARAMELIZED ONION SAUCE (PAGE 224)**
> **ROASTED SALMON WITH QUINOA AND CARROT OIL (PAGE 156)**
> **ANY VEGETABLE PUREE (SEE PAGE 134)**

8 ounces fresh shiitake mushrooms, caps only, cut into medium dice
8 ounces portobello mushrooms, caps only, cut into medium dice
¼ cup extra-virgin olive oil
¼ cup balsamic vinegar, preferably aged
Kosher salt and freshly ground black pepper

In a medium sauté pan, heat the olive oil over high heat until just smoking. Add the mushrooms and sauté until they begin to wilt, 2 to 3 minutes. Drizzle with the vinegar and sauté 1 minute longer. Season with salt and pepper. Serve warm.

MAKE-AHEAD NOTES

❧ The diced mushrooms can be refrigerated up to 1 day.

❧ The finished dish can be refrigerated up to 3 days; reheat over medium heat.

THE BEST CREAMED SPINACH

MAKES 2 CUPS, OR 4 SERVINGS

A spin on that creamy comfort food of our youths, fresh green spinach is combined with flavorful, finely diced sautéed vegetables and a light cream sauce. The whole dish is cooked in a flash.

The main flavor, of course, is spinach, but each bite gives you a taste of everything else in the mixture—garlic, shallots, scallions, mushrooms, and cream.

SERVE WITH:

SIMPLE ROASTED CHICKEN
(PAGE 204)
SADDLE OF LAMB
(SEE PAGE 218)
RACK OF LAMB (SEE PAGE 220)
PAN-ROASTED VEAL CHOPS
(SEE PAGE 224)
ROASTED SALMON
(SEE PAGE 156)

Spinach gives up so much water when it cooks that it dilutes the heavy cream, leaving just a delicate coating on the leaves. This is one of those dishes that will have you sneaking tastes in the kitchen—it's irresistible.

You can omit other ingredients if you want to, but keep the mushrooms and garlic!

1 tablespoon extra-virgin olive oil
¼ cup finely diced shallots
2 cloves Oven-Roasted Garlic (page 37)
⅔ cup finely diced mushrooms, domestic or wild (if wild, use caps only)
3 tablespoons finely sliced scallions, white part only

¾ cup heavy cream
5½ cups coarsely chopped spinach leaves (about 6 ounces)
1 teaspoon butter
Kosher salt and freshly ground black pepper

In a large sauté pan, heat the olive oil over medium heat until almost shimmering. Add the shallots and garlic and sauté until soft but not colored, 1 to 2 minutes. Add the mushrooms and scallions and sauté 1 minute. Add the cream, raise the heat slightly, and boil until slightly thickened, 1 to 2 minutes.

Add the spinach and stir until wilted. Add the butter and continue to stir until the spinach is soft, 1 to 2 minutes.

MAKE-AHEAD NOTE

The spinach can be refrigerated up to 3 days; reheat over low heat.

ROASTED GARLIC MASHED POTATOES

MAKES 6 SERVINGS

*M*ashed potatoes are a staple of French cuisine, and this is a delicious rustic version. Although creamy, rich, and smooth, these garlickly potatoes are more substantial in texture than a puree. With the mellow flavor and irresistible aroma of roasted garlic, they go well with lamb or chicken.

SERVE WITH:

SIMPLE ROASTED CHICKEN
(PAGE 204)
SADDLE OR RACK OF LAMB
(SEE PAGES 218, 220)
PAN-ROASTED VEAL CHOPS
(SEE PAGE 224)

Lighten the heavy cream with half-and-half or milk, depending on the richness desired.

3 large russet potatoes (about 2½ pounds), peeled and cut into medium dice
Kosher salt
½ cup heavy cream

4 tablespoons butter
2 teaspoons extra-virgin olive oil
8 cloves Oven-Roasted Garlic (page 37)
Freshly ground black pepper

Place the potatoes in a large saucepan with cold, salted water to cover and bring to a boil over high heat. Reduce the heat to medium and simmer until the potatoes are tender, 30 to 35 minutes; drain.

Meanwhile, in a small saucepan over medium heat, heat the cream, butter, and oil together until just simmering and remove from the heat.

In the bowl of an electric mixer with a whisk attachment (or with a hand-held electric mixer), beat the potatoes and garlic on low to medium speed. Slowly add the cream mixture and mix on medium speed, scraping the bowl occasionally, until smooth. Season with salt and pepper.

MAKE-AHEAD NOTE

The roasted garlic can be made up to 2 weeks in advance and refrigerated.

SWEET-POTATO PUREE

MAKES ABOUT 3 CUPS, OR 6 SERVINGS

Sweet potatoes make one of the smooth-est, creamiest, and prettiest purees of all. It compliments roasted poultry especially well, but it's also a good match for lamb. Try some of the variations that follow as well; they can be served with all the dishes suggested for sweet potato puree, as well as pan-roasted squab (page 212) or any of the lamb dishes in this book.

SERVE WITH:
SIMPLE ROASTED CHICKEN (PAGE 204)
ROASTED DUCK (PAGE 210)
SEARED AND ROASTED CHICKEN OR DUCK BREASTS (SEE PAGES 200, 202)
SEARED AND ROASTED TENDERLOIN OF PORK WITH APRICOTS AND PRUNES (PAGE 216)

3 medium to large sweet potatoes, peeled and sliced 1 to 2 inches thick
Kosher salt

4 tablespoons butter
¾ cup heavy cream, warmed
Freshly ground black pepper

Place the potatoes in salted water to cover in a large pot over high heat and bring to a boil. Reduce the heat to medium and simmer until very tender, about 20 minutes. Drain and place in a food processor. Pulse until almost pureed; then add the butter and cream and continue to pulse until smooth. Season to taste with salt and pepper.

MAKE-AHEAD NOTE

The puree can be refrigerated up to 2 days; reheat in a small pot over low heat, with a little cream, milk, or stock, stirring constantly.

VARIATIONS

For parsnip puree, substitute 2 pounds parsnips (9 or 10 parsnips), peeled and cut into 1-inch pieces, for the sweet potatoes. Use ½ cup heavy cream.

For celery root puree, substitute 2¾ pounds celery root (about 4), peeled and cut into 1½-inch pieces, for the sweet potatoes. Use ⅔ cup heavy cream.

HERBED SMASHED POTATOES

MAKES 3¼ CUPS, OR 6 SERVINGS

These potatoes are really easy: all you have to do is boil and dice them and then combine with fresh herbs. Because the dish is put together so quickly, the herbs and olive oil aren't cooked, and they retain their fresh flavors. Rich olive oil flavor is important here, and since the potatoes absorb all the oil, 6 tablespoons is not too much. If you are concerned about fat content (although olive oil is one of the "good" fats), or if you have extra-pungent and flavorful olive oil, you can reduce the amount by a tablespoon or two, but no more; just a drizzle of oil won't give you the right result.

SERVE WITH:
....
SIMPLE ROASTED CHICKEN
(PAGE 204)
SADDLE OF LAMB
(SEE PAGE 218)
RACK OF LAMB (SEE PAGE 220)
PAN-ROASTED VEAL CHOPS
(SEE PAGE 224)
ROASTED SALMON
(SEE PAGE 156)

The herbs provide a lot of the flavor, so this is a good showcase for any of your favorites. If you love tarragon, use it!

8 medium to large new potatoes (red-skinned, creamer, or fingerling), unpeeled

Kosher salt

6 tablespoons extra-virgin olive oil

2 tablespoons chopped fresh herbs (such as savory, thyme, oregano, and sage)

Cracked pepper

Place the potatoes and salted water to cover in a large pot over high heat and bring to a boil. Reduce the heat to medium and simmer until fork tender, about 20 minutes. Drain the potatoes, cut into medium dice, and toss with the olive oil, herbs, ¾ teaspoon salt, and pepper until slightly "smashed."

MAKE-AHEAD NOTE

The potatoes can be refrigerated up to 3 days; reheat in a little olive oil over low heat.

EGGPLANT PROVENÇAL IN ROASTED TOMATOES

MAKES 4 SERVINGS

ORDER OF PREPARATION

- Bake the eggplant.
- While the eggplant is baking, prepare the tomatoes for stuffing.
- Stuff the tomatoes with the eggplant and roast.

*I*n this simple dish, ripe tomatoes are stuffed with garlic and chopped baked eggplant. Then they are sprinkled with fragrant Provençal herbs and roasted. Eggplant and tomato are delicious separately, but this combination enhances their fresh flavors. Together, they make a very pretty package to serve with any lamb or chicken dish.

Cooking the eggplant takes about an hour. After the vegetables are combined, they need only 15 minutes of oven time.

SERVE:
....
AS A STUFFING FOR BELL PEPPERS; BAKE 25 MINUTES AT 350° F.

FOR THE EGGPLANT

1 large or 2 small eggplant, halved lengthwise
3 tablespoons extra-virgin olive oil, plus a few drops for oiling the baking sheet

1 teaspoon herbes de Provence
Kosher salt and freshly ground black pepper

Preheat the oven to 350° F.

Slash the cut surfaces of the eggplant in a crosshatch pattern, drizzle with the olive oil and herbs, and place on a lightly oiled baking sheet, cut-side up.

Bake until tender, about 1 hour. Scoop the flesh into a small bowl, mash lightly, and season to taste with salt and pepper.

TO SERVE

4 medium-size ripe tomatoes
4 cloves Oven-Roasted Garlic
   (page 37)
Extra-virgin olive oil, to drizzle
   over tomatoes

Kosher salt and freshly ground black
   pepper
2 tablespoons coarsely chopped
   parsley

Slice ½ inch off the top of each tomato and scoop out the seeds and loose flesh. Fill each with 1 clove roasted garlic and about ¼ cup eggplant (or enough to fill). Arrange on a baking sheet and drizzle with a little olive oil. Sprinkle each tomato with salt and pepper. Bake until softened and heated through, about 15 minutes. Sprinkle with chopped parsley and serve hot.

MAKE-AHEAD NOTES

✎ The roasted eggplant can be refrigerated up to 3 days.

✎ The stuffed, roasted tomatoes can be refrigerated up to 2 days; reheat in a low oven or in the microwave.

CONFIT BAYALDI

MAKES ONE 8 BY 8-INCH CONFIT, OR 6 SERVINGS

*I*n *this combination, Mediterranean vegetables are thinly sliced, layered, and then slowly cooked in the oven. This dish can be presented in two ways: Immediately after it has been cooked, it will be a loose, somewhat juicy vegetable mixture with a rustic appearance. If you refrigerate it overnight under a weight, to press out much of the moisture, you will have a firmly packed confit that makes a more refined presentation.*

> **SERVE WITH:**
> **ROASTED COD WITH CONFIT BAYALDI AND BASIL OIL (PAGE 173)**
> **GRILLED CHICKEN, FISH, OR LAMB**

The confit could be baked in individual tians (see page 130, for the method).

Slice all the vegetables as thin as possible.

1 tablespoon extra-virgin olive oil, plus extra for drizzling
1 tablespoon unsalted butter
1 medium onion, thinly sliced
2 cloves garlic, peeled and minced
Kosher salt and freshly ground black pepper
½ small eggplant, unpeeled, halved lengthwise and sliced ⅛ inch thick

1 medium zucchini, sliced crosswise on the bias ⅛ inch thick
1 tablespoon each minced fresh tarragon, sage, thyme, and parsley optional
1 medium yellow squash, sliced crosswise on the bias ⅛ inch thick
2 medium-size tomatoes, sliced ⅛ inch thick

Preheat the oven to 300°F. In a large skillet, heat the olive oil and butter together over medium-high heat until the butter has melted. Add the onion and garlic and cook until very soft and transparent, 10 to 12 minutes. Season with salt and pepper.

Season the vegetable layers generously with salt and black pepper.

Keep the proportions of vegetables fairly balanced (two-thirds tomatoes would be too wet).

Layer the vegetables and herbs in an 8 by 8-inch pan as follows: sautéed onions–garlic mixture; the eggplant drizzled with olive oil, and light salt and pepper; the zucchini sprinkled with half of the herbs, and light salt and pepper; the yellow squash, remaining herbs, and light salt and pepper; and the tomatoes. Drizzle olive oil over the top and cover tightly with foil. Place on a baking sheet to catch any overflowing juices, and bake 1½ hours, then remove the foil and bake another ½ hour.

Carefully pour off the juices and discard. The confit is ready to be served, but it will be loose. For a nicer presentation, cover the cooled confit with parchment or waxed paper and a pan of the same size, place 4 soup cans in the pan to weight it, and refrigerate for 1 day or overnight. The confit will be firm enough to slice easily.

MAKE-AHEAD NOTE

✍ The confit can be refrigerated overnight or up to 2 days; reheat over low heat for about 15 minutes. If it has been weighted, reheat in a 350° F. oven for about 15 minutes.

CAPONATA

Caponata is a Sicilian vegetable med-ley that usually is served as a cold hors d'oeuvre. It is similar to the French rata-touille, but more pungent, because of the olives and capers. I stray a bit from the classical treatment, adding carrots for sweetness and forgoing the usual anchovies and celery. Salt and pepper wake up the vegetable flavors, so season the individual ele-ments as you cook them, and then taste and reseason at the very end.

> **SERVE WITH:**
>
> **DOUBLE-CUT LAMB CHOPS AND POLENTA (PAGE 220)**
> **IN PLACE OF RATATOUILLE, WITH ANY DISH**
> **SEARED AND ROASTED CHICKEN BREASTS (SEE PAGE 200)**

7 tablespoons virgin olive oil

2 cloves garlic, minced

1 medium onion, cut into small dice

1 small or medium red onion, cut into small dice

2 medium-size tomatoes, quartered, squeezed, and seeded and cut into small dice

3 tablespoons tomato paste

8 leaves basil, cut in chiffonade

2 tablespoons chopped thyme leaves

1/2 cup Vegetable Stock (page 72), low-salt canned vegetable broth, or water

Kosher salt and freshly ground black pepper

2 medium carrots, peeled and cut into small dice

1 small red or orange bell pepper, cut into small dice

1/2 large eggplant, cut into small dice (about 3 cups)

1 medium zucchini, outside only cut into small dice

1 medium yellow squash, outside only, cut into small dice

15 cured black olives (such as Niçoise), pitted and cut into small dice

1 tablespoon crushed capers

1 tablespoon plus 1 teaspoon balsamic vinegar

Preheat the oven to 300° F.

In a large ovenproof saucepan or casserole, heat 2 tablespoons of the oil over medium heat until shimmering. Sauté the garlic, onion, and red onion until the onions are transparent, about 3 minutes. Add the tomatoes, tomato paste, basil, thyme, and stock and bring to a simmer. Season with salt and pepper and continue simmering.

Meanwhile, in a large skillet over high heat, heat 1 tablespoon oil and sauté the carrots and bell pepper until just tender, 3 minutes. Season them with salt and pepper and add to the simmering tomato mixture.

Add another 2 tablespoons of the oil, heat until smoking, and sauté the eggplant until just tender, about 2 minutes. Season with salt and pepper and add to the simmering tomato mixture.

In the same skillet you used for the eggplant, heat the remaining 2 tablespoons of oil over high heat until shimmering. Add the zucchini and yellow squash and sauté until tender, about 2 minutes. Season with salt and pepper and add to the simmering tomato mixture. Add the olives and capers and mix well. Cover and bake 1 hour. Add the vinegar, taste, and season with salt and pepper, if necessary.

MAKE-AHEAD NOTES

&. The cut vegetables can be refrigerated up to 1 day.

&. The finished Caponata can be refrigerated up to 3 days.

RATATOUILLE

Unlike some other versions of this popular vegetable medley, my ratatouille is a smooth, slowly cooked mixture of vegetables, with a fresh herb and tomato flavor and the texture of a thick sauce. It is delicious hot from the oven, and after a day or two or three, it tastes even better.

> **SERVE AS PART OF:**
> COD AND POTATO CAKES PROVENÇAL WITH RATATOUILLE AND BASIL OIL (PAGE 184)
> SADDLE OF LAMB WITH RATATOUILLE AND BASIL OIL (PAGE 218)

❧ Dice all the vegetables small so that they will cook in about the same time and melt together at the end.

❧ For a chunky ratatouille, cut the vegetables into large dice.

❧ Large chunks of zucchini will give the dish a pronounced zucchini flavor, rather than a dominant tomato flavor.

Substitute extra zucchini for yellow squash, yellow or orange bell peppers for red peppers (you can use green peppers, but the others are milder).

4 tablespoons virgin olive oil
1 medium onion, cut into small dice
1 medium red bell pepper, cut into small dice
1 clove garlic, minced
½ medium eggplant, cut into small dice
1 medium yellow squash, outside flesh only, cut into small dice
1 medium zucchini, outside flesh only, cut into small dice

4 medium-size ripe tomatoes, peeled, seeded, and cut into small dice
1½ tablespoons tomato paste
⅓ cup Chicken Stock (page 72), Vegetable Stock (page 72), or low-salt canned broth
1 bay leaf
1 teaspoon minced fresh thyme leaves
Kosher salt and freshly ground black pepper
Pinch of cayenne

Don't salt the eggplant before cooking; salting will just make it wetter. After its long, slow cooking with tomatoes and other vegetables, it won't taste bitter.

In a medium skillet, heat 1 tablespoon of the olive oil over medium-high heat until shimmering. Add the onion and bell pepper and sauté until softened, 4 to 5 minutes. Add the garlic and sauté 1 minute. Drain off the oil and transfer the vegetables to a medium casserole. Add the remaining 3 tablespoons olive oil to the skillet and heat until shimmering. Sauté the eggplant, squash, and zucchini until softened, 7 to 8 minutes, drain, and add to the onion mixture.

Preheat the oven to 275° F.

A parchment cover set right on top of the vegetables keeps them moist by preventing evaporation.

Place the onion–eggplant mixture over medium heat and add the tomatoes, tomato paste, stock, and herbs. Heat through, mixing well, and season with salt, pepper, and cayenne. Cover with a circle of buttered parchment paper and cook in the oven 1 hour; uncover and cook another 30 minutes, until thick and melted. Taste and adjust the seasoning. Remove the bay leaf before serving.

MAKE-AHEAD NOTES

The diced vegetables can be refrigerated up to 1 day.

The finished ratatouille can be refrigerated up to 3 days; reheat in a 275° F. oven or over low heat, or microwave.

CARAMELIZED ONION TARTS

MAKES 6 APPETIZER SERVINGS

ORDER OF PREPARATION

- Prepare the pâte brisée and refrigerate.
- Prepare the Chive Oil.
- Bake the tart shells.
- While the shells are baking, prepare the onion confit.
- Assemble the tarts.

This reminds me of a really good onion soup, with its sweet, cooked onions and deeply flavorful stock. Red onions, which caramelize especially well, are cooked with a little sugar until soft and then simmered until they turn into a golden, glossy confit. A touch of vinegar ensures that the tart filling is sweet without being cloying. Don't be surprised when you start with a large pile of raw onions in your pan—they will melt down a lot as they cook. In classic style, onions for confit are cooked in duck fat. If you want to substitute it for the olive oil, it is available in specialty food stores.

Caramelized Onion Tarts are the perfect appetizer to make ahead of time. The onion confit and the tart shells are prepared separately, and the baked shells are filled just before serving. You can make a single 9-inch onion tart, but it will be a little difficult to cut neatly; individual tarts are much easier to handle.

Serve onion confit under a seared and roasted fish steak or fillet (see page 151).

For caramelized onion and duck tarts, add 1 cup of braised duck meat (see page 64) to the onion confit.

FOR THE PÂTE BRISÉE

1¾ cups all-purpose flour	1 stick plus 7 tablespoons butter, at
½ teaspoon kosher salt	room temperature
½ tablespoon sugar	⅓ cup cold water

In the bowl of an electric mixer, use dough hook on low speed to combine the flour, salt, and sugar. Add the butter by chunks. When the mixture is the consistency of coarse meal, add the water and mix thoroughly, but do not overmix. The dough will be moist (but it will be tough if overmixed).

Gently shape the dough into a ball, wrap in plastic wrap, and refrigerate at least 4 hours or overnight.

When ready to bake, divide the dough into 6 equal pieces. On a lightly floured board, roll each piece ⅛ inch thick and press into a 4- to 4½-inch tart pan, making sure it extends ¾ inch up the sides of the pan. Refrigerate 1 to 2 hours.

Preheat the oven to 400°F. Line each shell with aluminum foil and fill with beans or pie weights. Bake 15 minutes, then remove the foil and beans,

This pâte brisée is good for sweet or savory tarts; it will make one 9-inch piecrust.

reduce the temperature to 375° F., and bake until light golden brown, about 10 minutes.

FOR THE ONION CONFIT

Substitute balsamic vinegar for sherry vinegar, Perfect Flaky Piecrust (page 254) or frozen purchased puff pastry for the pâté brisée.

3 tablespoons virgin olive oil
1 tablespoon butter
3 pounds red onions, peeled and very thinly sliced
4 tablespoons sugar

½ to ¾ cup Veal Stock (page 74), Vegetable Stock (page 72), or low-salt canned broth (optional)
3 to 4 tablespoons sherry vinegar
Kosher salt and freshly ground black pepper

In a large skillet, heat the oil and butter over high heat until shimmering. Add the onions, sprinkle with the sugar, and cook without stirring for 5 minutes. Stir, then continue to cook, stirring occasionally, for another 5 minutes. Reduce the heat to medium-high and cook 5 minutes more. Raise the heat to high, add ½ cup of stock, and boil for 1 minute. Add the vinegar and continue cooking 10 to 12 minutes, reducing the heat to medium-high as the onions begin to brown.

Taste and add stock if the onions are too tart, or vinegar if they are too sweet. Season with salt and pepper and keep warm.

TO SERVE

3 teaspoons minced chives
6 tablespoons Chive Oil (page 6), optional

Remove the shells from the tart pans. Spoon about ½ cup of the onions into each shell, sprinkle with the minced chives, and place on individual serving plates. Drizzle each plate with the optional chive oil.

MAKE-AHEAD NOTES

✎ The pâte brisée can be refrigerated as long as overnight; it can be frozen up to 1 month.

✎ The baked tart shells can be wrapped in plastic and kept at room temperature overnight or in the refrigerator up to 2 days.

✎ The Chive Oil can be refrigerated up to 2 days.

✎ The onion confit can be refrigerated up to 3 days.

CHAPTER 6

FISH AND

SHELLFISH

Perhaps it's my fondness for all things Mediterranean, or the fact that it's among the quickest foods to cook, but seafood of one kind or another seems to turn up on my dinner table on a nearly nightly basis. Oddly enough, it was during a period when I worked at a steak house that my appreciation for fish first came into full flower. Before I went on to shop at the wholesale meat markets on Washington Street, it became my habit to stop at Manhattan's Fulton Fish Market, where I chose the freshest, sweetest-smelling, most bright-eyed fish. This exposure to so many superb specimens of fish and shellfish opened my eyes to the myriad possibilities for preparation. I found fish to be light and versatile, providing a delicate backdrop for the fresh vegetables and herbs that inspire my cooking.

The way fish is cooked in restaurants and at home has changed considerably in the past twenty years. Only fairly recently have we begun to liberate fish from traditional butter and cream sauces and crumb or batter coatings. We now highlight the fine variations in texture and flavor among fish, from fragile sole to steak-like tuna, and use sauces to enhance, rather than hide, them. Yet despite its quick, easy preparation, people often seem afraid to buy and cook fish. This chapter is intended to take the mystery out of those processes and to demonstrate that nothing could be simpler or make a more lovely presentation.

The first thing to do is find a good fish market, even if it means you must pay more than supermarket prices. When you walk in, take a deep breath and a good look around: the store should be clean, without a fishy smell, and the fish should be displayed on ice, not wrapped in plastic. Whole fish should look shiny and moist, with firm, elastic skin. The eyes should be clear and the gills should be bright red. If the fish is fresh, it will almost look alive on its bed of ice. Fillets and steaks are better cut to order than precut, but either way, their flesh should not have any discoloration. I always ask to touch the fish, and if the answer is no, I ask the seller to press his own finger into the fish, so I can see that it is resilient and not mushy. And if I can smell the fish as it's coming toward my nose, I don't want it.

When you buy fish, have it wrapped in nonabsorbent paper and then store it that way in your refrigerator, to reduce the chances of its drying out. Refrigerate fish as soon as possible after buying and keep it below 40° F., preferably close to freezing, but not frozen. You can do this by setting the wrapped fish in a bowl with ice and resting the wrapped fish in it in your refrigerator. If it is really fresh, it should keep that way for up to four days; if you aren't sure of its freshness, don't keep it much longer than one day. You also may freeze fresh fish, but be sure to ask if the fish had been previously frozen.

Buy all shellfish as close to cooking time as possible. Choose clams and mussels with tightly closed shells that do not appear dry and that have no odor. The lobsters and crabs you want will show signs of vigorous movement when the fishmonger picks them up. Have them packed in moist newspapers or seaweed and refrigerate in the wrappings until you are ready to use them. Do not wrap them in plastic when you get them home, because they are alive and need to breathe.

Cooking Fish

Searing and roasting is my preferred technique for cooking fish steaks and fillets. Searing holds in the juices and produces an appetizing color and texture, and roasting surrounds the fish with heat and cooks it quickly. The fish is first seared briefly in a little hot oil, then quickly cooked through in a hot oven, and then seared on the other side in oil with a bit of butter added, to ensure a golden crust. This may sound time-consuming, but because of the high heat involved the whole process takes only minutes and the flavors and textures of the finished fish are unbeatable.

This technique also has the wonderful advantage of allowing you to cook fish ahead. Sear the fish on both sides, put it aside for an hour or more—it won't lose that color or that sear—and finish it in the oven later. Be warned, however, that as with any food, there will be some carryover cooking as the fish waits; when you are ready to complete the cooking, you will find it a bit closer to done than it was when it was set aside. So be sure to adjust the roasting time accordingly to avoid overcooking. Cooking ahead works best with thick cuts like salmon and swordfish, which give you some leeway if your judgment is not perfect. Thinner pieces of fish, like fillet of snapper, are better when seared minutes before starting dinner, rather than hours; but if you must cook ahead, do just a quick sear, leaving the fish almost raw, then roast as usual.

Related to searing but different in important ways is sautéing. When you sauté fish fillets or steaks, the important things to remember are high heat and little fat (too much oil will give you greasy fish). You must also use a pan large enough to hold the fish with space around it, so it doesn't steam.

Other methods I rely on for fish are pan-searing (that is, searing without the roasting step), grilling, roasting and baking in the oven, poaching, and, for a simple and delicious gravlax, curing. I describe all of them in this chapter.

Doneness

To me, the ideal degree of doneness for fish is medium-rare. Medium-rare fish is hot throughout and slightly firm but still juicy and moist. Here are the indications for medium-rare fish:

- When fillets are done, the flesh turns from translucent to just opaque and is juicy. They will feel lightly springy to the touch.
- When whole fish is done, the eyes are white, the juices run clear, and it is slightly firm to the touch.
- When fish cakes and crab cakes are done, they will be golden brown and cooked through.

However you cook your fish, keep testing it by pressing the flesh firmly—soon you will learn how your ideal state of doneness feels. Until you learn to judge by feel, you may want to actually see whether the fish is still bloody and raw in the middle. To do this, make a little incision, just deep enough to expose the inner flesh. Fish that is medium-rare will turn opaque; tuna will be light red in the middle.

More Recipes

Seared or grilled shellfish also make a delicious garnish for soups and add a bit of texture to salads and pasta dishes. See the recipes below for ideas on how to use the cooking techniques in this chapter to enhance every course of a meal:

- Celery Root Soup with Seared Bay Scallops (page 90)
- Broccoli Soup with Sautéed Shrimp, Mushrooms, and Roasted Garlic (page 102)
- Chilled Cucumber Soup with Grilled Shrimp and Caviar (page 98)
- Red Snapper Salad with Gazpacho Vinaigrette (page 50)
- Marinated Tuna Salade Niçoise (page 54)
- Warm Shrimp Salad with Artichokes and Cannellini Beans (page 58)
- Warm Scallop Salad with Parsnips and Wild Mushroom Vinaigrette (page 66)
- Seared Sashimi Tuna Two Ways (page 56)
- Sautéed Sea Scallops with Onion Confit and Beet Oil (page 61)
- Softshell Crab Salad with Fennel, Red Onion, and Kumquats (page 60)
- Rainbow Trout Salad with Kalamata Olives, Tomatoes, and Lemon Confit (page 52)
- Lobster Salad with White Beans and Fresh Thyme (page 59)
- Crab Salad with Ginger–Citrus Vinaigrette (page 49)

SEARING AND ROASTING

Searing and roasting is a great way to cook thick fish steaks like salmon, halibut, swordfish, tuna, and cod, as well as thinner fillets like snapper and bass. I use this method again and again because it is so flexible. You can sear ahead and roast later, and you can substitute fish as you like; any of the recipes will work with whatever fish looks best and freshest at the market.

As you will see in the recipes that follow, I love to serve seared and roasted fish on top of a bed of chewy grains or tender vegetables, surrounded by a drizzle of boldly flavored sauce. Each component enhances the others, giving a variety of tastes and textures in every bite. After you have served the combinations I suggest, try inventing your own compositions of fish and grains or vegetables. If you don't want to serve a sauce, drizzle a little flavored oil around the edges—preferably one that echoes or enhances the vegetables and herbs in the dish.

Make sure your skillet can go from the top of the stove to the oven. When cooking several pieces of fish, you can use more than one pan. At the point when one pan goes in the oven, another can go on the burner to heat up, for cooking the next batch. For each pan, use 1 tablespoon of oil.

METHOD

~ In a skillet over high heat, heat the oil until smoking.

~ Sear the fish flesh-side down until it gets a golden-brown crust, about 30 seconds.

~ Place the entire skillet into a very hot oven for a few minutes, cooking the fish about seven-eighths through.

~ Return the skillet to the stove top over high heat and add a little butter. Turn the fish and sear the skin side until crisp and colored, 30 seconds to 1 minute.

~ Turn again and remove from the skillet.

HALIBUT WITH TOMATO–CUMIN BROTH AND CURRIED COUSCOUS

MAKES 6 SERVINGS

ORDER OF PREPARATION

- Prepare the tomato–cumin broth and keep warm.
- Mix the Curried Couscous and let sit.
- While the couscous sits, sear and roast the fish.

These golden-crusted fillets are served on a mound of curry-scented couscous and surrounded by tangy orange-red broth. This unusual and versatile tomato broth has fresh herbal aromas of thyme and tarragon, along with the spicy flavor of cumin.

Best of all, the components are just quick enough for you to do right before serving.

SERVE TOMATO–CUMIN BROTH WITH:
....

GREEN AND YELLOW SQUASH RIBBONS (PAGE 128) ANY SEARED AND ROASTED OR GRILLED FISH GRILLED VEGETABLES (SEE PAGE 180) ROASTED FENNEL, TOMATOES, AND OLIVES (SEE PAGE 222)

FOR THE TOMATO–CUMIN BROTH

2 tablespoons butter

1½ medium onions, cut into medium dice

1 medium red bell pepper, seeded and roughly cut into 1-inch pieces

3 medium-size ripe tomatoes, roughly cut into 2-inch pieces

1 teaspoon finely chopped tarragon

1 teaspoon finely chopped thyme

2½ teaspoons ground cumin

2½ cups Chicken Stock (page 72), Vegetable Stock (page 72), or low-salt canned broth

Kosher salt and freshly ground black pepper

In a medium saucepan, melt the butter over medium heat and sauté the onions and bell pepper until soft, 12 to 14 minutes. Add the tomatoes, tarragon, thyme, cumin, and stock, raise the heat to high, and bring to a boil, then lower the heat to medium and simmer for 20 minutes. Strain through a coarse strainer, pushing down on the solids, and season with salt and pepper.

FOR THE HALIBUT

6 halibut steaks or fillets, about 8 ounces each

Kosher salt and freshly ground black pepper

1 tablespoon pure or virgin olive oil

1½ to 2 tablespoons butter

Preheat the oven to 400°F. Season the fish with salt and pepper.

In a large sauté pan, heat the oil over high heat until smoking. Add the fish flesh-side down and sear until golden, about 30 seconds. Place the pan in the oven for 4 to 5 minutes, or until the fish is nearly cooked to your preferred degree of doneness. Return the pan to the stove over high heat and add the butter. Turn the fish and cook until done, 1 to 2 minutes. Turn the fish back over and remove from the pan. (If the fish is difficult to turn, just leave it in the oven until done, another 1 to 2 minutes.)

TO SERVE

3 cups Curried Couscous (page 117)

Mound the couscous in the center of 6 serving plates and top with the fish. Spoon the broth around the couscous.

MAKE-AHEAD NOTES

&. The tomato–cumin broth can be refrigerated up to 3 days.

&. The Curried Couscous can be refrigerated up to 3 days. Rewarm over low heat or in a microwave.

VARIATION

For Halibut with Tomato–Cumin Broth and Seafood, in a large skillet or sauté pan over high heat, bring to a boil ½ cup combined stock, water, and wine. Add 18 cleaned clams or mussels, cover, and steam until they open, discarding any that do not. Scatter a few steamed clams or mussels around each serving of fish.

HERB-ROASTED HALIBUT
WITH A RAGOUT OF WILD MUSHROOMS,
LEEKS, AND POTATOES

MAKES 4 SERVINGS

ORDER OF PREPARATION

- Cook the potatoes, cool, and slice.
- Prepare the mushroom broth.
- Cook the leeks and mushrooms.
- When you are ready to sear the fish, combine the potatoes, leeks, and broth.
- While the broth warms, cook the fish.

A savory mushroom and potato ragout flavored with leeks, herbs, and stock provides the foundation for golden-seared halibut. This ragout could be made with ordinary chicken stock, rather than mushroom and herb-infused stock, and it would taste good. But in cooking, you often can take an extra step that elevates the food to a new level. Adding the mushrooms and thyme makes a noticeable difference in the finished dish—and it doesn't involve a lot of work.

An excellent idea for a dinner party, this allows you to prepare components ahead of time, even to sear the fish, then combine everything just before serving.

SERVE MUSHROOM RAGOUT WITH:

SNAPPER, INSTEAD OF POTATO GALETTE AND PORT WINE SAUCE (SEE PAGE **158**)
SALMON, INSTEAD OF LENTILS AND RED WINE SAUCE (SEE PAGE **160**)
ROASTED COD, INSTEAD OF CONFIT BAYALDI (SEE PAGE **173**)

FOR THE RAGOUT

The green part of leeks is tougher than the white, but cooking in stock will tenderize it. Leek greens taste less oniony than the white bulbs and add color to the ragout.

6 baby potatoes (creamers, red new potatoes, or Yukon golds)
Kosher salt
3 tablespoons virgin olive oil
8 ounces white domestic mushrooms, trimmed and cut into 1/4-inch slices
12 shiitake mushrooms, stems reserved and caps cut into 1/4-inch slices

1 3/4 cups Chicken Stock (page 72) or low-salt canned chicken broth
1 tablespoon chopped thyme leaves
2 leeks, green part only, well washed and cut on the diagonal into 1/2-inch slices
1 tablespoon butter
Freshly ground black pepper

Place the potatoes in a large saucepan with cold, salted water to cover and bring to a boil over high heat. Reduce the heat to medium and simmer until the potatoes are tender, 30 to 35 minutes. Cool and cut each potato into 6 pieces.

In a medium saucepan, heat 1 tablespoon of the olive oil over high heat until just smoking. Add the white mushrooms and shiitake stems and sauté for 1 minute. Add the stock and thyme and bring to a boil. Reduce the heat to medium and simmer about 15 minutes, until the broth is full-flavored. Strain the broth, discarding the solids.

In a medium sauté pan over medium heat, heat the remaining 2 tablespoons of olive oil until just smoking and sauté the shiitake caps until light golden brown, 1 to 2 minutes. Add the leeks and butter, cover, and cook until the leeks are tender, 6 to 7 minutes. Season with salt and pepper and remove from the heat.

Add the potatoes to the leek mixture, stir in the mushroom broth, and bring to a boil over high heat. Reduce the heat to medium and simmer 5 minutes. Taste and season with salt and pepper.

FOR THE HALIBUT

4 halibut steaks or fillets, 6 ounces each	2 teaspoons chopped fresh herbs (tarragon, savory, or parsley)
Kosher salt and freshly ground black pepper	1 teaspoon herbes de Provence
	2 tablespoons virgin olive oil

Preheat the oven to 400° F. Season the fish with salt and pepper and sprinkle on one side with the fresh herbs and herbes de Provence.

In a medium nonstick skillet, heat the olive oil over medium-high heat until shimmering. Add the fish, herb-side down, and sear until golden. Place in the oven and roast without turning until opaque and medium rare, 7 to 10 minutes, depending on thickness. Alternatively, you can continue to cook the fish on top of the stove, turning once, until medium-rare, 3 to 4 minutes on each side.

TO SERVE

Divide the ragout among 4 warm, shallow serving bowls and top with a halibut fillet. Serve immediately.

MAKE-AHEAD NOTES

&. The potatoes can be refrigerated up to 1 day (they will be easier to slice if they have been cooked and cooled).

&. The mushroom broth can be refrigerated up to 1 day.

&. The seared fish can be kept at room temperature on a lightly oiled baking sheet, herb-side up, for up to 1 hour; or refrigerated up to 3 hours and brought to room temperature before finishing in the oven.

ROASTED SALMON WITH QUINOA AND CARROT OIL

ORDER OF PREPARATION

- Prepare the Carrot Oil.
- Start the quinoa.
- While the quinoa is simmering, sear and roast the salmon.

These golden-brown seared and roasted fillets are especially good set atop a bed of grains, which adds contrasting flavors and textures to each mouthful. My choice here is super-nutritious quinoa mixed with pine nuts, diced mushrooms, onions, and carrots. Quinoa served this way is so delicious that it doesn't shout "health food." The carrot oil is luminous orange, with a concentrated carrot flavor. The dish looks especially pretty if you pack the quinoa into a 3-inch round ring mold, remove the mold, and place the fish on top of the grain.

If you don't want to fire up your oven, you can skip the roasting and simply sear this salmon, taking a little longer to cook it through on top of the stove.

FOR THE QUINOA

Good, chewy substitutes for quinoa: Wild Rice with Pine Nuts (page 119) or Curried Couscous (page 117).

4 tablespoons pine nuts

2 medium carrots, peeled and cut into brunoise

Kosher salt

1 tablespoon virgin olive oil

½ medium onion, diced fine

½ cup finely diced domestic or shiitake mushrooms

½ cup quinoa

1 cup Chicken Stock (page 72), low-salt canned chicken broth, or Vegetable Stock (page 72), plus a bit extra, if needed

Freshly ground black pepper

1 tablespoon minced parsley

Preheat the oven to 350°F. Spread the pine nuts on a baking sheet in 1 layer and toast until golden brown, 5 to 6 minutes. Chop medium-coarse and reserve.

In a small saucepan, combine the carrots with salted water to cover and bring to a boil over high heat. Boil them until tender, then drain and shock in a large bowl of ice water. Drain again and reserve.

In a medium skillet, heat the olive oil over medium heat until almost smoking and sauté the onion for 1 minute. Add the carrots and the mushrooms and sauté 1 minute. Add the quinoa and sauté 1 minute. Add the chicken stock, raise the heat to high, and bring to a boil. Reduce the heat to medium and simmer until the quinoa is tender, about 15 minutes, adding extra stock if it dries out. Transfer to a strainer if there is excess liquid, then return to the pot, season with salt and pepper, and stir in the nuts and parsley. Reserve, keeping warm.

FOR THE SALMON

For the fish, substitute boneless, skinless chicken breasts.

4 salmon fillets, 6 ounces each
Kosher salt and freshly ground black pepper

2 teaspoons vegetable oil
1 tablespoon butter

If you are going to finish the salmon in the oven, preheat to 400°F. Season the salmon with salt and pepper. In a large nonstick skillet, heat the oil over medium-high heat until shimmering. Add the salmon flesh-side down and sear 3 to 4 minutes, add the butter, turn over the fish, and cook another 3 to 4 minutes on the other side. Or sear flesh-side down, then place in the preheated oven until medium rare, about 5 minutes. Then add butter and sear the other side until brown. Remove from the pan.

TO SERVE

Substitutes for Carrot Oil: Basil Oil (page 5), Curry Oil (page 12)— especially nice if you substitute Curried Couscous, Beet Oil (page 9), or Roasted Garlic–Black Olive Oil (page 8).

½ cup Carrot Oil (page 10)

Mound about ½ cup of quinoa in the center of each warm serving plate. Place a portion of salmon on top of the quinoa and drizzle the carrot oil around the salmon.

MAKE-AHEAD NOTES

❧ The Carrot Oil can be refrigerated up to 2 days; bring to room temperature before serving.

❧ The quinoa can be refrigerated up to 5 days; rewarm over low heat or in a microwave, with a bit of stock.

SNAPPER WITH POTATO GALETTE AND PORT WINE SAUCE

MAKES 4 SERVINGS

ORDER OF PREPARATION

- Make the Port Wine Sauce and keep warm.
- Prepare the potato galettes and keep warm.
- Prepare the vegetables.
- While the vegetables are warming, sear and roast the fish.

Although this dish can be prepared just before serving, some of its components could be cooked ahead—potato galettes, blanched vegetables, and Port Wine Sauce—and then combined with fish that is quickly sautéed. Using components this way gives you a lot of room for creativity, and equally important, it simplifies life.

Potato galettes will flip easily and will stay together because of the starch in the potatoes. Idaho or baking potatoes, which are the starchiest, are the best to use. Brown them in clarified butter (see Basic Preparation Techniques, page xiv), which can be heated to a higher temperature than regular butter. This recipe calls for reheating the galettes at 450° F., since you will have the oven at that temperature to cook the fish, but you could reheat them at 200° to 350° F. for 2 to 3 minutes.

FOR THE VEGETABLES

Substitute zucchini for asparagus; string beans, wax beans, or a combination for haricots verts; a mixture of cherry, pear, and regular tomatoes for pear tomatoes.

Kosher salt
12 asparagus spears
12 haricots verts or thin green beans
1 tablespoon butter
2 tablespoons Chicken Stock (page 72) or low-salt canned chicken broth

12 morels, chanterelles, oyster mushrooms, or domestic mushrooms
8 pear or cherry tomatoes
Freshly ground black pepper

Fill a large pot with lightly salted water and bring to a boil over high heat. Blanch the asparagus until tender, about 2 minutes, then remove with tongs and plunge into ice water. Drain. Repeat with the haricots verts.

In a medium saucepan, heat the butter and stock over medium heat until simmering. Add the mushrooms and sauté until wilted. Add the tomatoes and the blanched asparagus and beans and toss until just warmed. Season to taste with salt and pepper.

Substitute bass or similar thin fillets for snapper.

1 tablespoon olive oil

4 snapper fillets, 6 ounces each

Kosher salt and freshly ground black pepper

1 teaspoon unsalted butter

Preheat the oven to 450° F.

In a large skillet or sauté pan, heat 1 tablespoon olive oil over high heat until it just begins to smoke. Season the flesh side of the fish with salt and pepper and place in the hot pan, flesh-side down. Immediately put the pan in the oven and cook 2 to 3 minutes, until rare to medium rare. Return the pan to high heat and add the butter. Then turn the fish and keep it over the heat just until it forms a crust on the skin-side, 30 to 45 seconds. Turn the fish skin side up again and remove from the pan.

TO SERVE

Substitute Red-Wine Salmon Sauce (page 36) for Port Wine Sauce; a drizzle of Basil Oil (page 5), Rosemary Oil (page 7), or Chive Oil (page 6) for the sauce.

4 potato galettes (see page 46)

½ cup Port Wine Sauce (page 31)

Place a potato galette on each plate. Top with the vegetables and then the fish, and drizzle the sauce around them.

MAKE-AHEAD NOTES

❧ The Port Wine Sauce can be refrigerated up to 1 week or frozen.

❧ The potato galettes can be wrapped tightly in plastic and kept at room temperature for several hours. Or, they can be refrigerated up to 1 day and reheated on a baking sheet in a 450° F. oven for about 30 seconds.

❧ The blanched vegetables can be refrigerated up to 1 day.

SALMON WITH LENTILS AND RED WINE SALMON SAUCE

MAKES 6 SERVINGS

ORDER OF PREPARATION

- Prepare the Red Wine Salmon Sauce.
- Cook the lentils.
- Combine the lentils with the shallots and garlic.
- While the lentils are warming, sear and roast the salmon.

A few recipes seem to ignore the rules of balance: all their components are full-flavored and no one ingredient plays second fiddle to another. Here is one of those combinations: lentils are flavored with bacon, garlic, and shallots and simmered in cream; salmon is naturally rich and oily; red wine sauce is intense. But despite their strength, these elements don't overpower one another. This is because fresh herbs reign in the strongly flavored lentils, the fish is simply seared and roasted, and the sauce is used sparingly, almost as an accent.

> **SERVE LENTILS WITH:**
>
> **SNAPPER, INSTEAD OF POTATO GALETTE AND PORT WINE SAUCE (SEE PAGE 158)**
> **ROASTED COD, INSTEAD OF CONFIT BAYALDI (SEE PAGE 173)**
> **SEARED AND ROASTED CHICKEN BREASTS (SEE PAGE 200)**

FOR THE LENTILS

French green lentils are the most flavorful and hold up the best when cooked.

Omit the bacon if you choose, although the lentils will lose their slightly smoky taste.

1 cup lentils, preferably French green lentils
6 cups water
2 tablespoons virgin olive oil
3 thick slices bacon, cut into small dice (about ½ cup)
3 medium cloves garlic, minced

2 large shallots, minced
¾ cup heavy cream
½ tablespoon minced fresh thyme leaves
1 teaspoon minced fresh marjoram
Salt and freshly ground black pepper

In a medium saucepan, combine the lentils and water and bring to a boil over high heat. Simmer until just tender, about 10 minutes, and drain.

In a medium saucepan over medium heat, heat the olive oil until almost smoking. Add the bacon and cook 1 minute. Add the garlic and shallots and cook, stirring, until the mixture is softened but not colored. Add the cream, bring to a boil, and cook until bubbly and slightly thickened, about 1 minute. Add the lentils, thyme, and marjoram, bring to a boil, and simmer until the lentils are heated through, about 10 minutes. Season with salt and pepper.

FOR THE SALMON

6 salmon fillets, 5 to 6 ounces each

Kosher salt and freshly ground black pepper

4 teaspoons olive oil

1 teaspoon unsalted butter

Preheat the oven to 400° F. Season the fillets with salt and pepper.

In a large skillet, heat the oil over high heat until smoking. Add the fillets and sear on the skin side. Place in the oven until the fish is medium rare, 3 to 4 minutes. Return the pan to high heat and add the butter. Turn the fish and sear the other side 30 to 45 seconds. Turn the fish back over and remove from the pan.

TO SERVE

¾ cup Red Wine Salmon Sauce (page 36)

Substitute Roasted Garlic Mashed Potatoes (page 132) for lentils, a drizzle of Basil Oil (page 5) for the sauce.

Divide the lentils among 6 warmed plates. Cover with a salmon fillet and drizzle about 3 tablespoons of the red wine sauce over and around the salmon. Serve immediately.

MAKE-AHEAD NOTES

✎ The Red Wine Salmon Sauce can be refrigerated up to 5 days or frozen.

✎ The lentils can be refrigerated up to 4 days.

✎ The seared fish can be kept at room temperature on a lightly oiled baking sheet, herb-side up, for up to 1 hour; or refrigerated up to 3 hours and brought to room temperature before finishing in the oven.

BASS WITH FLAGEOLETS, PANCETTA, AND THYME, IN RED WINE SALMON SAUCE

MAKES 4 SERVINGS

ORDER OF PREPARATION

- Prepare the Red Wine Salmon Sauce.
- Cook the flageolets.
- Combine with the leeks and pancetta, and cook.
- While the flageolets are simmering, sear and roast the bass.

A hearty, aromatic ragout serves as a bed for crisp-skinned seared and roasted fillets. It is a rich mixture of flavors and textures, with red wine, creamy cooked

SERVE THE BEAN RAGOUT WITH:
....
ROASTED SALMON
(SEE PAGE **156**)

beans, and smoky pancetta. Serve it in bowls for a beautiful and homey presentation.

I find flageolets have a more delicate and interesting flavor than other dried beans, yet they still give satisfying body to the sauce. The beans and sauce can both be made ahead of time; the fish will take only a few minutes to sear, just before serving.

FOR THE BEANS

Substitute Great Northern white beans for flageolets.

Substitute regular bacon for pancetta (a cured, unsmoked bacon).

¾ cup dried flageolets
Kosher salt
2 leeks, green part only, cut into ¼-inch diagonal slices
2 tablespoons pure olive oil
3 slices pancetta, ⅛ inch thick, cut into small dice

2 teaspoons butter
½ cup Chicken Stock (page 72) or low-salt canned chicken broth, plus extra as needed
½ cup Red Wine Salmon Sauce, plus extra as needed (page 36)
1 tablespoon chopped fresh thyme

Place the beans in a medium saucepan with cold salted water to cover by 2 inches and bring to a boil over high heat. Reduce the heat to medium and simmer until tender, about 45 minutes. Drain and reserve.

Over high heat, blanch the leek greens in a small saucepan of boiling salted water. Drain, then shock in ice water. Drain and reserve.

If the sauce seems too thick, add a little more red wine sauce or Chicken Stock.

In a medium saucepan, heat the olive oil over high heat until shimmering. Sauté the pancetta until just crisp, 1 to 2 minutes, and add the beans, leeks, butter, and stock. Bring the mixture to a boil and add the red wine sauce and thyme. Reduce the heat to medium and simmer 1 to 2 minutes. The mixture should be just thick enough to coat a spoon.

    4 fillets of striped or black sea bass,   1 tablespoon pure olive oil
        6 to 8 ounces each   2 teaspoons butter
    Kosher salt and freshly ground black
       pepper

Preheat the oven to 400° F. Season the fillets with salt and pepper.

In a large sauté pan or skillet, heat the olive oil until smoking. Add the fillets flesh-side down and sear until golden, 30 seconds. Place the pan in the oven and roast until the fish is almost opaque, 3 to 4 minutes. Remove from the oven and add the butter to the pan. Turn the fillets skin-side down and cook over medium-high heat for 1 minute. Turn the fish over again and remove from the pan; drain on a paper towel.

TO SERVE

Divide the beans and sauce among 4 shallow bowls, mounding them in the center. Place the fish on top and serve hot.

MAKE-AHEAD NOTES

∾ The Red Wine Salmon Sauce can be refrigerated up to 5 days or frozen up to 1 month.

∾ The flageolets can be refrigerated up to 2 days; reheat in the sauce.

SALMON WITH ONION CONFIT, WINTER VEGETABLES, AND RED WINE SALMON SAUCE

MAKES 6 SERVINGS

ORDER OF PREPARATION

- Prepare the Red Wine Salmon Sauce.
- While the sauce is simmering, prepare the onion confit.
- While the confit is cooking, prepare the winter vegetables.
- While the vegetables are cooking, sear and roast the salmon.

A crisp, herb-crusted salmon steak atop a cushion of melted onions, surrounded by fragrant roasted winter vegetables and a drizzle of red wine sauce, is absolutely ideal fare for holiday entertaining. Onion confit gives the dish richness and adds deep sweet and tart flavors. The roasted vegetables echo the sweetness of the confit, and add extra texture and color.

> **SERVE ONION CONFIT:**
>
> AS A BED FOR ANY SEARED AND ROASTED FISH STEAK OR FILET

Red Wine Salmon Sauce repeats the salmon flavor and adds leek and garlic essences to the oniony confit. Its blended flavors and dense texture bring the entire dish together. Any variety of fresh herbs or even a single herb can be substituted for the ones I suggest here.

FOR THE WINTER VEGETABLES

For the winter vegetables, substitute roasted carrots, parsnips, potatoes, or any other earthy-sweet root vegetables.

1 large or 2 medium beets
6 small new potatoes
½ small to medium butternut squash, seeded

1 medium turnip, halved and peeled
2 tablespoons plus 2 teaspoons butter
Kosher salt and freshly ground black pepper

In separate small saucepans, combine the beets and the potatoes with water to cover and bring to a boil over high heat. Reduce the heat to medium and cook until tender, 15 to 20 minutes, depending on their size. Drain. When the beets and potatoes are cool enough to handle, peel them and cut into small dice. Peel the squash and turnip and cut into small dice.

Melt 2 tablespoons of the butter in a large nonstick pan over medium-high heat. Season the potatoes, squash, and turnips with salt and pepper and sauté until golden brown, 5 to 6 minutes.

Meanwhile, melt the remaining 2 teaspoons butter in a medium nonstick pan over medium-high heat. Season the beets with salt and pepper and sauté them until heated through, 2 to 3 minutes. (Sautéing the beets separately ensures that all the vegetables won't turn beet red.)

Taste and reseason, if necessary. Cover with foil and keep warm.

1 tablespoon minced fresh savory

1 tablespoon minced fresh thyme

1 tablespoon minced fresh parsley

2 tablespoons minced fresh tarragon

6 salmon fillets, 5 to 6 ounces each

4 teaspoons olive oil

1 teaspoon unsalted butter

Preheat the oven to 400°F. Combine the minced herbs in a shallow dish or on a piece of waxed paper and coat the flesh side of each fillet with them.

In a large skillet, heat the oil over high heat until smoking and sear the fillets flesh-side down. Place the skillet in the oven and roast the fish until medium-rare, 4 to 5 minutes. Return the pan to high heat, add the butter, then turn the fish skin-side down and cook just until it forms a crust, 30 to 45 seconds. Turn the fish skin-side up again and remove from the pan.

TO SERVE

For onion confit, substitute Ratatouille (page 142).

3 cups onion confit (see page 145)

½ cup Red Wine Salmon Sauce (page 36)

Divide the onion confit among 6 warm plates and place a salmon fillet on top of each portion. Spoon the sautéed vegetables around the confit and ladle the red wine sauce around the vegetables.

MAKE-AHEAD NOTES

🐟 The Red Wine Salmon Sauce can be refrigerated up to 5 days or frozen up to 1 month.

🐟 The onion confit can be refrigerated up to 3 days.

🐟 The cooked and diced beets and potatoes and the uncooked diced squash and turnip can be refrigerated up to 2 days; sauté just before serving.

BLACK SEA BASS WITH CHANTERELLES AND LOBSTER ESSENCE

MAKES 4 SERVINGS

ORDER OF PREPARATION

- Prepare the Lobster Consommé.
- Cut and blanch the vegetables.
- Sear and roast the fish.
- Sauté the spinach.
- While the fish is cooking, add the butter and blanched vegetables to the lobster essence and keep hot.

*P*rimarily *for aesthetic reasons, many cooks skin fish fillets before cooking them or hide the skin on the serving plate, and few people consider it edible. What a waste! Leave the skin on this bass and let it show—it is dark, glistening, and beautiful and it's also delicious! If you insist on removing the skin, wait until the fish has been cooked, as the skin always helps hold fillets together during cooking.*

Lobster Consommé is the base of the deeply flavorful essence, scented with fresh thyme and loaded with spring vegetables, that surrounds the fish. The consommé is the only time-consuming part of the dish (and even that's a breeze if you've thought to make some up for the freezer) and serving couldn't be easier—just ladle the sauce over the fillets and their bed of fresh spinach.

> **SERVE CHANTERELLES AND LOBSTER ESSENCE WITH:**
> ....
> **ROASTED COD, INSTEAD OF CONFIT BAYALDI (SEE PAGE 173)
> ANY POACHED FISH (SEE PAGE 188)**

FOR THE LOBSTER ESSENCE

Substitute any wild mushrooms for the chanterelles.

2 cups Lobster Consommé (page 76)
6 tablespoons cold butter, cut into ½-inch pieces
1 tablespoon chopped fresh thyme leaves, or more, if desired
32 chanterelles, cleaned and halved
1 small or baby pattypan squash (about 3 ounces), blanched 1 to 2 minutes and quartered

1 small zucchini (about 3 ounces), blanched 1 to 2 minutes and quartered
1 pint red pear or cherry tomatoes, halved
Kosher salt and freshly ground black pepper

In a medium saucepan over high heat, bring the lobster consommé to a boil. Whisk in the butter piece by piece until incorporated.

Add the thyme, chanterelles, squash, and zucchini to the lobster essence and simmer until the chanterelles are tender, 3 to 4 minutes. Add the tomatoes and heat through. Season with salt and pepper.

FOR THE SEA BASS

Snapper may be substi-
tuted for the bass.

1 tablespoon pure olive oil

4 sea bass fillets with skin, 6 to 8
ounces each

Kosher salt and freshly ground black
pepper

1 teaspoon butter

Preheat the oven to 450° F.

In a large skillet, heat the olive oil over high heat until it just begins to
smoke. Season the flesh side of the fish with salt and pepper and place in the
hot pan, flesh-side down. Immediately put the pan in the oven and cook 3 to
4 minutes, until rare to medium-rare. Return the pan to high heat and add
the butter. Then turn the fish and keep it over the heat just until it forms a
crust on the skin side, 30 to 45 seconds. Turn it skin-side up while still in
the pan and remove (this is easier than flipping it onto the serving plate).

TO SERVE

Substitute fresh parsley
for the chervil.

2 tablespoons butter

12 ounces fresh spinach, washed and
stemmed

Kosher salt and freshly ground black
pepper

Fresh chervil, for garnish

In a medium skillet over medium heat, melt the butter and sauté the spinach
until wilted, 3 to 4 minutes. Season with salt and pepper and drain on paper
towels.

Divide the spinach among 4 shallow bowls. Place a fillet on top of the
spinach and surround with hot lobster essence and vegetables. Garnish with
sprigs of chervil.

MAKE-AHEAD NOTES

❧ The Lobster Consommé can be refrigerated up to 3 days; after that, boil
it every 2 days. Do not refrigerate longer than 7 days. It can be frozen.

❧ The blanched vegetables can be refrigerated up to 1 day.

❧ The seared fish can be kept at room temperature on a baking sheet for
up to 1 hour; finish cooking in a 400° F. oven for a few minutes. But it will
be much better if seared and roasted just before serving.

Pan searing without roasting works well for thicker pieces of fish and often is interchangeable with the sear-and-roast method. Unlike sautéing, pan searing doesn't involve stirring the food, although both methods use high heat and a small amount of fat. This method doesn't require that bit of butter when the fish is flipped, since there is no skin side that needs crisping, and the leaner fish, such as bass or snapper, generally aren't cooked this way.

Sear the fish exactly as you would if you were going on to roast it, simply cooking a little longer to ensure that the flesh is cooked through. Your skillet needn't be ovenproof, but it should be large and heavy.

METHOD

- Heat the olive oil in a skillet until smoking.
- Add the fish and cook until golden brown on one side, 1 to 2 minutes.
- Turn and continue to cook until golden brown and slightly firm to the touch, another 2 minutes.

SWORDFISH WITH ROSEMARY POLENTA, TOMATOES, AND FRESH HERBS

MAKES 4 SERVINGS

ORDER OF PREPARATION

- Prepare the tomato sauce.
- While the tomato sauce is simmering, cook the polenta.
- When the polenta has thickened, sear the swordfish.

This is a striking dish, with golden-seared swordfish resting on a pool of creamy yellow polenta, surrounded by a crimson tomato sauce studded with dark olives. The polenta's strong herbal flavor and fragrance enhance the seared fish and go well with the tomatoes, garlic, preserved lemon, and basil in the sauce. Both the sauce and the polenta can be prepared ahead of time, but the fish should be seared just before serving to ensure that it does not go beyond the point of just-done perfection.

SERVE TOMATO SAUCE OVER:

ANY PASTA OR COUSCOUS

FOR THE TOMATO SAUCE

Substitute oregano for rosemary(a good match for the Provençal flavors in the sauce), Vegetable Stock (page 72) or water for Chicken Stock, tomato–cumin broth (see page 152) for the sauce.

2 tablespoons virgin olive oil
2 medium onions, sliced ⅛ inch thick
4 cloves garlic, sliced thin
8 medium-size ripe tomatoes, cored and diced

1 tablespoon julienne lemon confit (see page 38)
12 Niçoise olives, pitted
8 leaves basil, julienned
Kosher salt and freshly ground black pepper

In a medium skillet, heat the olive oil over medium-low heat until almost shimmering. Slowly cook the onions and garlic until transparent but not colored. Add the tomatoes, lemon confit, and olives and cook until thick and bubbly, 30 to 40 minutes. Add the basil and season with salt and pepper. Keep warm.

FOR THE SWORDFISH

Substitute salmon, tuna, or cod for the swordfish.

4 pieces center-cut swordfish, 6 ounces each and about 1 inch thick

Kosher salt and freshly ground black pepper
1 tablespoon virgin olive oil

Season the fish with salt and pepper. In a large skillet, heat the olive oil over high heat until smoking. Add the fish and sear until golden brown on one side, 1 to 2 minutes. Turn and continue to cook until golden brown and slightly firm to the touch, another 2 minutes.

TO SERVE

2 cups Rosemary Polenta (page 122)

Divide the polenta among 4 warm plates or large, shallow bowls and top with a portion of swordfish. Surround with the tomato sauce.

MAKE-AHEAD NOTES

❧ The tomato sauce can be refrigerated up to 2 days; rewarm over low heat.

❧ The polenta can be kept in a covered bowl on a warm part of your stove for up to 1 hour. If you have any left over, it can be refrigerated up to 1 day and reheated over medium heat, mixed with a little stock or cream.

SESAME-CRUSTED SWORDFISH
WITH GINGER VINAIGRETTE

MAKES 4 SERVINGS

ORDER OF
PREPARATION

- Prepare the Ginger
  Vinaigrette.
- Boil and cool the
  potatoes.
- Sauté the potatoes and
  scallions.
- While the potatoes are
  cooking, sear the
  swordfish.

*S*esame is the unifying flavor in this dish. A coating of crisp sesame seeds helps these swordfish steaks sear to a dark golden brown and keeps them juicy under the seared crust. Their foundation, a mixture somewhat reminiscent of a warm German potato salad, combines sautéed potatoes and chunks of scallion with a vinaigrette that is fragrant with fresh ginger, shallots, and pepper. Black sesame seeds look especially pretty in this dish and are available in Oriental and gourmet markets.

This swordfish has been very popular in my cooking demonstrations. People seem to appreciate an exotic, impressive dish that can be put together so easily.

FOR THE POTATOES AND SCALLIONS

6 small purple or blue Peruvian potatoes	1 tablespoon sesame oil
6 small fingerling or creamer potatoes	1 bunch scallions, roots removed, cut 1 inch thick on the bias
Kosher salt	Freshly ground black pepper

Serve 4 large or 6 small baby beets, boiled until tender, peeled, and cut into small dice, alongside the potatoes.

Or roast 2 large beets in a 400° F. oven for 45 minutes to 1 hour, then peel and cut into small dice.

In a large pot over high heat, cover the potatoes with salted water, bring to a boil, and simmer until tender, about 15 minutes. Drain and cool in the refrigerator about 30 minutes.

When cool, cut in half, then slice about ⅛ inch thick.

In a medium nonstick pan, heat the sesame oil over medium-high heat until shimmering and sauté the scallions and the potatoes together until the scallions are tender and the potatoes are light golden brown, about 10 minutes. Season with salt and pepper and reserve, keeping warm.

FOR THE SWORDFISH

4 swordfish steaks, 6 to 8 ounces each and 1½ inches thick	Kosher salt and freshly ground black pepper
6 tablespoons sesame seeds, preferably black and white mixed	1 teaspoon vegetable oil

Coat the swordfish on both sides with the sesame seeds and season with salt and pepper.

In a large skillet over medium-high heat, heat the oil until just smoking and sear the swordfish on one side for 3 minutes. Turn over and sear until fairly firm to the touch, about 5 additional minutes.

TO SERVE

½ cup Ginger Vinaigrette (page 21)

Divide the potato mixture among 4 warm plates, place a piece of fish on top of each portion, and drizzle with the ginger vinaigrette.

MAKE-AHEAD NOTES

❧ The Ginger Vinaigrette can be refrigerated up to 2 weeks.

❧ The potatoes can be refrigerated up to 2 days. Slice and sauté just before serving.

❧ The swordfish can be coated with sesame seeds and refrigerated up to 2 hours.

Baking and Roasting

Baking in a moderate oven is ideal for a whole, stuffed fish, for thick cuts, or for fatty whole fish or steaks. Although this method takes a bit longer, and may not yield quite as crisp a result, the lower oven temperature allows the fish (or stuffing) to cook through without overcooking the exterior. A related technique, roasting in a high oven, is the perfect way to cook whole fish and thick steaks or fillets that should be served medium-rare. When a fish is roasted, dry, high heat sears the outside, forming a crisp crust that seals in juices.

If you are able to buy fish with the head and tail on, leave them that way when you roast or bake to preserve the juices. You can discard the head and tail when you serve the fish, if you prefer. The fish is done when juices begin to appear on the surface and no blood is visible near the backbone when you pierce it.

Method

⬩ Lightly oil a pan just large enough to contain the fish, or line it with foil or parchment.

⬩ Season the fish and brush with oil; stuff whole fish with herbs, if desired.

⬩ Bake in a preheated 350° to 400°F. oven; roast at 450°F., basting occasionally with pan juices or olive oil.

ROASTED COD WITH CONFIT BAYALDI AND BASIL OIL

MAKES 6 SERVINGS

ORDER OF PREPARATION
- Prepare the Confit Bayaldi.
- Prepare the Basil Oil.
- While the confit is reheating, roast the cod.

*H*ere's a recipe that really shows the beauty of having preassembled components at the ready to combine into showstopping—but practically effortless—dinners. Prepare the layered vegetable confit ahead of time, allowing its flavors to mellow, and then pair it with the crisp-skinned roasted fish at serving time. Add a drizzle of herbal green oil to pull all the elements together. Each plate will have generous amounts of fish and vegetables and an interesting contrast of textures.

FOR THE COD

For the cod, substitute 6 whole snapper, 1 to 1¼ pounds each, stuffed with 2 sprigs thyme each.

6 cod fillets, 6 to 8 ounces each and 1½ to 2 inches thick
3 tablespoons extra-virgin olive oil

Kosher salt and freshly ground black pepper

Preheat the oven to 450° F.

Rub the fish with olive oil, sprinkle with salt and pepper, and place in a lightly oiled pan.

Place the pan in the middle or upper third of the oven and roast 12 to 15 minutes, depending on thickness.

TO SERVE

Confit Bayaldi, made in an 8 by 8-inch pan and pressed (page 138)

6 tablespoons Basil Oil (page 5)

Divide the confit into 6 portions and place on serving plates. Place a cod fillet on top of each portion and drizzle 1 tablespoon basil oil around it.

MAKE-AHEAD NOTES

☙ The Basil Oil can be refrigerated up to 2 days.

☙ The Confit Bayaldi can be refrigerated 8 hours, overnight, or up to 2 days; reheat over low heat for about 15 minutes.

BAKED RAINBOW TROUT WITH LEEKS, APPLES, AND WALNUTS

MAKES 4 SERVINGS

ORDER OF
PREPARATION
- Cook the leeks.
- While the leeks are simmering, put the trout in the oven.
- When the fish is almost done, sauté the apples and walnuts.

*I*n a dish that will wake up your table, trout is served on a bed of pale green, silky leeks and topped with aromatic, butter-infused apples and walnuts. This combination may look totally unfamiliar and even a little odd (though beautiful), but wait until you taste it! The sweet, wilted leeks marry perfectly with the flavors of fruit, nuts, brown butter, and trout. Only the green portions of the leeks are used here; save the white parts for another recipe.

SERVE LEEKS, APPLES, AND
WALNUTS WITH:

SNAPPER WITH POTATO GALETTE
INSTEAD OF PORT WINE SAUCE
(SEE PAGE 158)
SALMON WITH LENTILS INSTEAD
OF RED WINE SAUCE
(SEE PAGE 160)
ROASTED COD INSTEAD OF
CONFIT BAYALDI
(SEE PAGE 173)

☙ *Ask your fishmonger to bone the trout; it will make serving easier.*

FOR THE LEEKS

2 tablespoons butter

4 cups leek greens, cut on the diagonal into ½-inch slices (2 to 3 leeks)

½ cup Chicken Stock (page 72) or low-salt canned chicken broth, plus extra, if needed

Kosher salt and freshly ground black pepper

In a large skillet or sauté pan, melt the butter over medium-high heat and sauté the leeks 2 to 3 minutes. Add the chicken stock and simmer, covered, until tender, 6 to 8 minutes, adding a little more stock if the leeks dry out. When done, drain off any excess stock. Season the leeks with salt and pepper and keep warm.

FOR THE TROUT

Substitute any mild fish, such as coho salmon, cod, or snapper

4 rainbow trout, 8 to 10 ounces each, cleaned and boned head and tail on, if possible

Kosher salt and freshly ground black pepper

Preheat the oven to 400° F. Season the trout inside with salt and pepper and place on a lightly oiled baking sheet. The fish is done when the eyes are white, the juices run clear, and it is slightly firm to the touch, 12 to 15 minutes.

FOR THE APPLES

6 tablespoons butter

2 large Granny Smith apples, peeled, cored, and thinly sliced (about 2 cups)

1 cup coarsely chopped walnuts

Few drops of fresh lemon juice

1 tablespoon finely chopped parsley

Kosher salt and freshly ground black pepper

A few minutes before you are ready to serve the dish, place the butter in a medium skillet over high heat. When it begins to bubble, add the apples and walnuts. Cook until the butter begins to brown and the apples and nuts give off a nutty aroma, 2 to 3 minutes. Add the lemon juice and parsley. Sprinkle with salt and pepper.

TO SERVE

Trout is not forgiving; you must serve it as soon as it is cooked.

Remove and discard the fish head and tail.

Divide the leeks among 4 serving plates. Place a portion of fish on top and spoon the apple–walnut mixture over all. Serve immediately.

MAKE-AHEAD NOTE

The sliced apples can be refrigerated up to a few hours. Sprinkle with a few drops of lemon juice so they do not turn brown.

BAKED RAINBOW TROUT
WITH LEEKS AND THYME

MAKES 4 SERVINGS

ORDER OF PREPARATION

- Prepare the thyme crème fraîche sauce.
- While the sauce is simmering, prepare the leek strips and the stuffing.
- Stuff, tie, and roast the trout.

For this recipe, small whole fish are stuffed with a vegetable–herb stuffing and then tied with strips of leek. Don't let the process intimidate you. It's really the same as tying a roast or a package with string—the leeks are that flexible. The stuffed fish can be served whole or it can be cut into medallions. Either way, it makes a beautiful dish. The simple thyme sauce, enriched with a little Crème Fraîche, repeats the flavors of fish, vegetable, and herb.

> **SERVE WITH:**
> ....
> **ROASTED GARLIC MASHED POTATOES (PAGE 132)**
> **HERBED SMASHED POTATOES (PAGE 135)**

FOR THE THYME CRÈME FRAÎCHE SAUCE

Substitute Red Wine Salmon Sauce (page 36) or a flavored oil for the thyme crème fraîche sauce.

2 cups Fish Stock (page 71) or Lobster Stock (page 75)

3 tablespoons finely diced shallots (2 medium)

2 sprigs fresh thyme, plus 2 teaspoons thyme leaves

½ teaspoon cracked black pepper

½ cup Crème Fraîche (page 39) or heavy cream

Kosher salt and freshly ground black pepper

Combine the stock, shallots, thyme sprigs, and pepper in a medium saucepan and bring to a boil over high heat. Reduce until thick and syrupy, about 40 minutes. Reduce the heat to medium, add the crème fraîche, and bring to a boil. Simmer until bubbly and slightly thickened, about 3 minutes. Strain through a fine strainer and season with salt (if needed) and pepper.

Stir the thyme leaves into the reduced stock mixture and keep warm.

FOR THE LEEK STRIPS AND STUFFING

3 leeks, rinsed well, roots cut off

Kosher salt

1 tablespoon unsalted butter

½ cup Chicken Stock (page 72) or low-salt canned chicken broth

1 teaspoon chopped fresh thyme leaves

Freshly ground black pepper

Cut each leek lengthwise through the outer 1 or 2 layers only and remove those layers. Flatten and cut lengthwise into ¼-inch-wide strips (you will

Substitute mushrooms or small-diced vegetables for leeks in the stuffing.

Serve the stuffing as a foundation for any fish fillet or fish steak, and drizzle with any sauce or flavored oil.

need about 20). In a large pot of boiling salted water, blanch the strips for 30 seconds. Shock in a bowl of ice water and drain.

Cut the remaining white part of the leeks in half lengthwise and then slice crosswise into ¼-inch half-moons. In a small skillet, heat the butter over medium-high heat until bubbling. Add the sliced leeks and cook until tender, 3 to 4 minutes. Raise the heat to medium-high, add the stock and thyme leaves, and cook until the leeks are soft and the stock is reduced to less than a tablespoon. Season with salt and pepper, drain and cool at room temperature.

FOR THE TROUT

Substitute coho salmon (or a larger fish, increasing the stuffing and the cooking time) for rainbow trout.

4 rainbow or brook trout, 8 to 10 ounces each and 8 to 10 inches long, butterflied and boned (the fishmonger will do this), with head and tail left on

Kosher salt and freshly ground black pepper
2 tablespoons vegetable oil

Preheat the oven to 350° F.

Lay 5 leek strips crosswise on a flat surface, spacing them every 1½ to 2 inches. Open a trout flat and season lightly with salt and pepper. Place over the strips lengthwise, and stuff with leek and thyme stuffing. Close the fish over the stuffing, and tie each strip around the fish, knotting it on top. Repeat with the remaining fish, leek strips, and stuffing.

Place the stuffed fish on a lightly oiled baking sheet and bake until medium-rare, 25 to 30 minutes.

TO SERVE

With a sharp knife, slice the fish between the ties to make 3 medallions, each one wrapped with a leek strip, discarding the head and tail portions. Spoon some thyme sauce onto each plate and place 3 medallions on top. Or serve whole, accompanied by the sauce.

MAKE-AHEAD NOTES

🍃 The thyme sauce can be refrigerated up to 3 days; rewarm over medium heat.

🍃 The leek strips can be refrigerated up to 1 day.

🍃 The stuffing can be refrigerated up to 2 days; rewarm over low to medium heat with a little stock or butter.

GRILLING

Charcoal, wood, electric, or gas fires cook fish quickly and form a crisp crust that seals in the natural juices of fish. This method works best with thick, fatty fish steaks, such as tuna, swordfish, salmon, halibut, and mackerel; thin or dry fish have a tendency to stick to the grill or break apart. I reserve the grill for heartier fish for another reason, too: The smoky flavor grilling imparts can overwhelm the flavor of more delicate fish.

Before cooking, cut the fish into even pieces so it grills evenly. Marinate in any vinaigrette up to 3 hours, or simply brush with olive oil and season. Make sure the grill rack is clean, and oil it lightly.

As an alternative to grilling, you can brush thick fish steaks with oil, season them, and broil, turning to brown both sides. Thin fillets can be broiled, too. They will take only a very short time and need not be turned. Place them close to the heat so they will brown quickly.

METHOD

- Prepare a charcoal or wood fire and let it burn down to embers. Lightly oil a grill rack.
- Season fish with salt and pepper.
- Place on the rack and grill until crusted, about 5 minutes, brushing with olive oil.
- Turn and grill another 3 to 4 minutes, brushing with olive oil.

For a rich but delicious and unusual luncheon salad, cut gravlax (see page 186) into 5- to 6-ounce fillets and grill, then serve over greens.

BALSAMIC-GLAZED GRILLED SALMON

MAKES 6 SERVINGS

ORDER OF PREPARATION

- Prepare the marinade and marinate the salmon.
- Grill the salmon.

*T*art and sweet, a marinade based on the mellow flavor of balsamic vinegar cuts through the richness of salmon and enhances its flavor, and also helps the fish brown beautifully on the grill. Make sure your grill is really hot, and then cook the salmon to perfection in a matter of minutes.

SERVE WITH:

ANY SIMPLE GREEN SALAD
GRILLED VEGETABLES (SEE PAGE 180)
ROSEMARY POLENTA (PAGE 122)

For the salmon, substitute tuna or swordfish.

1 cup balsamic vinegar
2 tablespoons honey
2 teaspoons fresh lime juice
4 salmon steaks, 6 to 8 ounces each and 1 inch thick

Olive or vegetable oil, for the grill
Kosher salt and freshly ground black pepper
2 tablespoons julienne Lemon Confit (page 38), for garnish

In a small pan or bowl, combine the vinegar, honey, and lime juice. Add the salmon, coat with the mixture, and marinate in the refrigerator for 30 to 40 minutes.

Prepare a charcoal or wood fire and let it burn down to embers; lightly oil a clean grill rack.

Remove the salmon from the marinade and season with salt and pepper. Grill 2 minutes; turn slightly (to create a cross-hatch pattern) and grill another 2 minutes. Carefully turn the steaks and grill 2 more minutes on the second side, or until done.

Place each grilled fish steak on a serving plate and garnish with the lemon confit.

MAKE-AHEAD NOTES

✍ The marinade can be refrigerated up to 3 days; whisk to recombine before using.

TUNA WITH GRILLED VEGETABLES AND PROVENÇAL VINAIGRETTE

MAKES 4 SERVINGS

ORDER OF PREPARATION

- Prepare the Provençal Vinaigrette.
- Roast the tomatoes.
- After the tomatoes have cooked about 25 minutes, briefly grill the fennel and put it in the oven.
- When the tomatoes and fennel are almost done, grill the zucchini and yellow squash.
- Immediately after they are done, grill the tuna.

*T*his is a dish that makes optimal use of your grill, with a little help from your oven. The palette of colors is striking, with the rich greens, yellows, and whites of the vegetables, dark-brown grill marks of the fish, and the pale orange-pink vinaigrette.

The vegetables are cooked in stages, with the tomatoes taking longest, until they are softened, but not dry. The fennel and leeks should be cooked until tender, as should the zucchini and yellow squash (the last will take just a couple of minutes).

❧ *To cut tomatoes into petals, blanch whole tomatoes in boiling water 10 seconds and shock in ice water. Cut into quarters and remove the ribs and seeds. The remaining shells are petals.*

> **SERVE GRILLED VEGETABLES WITH:**
> ....
> ANY SEARED AND ROASTED FISH (SEE PAGE 151)
> SEARED AND ROASTED CHICKEN BREASTS (SEE PAGE 200)
> SIMPLE ROASTED CHICKEN (PAGE 204)
> SADDLE OF LAMB INSTEAD OF RATATOUILLE (SEE PAGE 218)
> DOUBLE-CUT LAMB CHOPS INSTEAD OF CAPONATA POLENTA (SEE PAGE 220)
> DRIZZLE WITH A LITTLE BASIL OIL (PAGE 5)

FOR THE GRILLED VEGETABLES

For grilled vegetables, substitute Ratatouille (page 142) or Confit Bayaldi (page 138).

Vegetable oil
4 medium-size tomatoes, peeled, seeded, and cut into petals
3 tablespoons virgin olive oil
Pinch of ground cumin
Pinch of curry powder
4 bulbs fennel, halved lengthwise and cored

Kosher salt and freshly ground black pepper
4 leeks, white part only
1 medium zucchini, washed, sliced ⅛ inch thick
1 medium yellow squash, washed, sliced ⅛ inch thick

Preheat the oven to 300°F. Prepare a charcoal or wood fire and let it burn down to embers, and lightly oil a clean grill rack.

Lightly grease 2 baking sheets with vegetable oil.

Drizzle the tomatoes with 1 tablespoon of the olive oil and sprinkle with the cumin and curry powder. Place on a prepared baking sheet and roast until softened and somewhat shrunken, about 40 minutes.

Rub the fennel with olive oil, season with salt and pepper, and grill just until marked on both sides. Drizzle the leeks with another tablespoon of olive oil and season with salt and pepper. Place the fennel and leeks on a prepared baking sheet, season, and bake until soft, about 15 minutes.

While the fennel and leeks are baking, rub the zucchini and yellow squash with the remaining tablespoon of olive oil, season with salt and pepper, and grill until marked on both sides and tender, 1 to 2 minutes per side.

FOR THE TUNA

For tuna, substitute bass or cod.

4 center-cut tuna steaks, 6 to 8 ounces each and 1 inch thick

Kosher salt and freshly ground black pepper

Olive or vegetable oil for the grill

Season the fish with salt and pepper and place on the oiled grill rack. Cook until golden brown, about 5 minutes. Turn and cook until done, 3 to 4 minutes more.

TO SERVE

½ to ¾ cup Provençal Vinaigrette (page 24)

Divide the grilled vegetables and roasted tomatoes among 4 serving plates. Arrange a portion of fish on top and drizzle with the vinaigrette.

MAKE-AHEAD NOTES

∼ The Provençal Vinaigrette can be refrigerated up to 2 weeks; whisk to recombine before serving.

∼ The grilled vegetables can be refrigerated up to 1 day; reheat in a 250°F. oven, or microwave.

PANFRYING

Panfrying requires more oil than searing or sautéing—but there are some things that can't be cooked in just a bit of oil. If you brown one side of a thick crab cake, flip it over, and then brown the other side, it will still have an uncooked ring around the middle. You have to surround the cake with fat to crisp and brown it on all sides and seal in the juices and flavor. Watch for oil splatters, and for safety, turn the skillet handle to the side, rather than letting it extend out over the front of the stove.

This is the best way to cook fish cakes and crab cakes, and it is not complicated. Simply dredge them lightly in flour or cornmeal and cook them in a pan filled with enough hot oil to come one quarter to halfway up their sides. Keep the heat medium-high; the oil should sizzle when food hits it, but should not be so hot that it browns the food right away without cooking it through. Test the temperature by tossing in a few crumbs and if they burn, lower the heat.

METHOD

- Coat the food lightly with breadcrumbs and refrigerate to set.
- Fry in oil over medium-high heat until golden brown on all sides.
- Drain on paper towels.

CRAB CAKES

*T*hese golden, crisp cakes are intensely flavored and have the spicy kick of French Dijon mustard (I prefer Maille; if it is not available, use the best brand you can find). They are mainly crabmeat, with no vegetable filler to detract from the fresh crab taste. The eggs make them puff up a bit, like little soufflés. If you like, make smaller cakes to serve as an appetizer or hors d'oeuvre.

> **SERVE CRAB CAKES WITH:**
> **RATATOUILLE (PAGE 142)**
> **GREEN AND YELLOW SQUASH RIBBONS (PAGE 128)**
> **ANY GREEN SALAD**
>
> **DRIZZLE WITH:**
> **BASIL OIL (PAGE 5)**
> **CHIVE OIL (PAGE 6)**

For breadcrumbs, tear 4 slices of bread, crusts removed, into 1-inch pieces. Pulse in the food processor until the crumbs are medium-fine.

2 large eggs
½ cup mayonnaise, fresh (page 27) or good-quality purchased
1 to 2 tablespoons French Dijon mustard
1 pound excellent-quality lump crabmeat, cartilage removed
2 tablespoons chopped parsley
¼ cup finely chopped scallions
2 teaspoons capers, crushed
1 tablespoon finely chopped cornichons
2 cups fresh breadcrumbs
1 teaspoon Old Bay Seasoning
Pinch of cayenne
Vegetable oil

In a mixing bowl, lightly beat the eggs, add the mayonnaise and mustard, and combine. Add the crabmeat and toss lightly. Add the parsley, scallions, capers, and cornichons and mix. Gently fold in 1½ cups of the breadcrumbs. Add the Old Bay Seasoning and the cayenne. Form into 2-inch cakes and coat lightly with the remaining ½ cup of breadcrumbs. Refrigerate 1 hour.

In a large skillet, heat the oil until shimmering over medium-high heat. (The oil should come one third of the way up the crab cakes.) Fry the cakes until golden brown and drain on paper towels. Serve hot.

MAKE-AHEAD NOTES

&. The Crab Cakes can be cooked until just golden on each side, drained, and kept at room temperature or refrigerated up to 1 hour. Just before serving, finish cooking in a 350°F. oven.

&. Finished Crab Cakes can be refrigerated up to 1 day.

COD AND POTATO CAKES PROVENÇAL WITH RATATOUILLE AND BASIL OIL

MAKES 4 MAIN-COURSE OR 8 APPETIZER SERVINGS

ORDER OF PREPARATION

- Prepare the Basil Oil.
- Prepare the Ratatouille.
- While it cooks, boil and dry the potatoes; simmer the codfish.
- Form the cakes and refrigerate.
- Panfry the cakes.

I love the delicate flavor of cod; because it's a little plain, it marries well with strong flavors such as garlic, thyme, basil, and Ratatouille. These old-fashioned savory cakes are chunky with potatoes and fish and juicy under a crisp golden crust.

Once the potatoes have been cooked, it's important to dry them out a little bit. Then mash with a fork until the big lumps are gone, leaving a coarse texture. Don't use a ricer or electric mixer, because you want little chunks of potato and cod, not a puree. Mashing the potatoes, flaking the cod, and mixing them to just the right consistency is a great example of the tactile side of cooking.

FOR THE COD AND POTATO CAKES

For cod, substitute halibut, snapper, or bass.

3 medium Idaho potatoes, peeled and cut into about 8 chunks each

Kosher salt

2 cups dry white wine

2 cups water

10 sprigs fresh thyme

3 cloves raw garlic

2 pounds cod fillet

4 cloves Oven-Roasted Garlic (page 37)

6 tablespoons extra-virgin olive oil

1⅓ cups milk

Freshly ground black pepper

Flour for dredging (I prefer Wondra)

Vegetable oil to a depth of ¼ inch in the sauté pan

Place the diced potatoes in a saucepan of cold, salted water over high heat and bring to a boil. Reduce the heat to medium and simmer until the potatoes are fork tender, 20 to 25 minutes.

Preheat the oven to 350°F. Drain the potatoes, spread them out in one layer on a baking sheet, and place in the oven until dry, 5 to 6 minutes.

Meanwhile, place the wine, water, thyme, and raw garlic in a large skillet over medium-high heat and bring to a boil. Reduce the heat to medium, add the cod, and simmer until opaque, 6 to 8 minutes. Drain the fish on a cloth towel and, using your fingers, flake it into a bowl.

Mash the roasted garlic and combine with the olive oil and milk. In a mixing bowl, mash the dried potatoes with a fork, slowly adding the garlic mixture and mixing until it is incorporated. The potatoes should be slightly lumpy. Add the flaked cod and mix well. Season with salt and pepper. Form the mixture into 8 cakes, dredge in flour, and refrigerate for at least 1 hour and up to 24 hours.

When ready to serve, heat the oil until shimmering in a medium skillet over medium heat and cook the cakes until golden brown, about 2 minutes on each side. Drain on paper towels.

TO SERVE

For Ratatouille, substitute Confit Bayaldi (page 138), Caponata (page 140), Green and Yellow Squash Ribbons (page 128), or any green salad.

2⅔ cups Ratatouille (page 142)   5 to 6 tablespoons Basil Oil (page 5)

Divide the ratatouille among 4 (or 8) warm plates. Place 2 (or 1) cod and potato cakes on top and drizzle the basil oil around.

For Basil Oil, substitute Chive Oil (page 6), Roasted Garlic–Black Olive Oil (page 8), or rouille (see page 195).

MAKE-AHEAD NOTES

❧ The Basil Oil can be refrigerated up to 2 days.

❧ The Ratatouille can be refrigerated up to 3 days. Reheat in a 275°F. oven or over low heat, or microwave.

❧ The panfried cod and potato cakes can be kept at room temperature up to 1 hour. Reheat on a lightly oiled pan in a 375°F. oven.

GRAVLAX WITH MUSTARD–DILL SAUCE AND MARINATED CUCUMBER

MAKES 8 APPETIZER SERVINGS

ORDER OF PREPARATION

- Prepare the spice mixture.
- Sprinkle the salmon with the spice mixture and refrigerate.
- Marinate the cucumber.

*T*he finished salmon is opaque and slightly sweet, salty, and flavored with dill. The thinly sliced cucumber is softened by its marinade and has a sweet-and-sour flavor with hints of lemon, dill, and juniper. Mustard–Dill Sauce is the classic accompaniment to gravlax, repeating the sweet, spicy, and dill flavors.

SERVE GRAVLAX:

ON A BED OF MIXED GREENS;
ON DARK BREAD OR CRACKERS,
AS A CANAPÉ;
CUT INTO 5- OR 6-OUNCE
FILLETS AND GRILLED, OVER
GREENS

This recipe uses 1$\frac{1}{2}$ pounds of salmon; if you want to double it, the curing process will require 2 to 4 days. The spice mixture is enough to cure one whole side of salmon; use what you need and keep the rest for another time.

*For salmon, substitute
tuna or striped bass.*

*If you have made
Lemon Confit (page 38),
sprinkle some of the
lemon-flavored salt over
the salmon.*

²⁄₃ cup sugar

½ cup kosher salt

2 tablespoons cracked or coarsely
ground black pepper

1 tablespoon crushed, dried juniper
berries

½ cup coarsely chopped dill, tops and
stems

¼ cup coarsely chopped cilantro, tops
and stems, optional

¼ cup coarsely chopped fennel greens,
tops and stems (optional)

1 (1½-pound) salmon fillet

Peel of 2 lemons, cut in approximately
½-inch pieces

2 tablespoons olive oil

Three days before serving, combine the sugar, salt, pepper, juniper berries,
and herbs in a small bowl. Place the salmon skin-side down in a pie tin, cover
with the lemon peel, and sprinkle evenly with the spice and herb mixture.
Cover the salmon completely, so it doesn't show through the mixture. Rub
with the olive oil. Cover with plastic wrap and weigh down with another pie
tin and a few heavy cans (juice cans are good). Refrigerate and begin to check
for doneness after 2 days; allow to cure up to 3 days. When done, the fish will
be firmer to the touch and slightly darker than when raw. Pour off excess liquid daily, if necessary.

TO SERVE

1 cucumber, cut into ⅛-inch slices
and marinated (page 57)

½ cup Mustard–Dill Sauce (page 28)

Scrape off the cure and cut the salmon on the diagonal in very thin, skinless slices, as you would smoked salmon. Place 3 slices on each chilled
plate, along with a small mound of cucumber. Serve the mustard–dill sauce
on the side.

MAKE-AHEAD NOTES

☙ The spice mixture without the fresh herbs can be stored in a tightly
covered jar at room temperature for up to 1 month. Add the fresh herbs
when you are ready to use.

☙ The salmon, sprinkled with the spice mixture, should be refrigerated for
2 to 3 days. After curing, it may be refrigerated up to 4 days more.

☙ The cucumber should marinate for 30 minutes at room temperature.
After marination, it can be refrigerated up to 1 day.

POACHING AND BOILING

Poaching fish is the simple technique of cooking in liquid at a gentle simmer, on the stove or in the oven. I prefer the oven method because it gives more even heat, but if you would rather not use your oven, stove-top poaching works well (see Bouillabaisse, page 194).

Since the poaching liquid can be reduced to make a wonderful sauce, don't bother using water, which doesn't reduce to anything. Chicken Stock, a combination of Chicken Stock and Fish Stock, or a combination of white wine and water all are good. I don't, however, like to use pure Fish Stock, which tastes too strongly fishy when reduced.

Thin fillets such as sole and trout will poach in about 5 to 7 minutes; thicker fillets such as salmon will take about 8 minutes. In terms of cooking time, salmon and similar fat fish are the most forgiving.

To make a simple sauce, reduce the poaching liquid almost to a syrup and stir in a few drops of fresh lemon juice, a little butter, and a sprinkling of chopped herbs. Taste and season with salt and pepper. (See Poached Salmon with Lemon Butter Sauce, page 190; and Roasted Garlic–Almond Butter for shellfish, page 34.) Or, let the liquid cool down and then refrigerate and reserve it for further poaching. You may refrigerate poaching liquid for up to 4 days or freeze it.

While poaching is good for fragile fillets, boiling is my method of choice for cooking lobster. Cook the lobster in salted water at a rapid boil, not at a simmer (see page 192).

METHOD

∾ Put the seasoned fish skin-side down in a lightly oiled pan that fits it snugly and cover by seven eighths with cold liquid.

∾ Heat almost to a simmer on the stove; then place on the middle rack of a preheated oven.

∾ Simmer very gently, uncovered, until opaque and firm to the touch. Be sure the liquid does not boil.

SNAPPER AU PISTOU

ORDER OF
PREPARATION
• Prepare the Soupe au
Pistou.
• While the pistou is
cooking, prepare the
Basil Pesto and poach
the snapper.
• Bring the pistou to a
boil and add the pesto.

*B*uy really fresh, beautiful fish for this dish, because you will be cooking it very quickly and placing it right on top of all the vegetables—nothing will cover it up.

Every element of the dish should be well seasoned: salt and pepper really wake up the flavors. The pesto will be slightly garlicky and the pistou—that wonderful Provençal soup, used here as a sauce—will have lots of color and small chunks of vegetables. Because the pistou is not made from the poaching liquid, it can be done ahead of time, but stir in the pesto at the last moment before serving, so it stays nice and green.

FOR THE SNAPPER

For the snapper, substitute any fish fillets, or steamed mussels or clams (see page 196).

Instead of poaching the snapper, you can sear and roast it (see page 151).

4 fillets of snapper, 4 ounces each
Kosher salt and freshly ground black
pepper

Chicken Stock (page 72), low-salt
canned chicken broth, or white
wine, to cover

Preheat the oven to 450°F. Season the fillets on the flesh side with salt and pepper, place skin-side up in a shallow pan, and cover by seven eighths with chicken stock or wine. Place in the oven for 5 minutes, or until rare.

TO SERVE

4 cups Soupe au Pistou (page 78)
½ cup Basil Pesto (page 26), at room
temperature

Kosher salt and freshly ground black
pepper
Fresh chervil or parsley, for garnish

Bring the soup to a boil, mix in the pesto, and season with salt and pepper, if necessary. With a slotted spoon, scoop out the vegetables and divide them among 4 bowls. Place a piece of fish on top of the vegetables in each bowl. Ladle the hot broth and pesto over all, catching plenty of the basil in each ladleful. Garnish with the chervil or parsley.

MAKE-AHEAD NOTES

❧ The Soupe au Pistou can be refrigerated up to 3 days; reheat over medium to high heat.

❧ The Basil Pesto can be brushed lightly with oil, covered, and refrigerated up to 1 week or frozen.

POACHED SALMON WITH LEMON BUTTER SAUCE

MAKES 4 SERVINGS

ORDER OF PREPARATION

- Poach the salmon and keep warm.
- Prepare the lemon butter sauce with the poaching liquid.

*S*almon *fillets take to poaching beautifully, and it is a snap to turn the poaching liquid into a glossy, buttery sauce. For extra flavor, sprinkle the fish with 1 to 2 teaspoons chopped herbs (dill, tarragon, or chervil, or a mixture of these) before poaching, and add a bit of lobster syrup (see page 25) to the poaching liquid. This sauce is lighter than a classic French beurre blanc, which it resembles.*

This preparation may be used as well for cod, halibut, and other fish steaks or whole fish, and scallops.

FOR THE SALMON

4 salmon fillets, 6 to 8 ounces each

Kosher salt and freshly ground black pepper

Poaching liquid to nearly cover fish, such as Chicken Stock (page 72),

Lobster Stock (page 75), half Chicken Stock and half Fish Stock (page 71), or half water and half wine

Preheat the oven to 375° F. Season the fish with salt and pepper.

Place the fish in a medium to large roasting pan or ovenproof casserole and add the liquid to come seven eighths of the way up the sides of the fish. Place in the oven for 8 to 10 minutes, depending on thickness of the fillets. When done, the salmon should be opaque and firm to the touch. Remove from the liquid and cover with foil to keep warm, reserving the poaching liquid for the lemon butter sauce.

FOR THE LEMON BUTTER SAUCE

2 to 3 tablespoons finely diced shallots

Poaching liquid (above)

2 to 3 tablespoons cold butter

Few drops of lemon juice

1 to 2 teaspoons chopped dill, tarragon, or chervil, or a mixture of these (optional)

Kosher salt and freshly ground black pepper

In the same pan the fish was cooked in, add the shallots to the poaching liquid. Over medium-high heat, bring to a boil and reduce until slightly syrupy, 12 to 15 minutes. Whisk in the butter, lemon juice, and optional herbs. Taste and season with salt and pepper.

To serve, place a fillet on each serving plate and spoon the lemon butter sauce on top.

For cold poached salmon:
- cool the poached fish at room temperature
- place it on a rack or plate, cover with plastic wrap, and refrigerate until chilled through, from 1 hour to overnight
- serve with Mustard–Dill Sauce (see page 28)

Lemon butter sauce can be thick or thin, depending on the ratio of stock to butter. For a thicker sauce, use 3 tablespoons stock and 4 to 6 tablespoons butter.

Lemon butter sauce additions:
- 2 to 3 tablespoons diced tomatoes, roasted bell peppers, or blanched carrots
- 2 tablespoons roughly chopped pale green celery leaves
- 2 tablespoons sliced scallions
- 2 to 3 mashed roasted garlic cloves
- 1 to 2 tablespoons French Dijon or whole-grain mustard (especially good with scallops, skate, salmon, or swordfish)

LOBSTER WITH CURRY SAUCE

MAKES 4 SERVINGS

ORDER OF PREPARATION

- Prepare the Curry Sauce.
- Boil the lobsters and remove the meat from the shells.
- Reheat the lobster meat in Chicken Stock.
- Arrange the lobster meat on plates, spoon Curry Sauce on top, and garnish with herbs.

Because the lobster is cooked first, then napped with Curry Sauce, its meat remains tender and delicate. This was the most popular lobster dish during my time at Montrachet, and the sauce, incorporating the sweet spiciness of curry, is one of my favorites.

Even live lobsters in tanks may not be fresh from the ocean, so be sure that those you buy are lively and active. Ask for female lobsters; they have bigger tails than the male lobsters do, and under the tail, the first spinnerets are soft and fringed, while the males' are smooth and harder. Females will give you more tail meat, as well as a bonus: delicious tomalley and coral.

Boiling lobster is easier and more humane than steaming. It also allows you to cook several lobsters in one pot, while it is hard to find a pot and rack large enough to steam more than 2 lobsters at a time. For those who won't have their lobster any other way, however, I include steaming as an alternative.

> SERVE COOKED LOBSTER MEAT
> WITH:
>
> RED WINE SALMON SAUCE
> (PAGE 36)
> PESTO VINAIGRETTE (PAGE 22)
> LOBSTER VINAIGRETTE
> (PAGE 25)
> RED-CHILI VINAIGRETTE
> (PAGE 20)
> LOTS OF MELTED BUTTER
>
> SERVE IN:
>
> CORN–LOBSTER SOUP
> (PAGE 101)
> PENNETTE WITH MUSHROOM
> CREAM, LOBSTER, AND
> ASPARAGUS (PAGE 112)

Lobsters are sold by weight, with corresponding names:
¾ to 1 pound: chicken
1 to 1¼ pounds: quarter
1½ to 2 pounds: select
2 pounds or over: jumbo
1 or 2 claws missing: cull

1 tablespoon kosher salt per quart of water
4 lobsters, 1½ pounds each, female, if possible

6 cups Chicken Stock (page 72) or low-salt canned chicken broth

Fill a stockpot or 8-quart pot with salted water and bring to a boil over high heat. Plunge the lobsters headfirst into the boiling water, cover, and cook 12 to 14 minutes. Carefully remove the lobsters from the pot. Allow them to cool somewhat, and remove the meat from the shells (see opposite).

Before serving, in a medium saucepan, heat the stock over medium-high heat until it is hot to the touch but not boiling. Add the lobster meat and heat through, 5 to 10 minutes, and drain. Be careful not to overheat; if the meat gets too hot, it will curl up.

TO SERVE

1 cup Curry Sauce (page 29)   Sprigs of thyme, tarragon, or sage
                                     (optional)

Bring the curry sauce to a boil over medium heat.

Divide the heated lobster meat among 4 plates and spoon curry sauce on top. Garnish with the herbs, if desired.

MAKE-AHEAD NOTES

∼ The Curry Sauce can be refrigerated up to 3 days; do not freeze. Reheat over medium heat or in a microwave.

∼ Lobster meat can be refrigerated up to 12 hours.

To steam lobsters:

∼ bring 2 inches of water to a boil over high heat in a large pot and place a wire rack or steamer tray in the pot

∼ place 2 lobsters (about 2¼ pounds each) on the rack, cover the pot with a lid, and steam until done, 18 to 20 minutes

To remove lobster meat from the shells after cooking:

∼ separate the tail from the rest of the body

∼ halve the tail lengthwise and remove the meat

∼ twist off the claws, then separate the knuckles from the claws

∼ crack the knuckles with the back of a knife and remove the meat. Crack the claws just below the joint with a knife, break open with your fingers, and remove the meat

For salads or soups, refrigerate cooked lobster meat up to 12 hours in plastic wrap (discard the shells or freeze and save them for stock).

BOUILLABAISSE

ORDER OF PREPARATION

- Prepare the bouil-labaisse broth.
- Prepare the rouille syrup and rouille.
- Prepare the vegetables.
- Make the croutons.
- Heat the broth and vegetables and cook the fish and shellfish.

MAKES 6 SERVINGS

*S*teaming golden broth with the flavor of the sea and the fragrance of saffron and garlic marks this Marseillaise classic brimming with fresh fish and shellfish, potatoes, leeks, and fennel. Crisp toasted croutons and the fiery garlic mayonnaise known as rouille garnish the dish.

Once you have prepared the broth and the rouille syrup, the rest of the cooking goes very quickly. I prefer to cook the fish, shellfish, and vegetables in separate pots of broth, so components can be done ahead and combined just before serving, simplifying this complex dish enormously! If you prefer the traditional method, you can bring to a boil a large pot of broth and add the shellfish and fish in order of thickness, cooking them all together.

FOR THE BOUILLABAISSE BROTH

For Chicken Stock, substitute Lobster Stock (page 75), or half each chicken and lobster stocks.

For black pepper, substitute ¹/₂ teaspoon chili pepper flakes or 2 pinches of cayenne.

6 tablespoons pure olive oil
3¹/₂ pounds fish bones, such as flounder, sole, or salmon, coarsely chopped and rinsed well
3 lobster bodies or 2 cups shrimp shells
2 leeks, white parts only, washed and cut into ¹/₄-inch-thick slices
1 large onion, cut into medium dice
1 stalk fennel, cut into medium dice

1 tablespoon saffron threads
³/₄ cup Pernod or Ricard
2¹/₂ to 3 quarts Chicken Stock (page 72) or low-salt canned chicken broth
¹/₄ jalapeño pepper, finely diced
2 large tomatoes, coarsely chopped
Zest of 1 orange
Kosher salt and freshly ground black pepper

This recipe makes 12 cups of broth and you will need 6, or possibly a little more; if you refrigerate or freeze half, there will still be more than enough broth to cook everything, even allowing for evapo-ration and absorption.

In 2 large, shallow pans, heat 3 tablespoons of the oil over high heat until smoking. Add the fish bones and lobster bodies or shrimp shells in a single layer and sauté until light golden brown. It is important that they be spread in one layer; if they are packed too close together, they will steam, not brown. Add half the leeks, onion, fennel, and saffron to each pan and sauté until soft-ened, 3 to 4 minutes.

Add 6 tablespoons of Pernod to each pan, pouring it in carefully since it may ignite, and mix, scraping the bottom of the pans. Combine the mixture in a large stockpot. Add the chicken stock, jalapeño pepper, tomatoes, and orange zest, lower the heat to medium, and simmer until reduced by one third, about 1¹/₄ hours, stirring occasionally. Strain through a fine strainer, dis-carding the bones and vegetables, and season the broth with salt and pepper.

FOR THE ROUILLE

1½ cups bouillabaisse broth

1 teaspoon saffron threads

¼ jalapeño pepper, finely chopped

3 cloves garlic, peeled

3 large egg yolks

2 cloves Oven-Roasted Garlic
   (page 37)

1 cup pure olive oil

Kosher salt and freshly ground black
   pepper

Dash of cayenne

Rouille should have a consistency similar to mayonnaise; thin with a few drops of water or lemon juice, if needed.

In a medium saucepan, combine the broth, saffron, jalapeño, and raw garlic and bring to a boil over medium-high heat. Cook until reduced to a syrup, 25 to 30 minutes, taking care that it does not burn. Strain through a fine strainer, pushing down on the solids, and cool to room temperature.

Place the yolks and roasted garlic in the bowl of an electric mixer and beat until the mixture is pale yellow. Drizzle in ¼ cup of the olive oil. Begin adding 2 to 3 tablespoons of the syrup, 1 tablespoon at a time, alternately with the rest of the oil. The sauce should be thick and smooth. Check the seasonings and add the cayenne.

FOR THE VEGETABLES

Kosher salt

6 small to medium potatoes (new,
   Yukon gold, or creamer), unpeeled

2 bulbs fennel, cored and cut into
   ⅛-inch slices

1 tablespoon butter

2 leeks, white part only, halved
   lengthwise, and sliced ¼ inch thick

3 to 5 tablespoons bouillabaisse broth

½ pint (about 12) red pear or cherry
   tomatoes, halved

Freshly ground black pepper

Bring a large pot of salted water to a boil; boil the potatoes until tender, 20 to 25 minutes. Drain and halve or quarter, depending upon size.

In a large pot of boiling salted water, blanch the fennel until almost tender, about 1 minute. Drain and rinse under cold running water.

In a large skillet, melt the butter over medium heat and sauté the leeks until almost tender. Add the fennel and a few tablespoons bouillabaisse broth. Add the tomatoes, heat through, and season with salt and pepper.

FOR THE CROUTONS

18 slices French bread, ¼ inch thick

Extra-virgin olive oil (optional)

Preheat a broiler and arrange the bread slices in 1 layer on a baking sheet. Drizzle with oil, if desired. Toast on both sides until golden brown.

FOR THE FISH AND SHELLFISH

6 fillets of bass, snapper, tilefish, or monkfish, 3 to 4 ounces each	12 to 18 medium to large shrimp, shelled
Kosher salt and freshly ground black pepper	12 to 18 scallops
6 cups bouillabaisse broth, or as needed	12 to 18 mussels, rinsed in cold running water and debearded
	18 to 24 clams, scrubbed and rinsed in cold running water

Let the poached fish sit in its broth while you cook the shellfish, rather than risking breaking it by lifting it out. Instead, strain the cooked shellfish out of their broth and add them to the pot with the fish. Before serving, combine the broths you used to steam the fish and shellfish; they will be full of intense flavor.

Season the fish with salt and pepper. In a large pot, cover the fish by seven eighths with cold broth and bring almost to a simmer over medium heat. Poach the fish until just opaque, 5 to 6 minutes. Set aside the fish and broth. Fill a medium pot or sauté pan halfway with broth and bring to a boil over medium heat. Add the shrimp and scallops and simmer just until opaque, 2 to 3 minutes. Return the leftover steaming liquid to the pot of broth and set the shrimp and scallops aside.

Place the mussels and clams in a shallow pan, cover with cold broth, and bring to a boil over high heat. Steam until the shellfish pop open, 6 to 8 minutes, and discard any that do not. Return the leftover steaming liquid to the pot of broth and add the shellfish to the shrimp.

TO SERVE

Bring the large pot of broth to a boil. Divide the vegetables among 6 shallow soup bowls. Use a slotted spoon to transfer a piece of fish to each bowl, and arrange some of the shellfish over the vegetables as well. Ladle the boiling broth over all, and garnish with croutons and rouille.

MAKE-AHEAD NOTES

✺ The bouillabaisse broth can be refrigerated up to 7 days; bring it to a boil every 2 days, to kill any bacteria that may form. It can be frozen.

✺ The rouille syrup can be refrigerated up to 10 days or frozen.

✺ The rouille can be refrigerated up to 10 days.

✺ The cooked vegetables can be refrigerated in the broth up to 3 days.

✺ The croutons can be wrapped and kept at room temperature for 1 day.

CHAPTER 7

POULTRY AND
MEAT

One of my earliest restaurant jobs was at Dennis Foy's elegant steak house, Toto, where I worked for two years and learned many valuable lessons. The primary focus of the menu was meat: filet mignon, strip steak, Delmonico steak, and prime ribs were among the most requested main courses. In the years subsequent to that job, I have moved pretty far from that list, preferring lighter, more refined fare that showcases my beloved herbs and vegetables. But I haven't turned away from meat entirely; now, rather than pricey filet mignon, I'm more likely to prepare inexpensive, less tender cuts such as lamb shanks, oxtails, and veal shoulder, breast, and shanks. To me, they are much more flavorful than steaks, and they allow me to use herbs, stocks, and fruit the way French country cooks do. These more humble cuts produce the kinds of dishes I so admired in the little family-owned restaurants of Provence, such as blanquette de veau and lamb shanks with rosemary—slow-cooked, cool-weather food that fills the kitchen with warm, promising aromas. Although a braised dish can call for many ingredients, once the ingredients are combined, the dish practically cooks itself and has a finished flavor that needs no other sauce or embellishment. It also pleases me, when I'm shopping at the supermarket, to see that I can make a great meal out of a piece of meat that costs a dollar-something a pound!

Fairly small cuts of lamb, beef, and pork, such as tenderloin, saddle, and rack, as well as veal, lamb, and pork chops, are the easiest to cook for family dinners. The versatile sear-and-roast technique, so indispensable for cooking fish, works well for these cuts too, as does pan-roasting. Both techniques allow you to create delicious pan sauces, which can be the most exciting part of a dish—and certainly are the most fun to experiment with. I very much prefer them to the classic brown sauces I was taught as a beginning chef; they cook in just a few minutes, while the meat rests before carving, and they are deeply flavored with cooking juices and stock.

The key to great pan sauces:

🍃 Set the meat aside, keeping it warm, and pour the fat off the cooking juices.

🍃 Over medium-high heat, add liquid (port, wine, or stock) to the juices in the pan, being careful that the alcohol doesn't ignite.

🍃 Stir, scraping off any bits of food from the bottom (these will add flavor and texture).

🍃 Bring the liquid to a boil and quickly reduce to a syrup over high heat.

🍃 As the sauce thickens, lower the heat, taste, and season. Add herbs if desired.

Pan sauces are also a natural when you cook poultry, which, these days, seems to be more of a menu staple than meat in most kitchens. In addition to the methods mentioned above, I favor oven roasting for poultry; roasting a whole chicken or duck in a high oven ensures a crisp skin that holds in the juices. (At Montrachet, diners were surprised by the crispness and tenderness of our roasted chicken. Some claimed it was so different from the usual bird it almost seemed like a new kind of food.) And because easy-to-buy and prepare chicken, Cornish hens, quail, and duck all take well to the fruits and herbs that enliven French provincial cooking, it's no surprise that they're among the things I most enjoy preparing.

Everyone knows how simple chicken is to cook; the surprise is that duck can be just as easy. The recipes in this chapter should demystify preparation of that flavorful bird, whether you choose to roast it whole or to sear and roast just the breasts. For either chicken or duck breasts, a modification of the sear-and-roast technique used for fish works beautifully; marinating in an herbal oil or a vinaigrette adds extra flavor.

Additional poultry recipes can be found in the salad chapter. See:

🍃 Grilled Quail Salad with Provençal Vegetables and Balsamic Vinaigrette (page 63)
🍃 Warm Duck Salad with Cranberries and Walnuts (page 64)

Chicken or duck breasts take to my favorite cooking method as easily as fish steaks do, and while they need a bit more oven time, they don't require a second sear afterward. Like fish, they can be seared ahead and finished later, but they cook so quickly and are so delicious fresh from the pan, I rarely bother.

METHOD

❧ In a hot pan, over high heat, sear the breasts skin-side down in a little oil for at least 30 seconds.

❧ Transfer the pan to a hot oven and roast skin-side down for 8 minutes (the meat will be opaque and slightly underdone).

❧ Turn and roast 2 to 3 minutes longer.

❧ Let rest, preferably on a rack over a platter (so it doesn't sit in its own juices and lose its crisp sear), 5 minutes before serving. Cover lightly with aluminum foil, if desired.

While the meat roasts, you can make a quick herbal pan sauce with chicken stock (see the recipe that follows), if you like. But often, if you use a vinaigrette marinade before cooking, you may choose to skip a sauce; there will be plenty of flavor in the meat itself.

SEARED AND ROASTED CHICKEN BREASTS WITH LEMON AND THYME

MAKES 4 SERVINGS

ORDER OF PREPARATION

- Prepare the marinade and marinate the chicken.
- Sear and roast the chicken.
- While the chicken is resting, prepare the sauce.

Like most people, I've always been partial to the pairing of lemon and chicken. Here, the chicken picks up lemon and thyme flavors from its marinade and the pan sauce echoes them. You'll note I don't suggest any variations or substitutions for this recipe: When you have something that tastes so good and is so easy, why change it?

SERVE WITH:

GREEN AND YELLOW SQUASH RIBBONS (PAGE 128) OR ANY ZUCCHINI DISH; THYME AND ZUCCHINI ARE A SUPERB COMBINATION
HERBED SMASHED POTATOES (PAGE 135)
CONFIT BAYALDI (PAGE 138)

FOR THE CHICKEN

Juice of 1 lemon

5 tablespoons virgin olive oil

4 chicken breasts

Zest of 1 lemon, in strips

8 sprigs thyme

½ teaspoon cracked black pepper

Kosher salt and freshly ground black
pepper

Combine the lemon juice and 4 tablespoons of the olive oil in a small bowl. Place the chicken breasts in a shallow pan and pour the lemon mixture over them, coating both sides. Scatter the zest, thyme, and pepper over both sides. Cover and refrigerate for 3 hours or up to 1 day.

Preheat the oven to 400° F. Season the chicken with salt and pepper.

In a large skillet, heat the remaining tablespoon of oil until smoking over high heat. Add the chicken, skin-side down, then immediately transfer the pan to the oven and roast the chicken for 8 minutes. Turn and continue roasting until just cooked through, 2 to 3 minutes more. Remove from the pan and let rest at room temperature for 5 minutes, keeping warm.

FOR THE SAUCE

1 tablespoon pure olive oil

1 large shallot, minced

1 cup Chicken Stock (page 72) or
low-salt canned chicken broth

Juice of ½ lemon, plus a few drops

1 teaspoon finely chopped thyme
leaves

3 tablespoons cold butter

Kosher salt and freshly ground black
pepper

Pour off any grease and return the skillet to medium heat. Heat the olive oil until shimmering, then sauté the shallot for 1 minute. Add the stock and bring to a boil, stirring and scraping up any browned bits. Add the lemon juice and thyme, reduce the heat to medium-high, and boil gently until reduced by a little more than half. Reduce the heat to medium and whisk in the butter.

Taste and add more lemon juice if needed. Season with salt and pepper.

TO SERVE

Cut each breast on the bias into ½-inch slices. Place on a warm serving plate and spoon the sauce on top, to taste.

MAKE-AHEAD NOTES

❧ The chicken in its marinade can be refrigerated 3 hours or up to 1 day.

❧ The seared and roasted chicken can be kept at room temperature, in the baking pan, up to 1 hour.

SEARED AND ROASTED DUCK BREASTS WITH GREEN PEPPERCORN SAUCE

MAKES 4 SERVINGS

ORDER OF PREPARATION

- Sear and roast the sea-soned duck; let rest at room temperature.
- While the duck is rest-ing, prepare the sauce.

*D*uck breasts are much easier to cook than a whole duck; in fact, they are as easy as chicken breasts. The sear-and-roast method will give them crisp, golden-brown skin and juicy meat. Season the duck breasts well since they will lose a lot of salt and pepper with the fat when they are seared. The peppery pan sauce is a quick reduction of the duck juices with stock, port, and wine.

SERVE WITH:

WILD RICE WITH PINE NUTS (PAGE 119)

THE BEST CREAMED SPINACH (PAGE 132)

SERVE THE PEPPERCORN SAUCE WITH:

SEARED AND ROASTED CHICKEN BREASTS (SEE PAGE 200)

FOR THE DUCK BREASTS

Veal Stock makes the richest sauce, but, if necessary, substitute Duck Stock (page 73), Vegetable Stock (page 72), or Chicken Stock (page 72).

4 duck breasts, about 8 ounces each

Kosher salt and freshly ground black pepper

Preheat the oven to 400° F. With a sharp knife, cut the flesh side of the duck breasts in a shallow crosshatch pattern. Season with salt and pepper.

Place a large skillet over medium-high heat until the pan begins to smoke and sear the duck, fat-side down, 2 minutes. Pour off the grease and place the pan in the oven until the duck is medium-rare, 10 to 12 minutes. Turn and cook the other side 1 minute. Remove from the pan and pour off the grease. The duck breasts will retain their heat while you prepare the sauce.

FOR THE GREEN PEPPERCORN SAUCE

For green peppercorn sauce, substitute Ginger–Orange Sauce with Candied Ginger (page 30).

¼ cup port
¼ cup red wine
1 tablespoon green peppercorns (available canned)

1 cup Veal Stock (page 74)
1 teaspoon butter
Kosher salt and freshly ground black pepper

Place the pan the duck was roasted in over high heat and add the port and wine to the duck juices (be careful—they may ignite). Add the peppercorns and any juices that have accumulated around the cooked duck breasts and scrape the bottom of the pan, bringing up the browned bits and incorporating them into the juices. Boil for 2 minutes, then add the veal stock and boil gently 5 to 6 minutes. Swirl in the butter and season with salt and pepper.

TO SERVE

Cut each duck breast on the bias into 8 to 10 slices and arrange on individual plates. Spoon about 2 tablespoons of the sauce, or to taste, over the duck and serve immediately.

If you can't buy duck breasts:

ℑ remove breasts from two 5-pound ducks

Use the legs for:

ℑ braised duck legs in Warm Duck Salad with Cranberries and Walnuts (page 64)

ℑ Caramelized Onion Tarts (page 144) with added braised duck

When chicken or other poultry is roasted, it cooks at a high temperature until its skin is crisp; then the temperature is lowered slightly to allow the flesh to cook slowly. It emerges from the oven finely textured and full of concentrated flavor.

A hot oven is essential to roasting. At a lower temperature, the bird would bake, not roast, and would not come out crisp-skinned and juicy.

The juices produced by a roasting bird give you the base for a simple pan sauce. While the meat rests for a few minutes before carving, reduce the pan juices with stock and deglaze the roasting pan.

METHOD

- Place the chicken, breast-side up, over a bed of diced vegetables in a roasting pan, season, and brush with melted butter and olive oil.
- Roast in a hot oven, turning as each side becomes crisp.
- Turn breast-side up again and finish roasting at lowered heat, basting.
- Remove from the pan and let rest 5 minutes before carving.

SIMPLE ROASTED CHICKEN

MAKES 2 OR 3 SERVINGS

ORDER OF PREPARATION

- Dice the vegetables.
- Roast the chicken.
- Remove the chicken from the oven and let rest.
- While the chicken is resting, prepare the pan sauce.

Brushed with a mixture of olive oil and butter, stuffed with fresh herbs and garlic, and roasted on a bed of aromatic vegetables, this chicken has crisp, golden skin and juicy meat. The easy-to-prepare pan sauce is slightly thickened and full of herbal and chicken flavor.

Versatile roasted chicken would go nicely with almost any roasted or pureed vegetables in addition to the suggestions at right. Substitute herbs freely—add some tarragon to the mix or substitute it for any of the herbs called for.

SERVE WITH:

ROASTED-GARLIC MASHED POTATOES (PAGE 132)
ROSEMARY POLENTA (PAGE 122)
SWEET-POTATO PUREE (PAGE 134)
WILD RICE WITH PINE NUTS (PAGE 119)
THE BEST CREAMED SPINACH (PAGE 132)
CONFIT BAYALDI (PAGE 138)
EGGPLANT PROVENÇAL IN ROASTED TOMATOES (PAGE 136)

Use fresh rosemary, thyme, sage, oregano, or any other herbs you prefer.

2 tablespoons butter
2 tablespoons virgin olive oil
1 chicken, 2½ to 3 pounds
Kosher salt and cracked black pepper
6 to 8 sprigs fresh herbs
3 cloves garlic, peeled

1 small onion, cut into medium dice
2 medium carrots, peeled and cut into
    medium dice
2 stalks celery, cut into medium dice
½ teaspoon herbes de Provence

Preheat the oven to 475° F. In a small pot over medium-low heat, melt together the butter and olive oil.

Rinse the chicken well and pat dry with paper towels. Season the cavity with salt and pepper and stuff with the fresh herbs and garlic cloves.

If desired, strip the leaves from a sprig of rosemary and sprinkle over the chicken before roasting.

Arrange the diced vegetables in an even layer on the bottom of a roasting pan just big enough to accommodate the chicken (13 by 9 by 2 inches). Place the chicken breast-side up on top of the vegetables and brush with the butter mixture. Sprinkle on all sides with salt and pepper and herbes de Provence.

Roast 15 minutes, then turn the chicken on its side, brush with the butter mixture, and roast 10 minutes. Turn, brush, and roast on the other side, about 8 minutes.

Reduce the oven to 400° F. Turn the chicken breast-side up and roast 18 to 20 minutes more, basting 2 or 3 times with pan juices and butter; the juices should run clear when the chicken is pierced at the junction of the leg and thigh. Remove from the pan and let rest 5 minutes before carving.

FOR THE PAN SAUCE

2 cups Chicken Stock (page 72) or
    low-salt canned chicken broth
2 teaspoons butter

Salt and freshly ground black pepper
½ teaspoon chopped tarragon, savory,
    chives, or rosemary (optional)

Spoon or pour off the grease from the roasting pan. Place the pan over high heat, add the stock, and cook, scraping up the cooked-on bits from the bottom of the pan. Bring to a boil and reduce to one third of its original volume. Whisk in the butter. Season to taste and stir in the optional herbs.

TO SERVE

It is easiest to carve a chicken for 2, with equal portions of light and dark meat, but this size chicken yields meat for 3.

Carve the chicken and serve with the pan sauce.

MAKE-AHEAD NOTE

❧ The diced vegetables can be refrigerated up to 2 days.

STUFFED CORNISH HENS
WITH CRANBERRY SYRUP

MAKES 4 SERVINGS

**ORDER OF
PREPARATION**

- Prepare the stuffing.
- Stuff the hens and roast immediately.
- While the hens are roasting, prepare and cool the cranberry syrup.

A brown, crisp-skinned little hen makes an elegant portion for one: Each diner gets two small legs and breasts. This stuffing is a recipe I have always loved, a great combination of sage, sausage, apples, and crunchy walnuts, with the juices from the hens cooked in. The savory hens seem to cry out for cranberries: A drizzle of this refined and pretty syrup highlights their crispness and flavor in an elegant way.

The roasting method is a slight modification of the basic chicken roasting technique.

> **SERVE THE
> CRANBERRY SYRUP WITH:**
>
> **SEARED AND ROASTED CHICKEN
> OR DUCK BREASTS
> (SEE PAGES 200, 202)
> ROASTED TURKEY
> (SEE PAGE 208)**

FOR THE STUFFING

For the stuffing, substitute My Dad's Thanksgiving Stuffing (see page 208).

6 ounces good-quality pork sausage meat

2 tablespoons finely chopped fresh sage

4 slices country white bread or brioche, cut into ½-inch pieces

1 medium Granny Smith apple, peeled and finely diced

¼ cup coarsely chopped walnuts

Kosher salt and freshly ground black pepper

In a medium skillet over medium-high heat, sauté the sausage until cooked through. With a fork, break up the meat into small pieces and mix in the sage.

Meanwhile, in a large bowl, combine the bread with the apple and nuts. Add the sausage and any accumulated fat, mix well, and season with salt and pepper. Cool to room temperature.

This amount of stuffing is also enough for 4 pounds of chicken.

FOR THE HENS

4 Cornish hens, about 1½ pounds each

2 tablespoons virgin or pure olive oil

2 tablespoons butter, melted

Kosher salt and freshly ground black pepper

Preheat the oven to 425°F. Rinse the hens with cold water inside and out and pat dry. Remove any excess fat. Stuff each hen with about 1 cup of stuffing and tie the legs together with kitchen string.

If you roast the hens unstuffed, subtract 15 minutes from the cooking time.

Arrange breast-side up in 2 pans that each accommodates 2 hens (13 by 9 by 2-inch size works well). Combine the oil and melted butter in a small bowl. Brush the hens with the butter mixture, season with salt and pepper, and roast for 30 minutes. Reduce the oven temperature to 350° F., and roast 30 minutes longer, or until the juices run clear when the hen is pierced at a joint. You need not turn the hens.

FOR THE CRANBERRY SYRUP

1 cup fresh cranberries
½ cup orange juice, fresh or
   good-quality purchased

3 tablespoons sugar

When you strain the cranberry juice, save the cranberries to add to your favorite muffin batter.

Combine the ingredients in a small saucepan and bring to a boil over high heat. Reduce the heat to medium and boil until thick and syrupy, about 7 minutes. Strain through a fine strainer, reserving the cranberries for another use or discarding.

TO SERVE

Remove the stuffing from the hens and divide among 4 warmed plates. Carve the hens and arrange 2 legs and 2 breasts around the stuffing on each plate. Drizzle the cranberry syrup around each serving.

MAKE-AHEAD NOTES

ᔐ The cranberry syrup can be refrigerated up to 1 week or frozen. Bring to room temperature before serving.

ᔐ The stuffing can be refrigerated up to 2 days. (Once the hens have been stuffed, they must be cooked immediately.)

To carve the hens:

ᔐ place on a cutting board

ᔐ sever the legs where they join the body (you almost will be able to pull them off)

ᔐ cut down the breastbone and remove each breast

ᔐ as you carve, place the pieces on a baking sheet and keep warm in a 200° F. oven so you can fill and serve all plates at once

ROASTED TURKEY WITH MY DAD'S THANKSGIVING STUFFING

MAKES 12 TO 15 SERVINGS

ORDER OF PREPARATION
- Prepare the stuffing.
- Stuff the turkey and roast immediately.

*T*here is not a hint of France here, but even chefs appreciate a time-honored family recipe. Our Thanksgiving turkey sometimes seems to be just an excuse for making the Ponzek family stuffing, a recipe passed down to my father by his mother. Chunky with potatoes, sausage, and beef, this robust mixture starts out with a lot of flavor and absorbs delicious juices as the turkey roasts. Don't bake the stuffing separately—the poultry juices are a necessary ingredient. The turkey itself is brown-skinned and succulent, a perfect backdrop for the spicy stuffing.

This turkey is not roasted at high heat, but the long oven time will ensure a crisp, brown skin, even at a moderate temperature.

FOR THE STUFFING

Leaves from 1 bunch celery (about
$\frac{1}{2}$ cup)

1 small onion, cut into small dice

2 large potatoes, peeled and quartered

Kosher salt

3 slices white bread, held briefly
under running water to moisten

$\frac{1}{2}$ pound good-quality pork sausage,
casings removed

1 pound lean ground beef

Cracked or coarsely ground black
pepper

In a small saucepan over medium-high heat, simmer the celery leaves and onion in $1\frac{1}{2}$ cups water until about $\frac{1}{4}$ cup liquid remains, about 15 minutes.

Place the potatoes in a medium saucepan over high heat, cover with salted water, and bring to a boil. Reduce the heat to medium, simmer until tender, 20 to 25 minutes, and drain. Place in a large bowl and mash lightly with a fork, leaving some lumps. Crumble the bread into the potatoes and add the celery mixture.

Leftover stuffing is a great addition to a turkey sandwich.

Meanwhile, cook the sausage in a large skillet over medium-high heat until cooked through, 5 to 6 minutes. Add the beef and continue cooking until cooked through, 6 to 8 minutes. Drain well in a colander and add to the mashed potatoes and celery. Season to taste with salt and pepper and cool to room temperature.

FOR THE TURKEY

1 (14- to 16-pound) turkey, giblets removed, washed with cold water and patted dry	Kosher salt and freshly ground black pepper
Virgin olive oil	7 cups stuffing (above), at room temperature

Preheat the oven to 325°F. Place a rack in the bottom third of the oven.

Brush the turkey with a little olive oil and sprinkle with salt and pepper inside and out. Turn it breast-side up and loosely pack stuffing into the neck cavity. With a skewer, secure the end of the neck skin to the backbone. Turn the turkey over and stuff the main cavity loosely; close with a skewer. Tie the drumsticks together close to the body with kitchen string or twine tied once or twice around the whole bird.

Place the stuffed turkey breast-side up in a roasting pan that fits it snugly and place in the preheated oven.

When the turkey is done, a thermometer inserted into the stuffing should read 160°F. If the temperature is lower, scoop the stuffing into a baking dish and continue baking, or microwave it, until that temperature is reached.

Roast about 4 hours, until the juices run clear when you pierce the flesh with a knife and the drumstick can easily be moved up and down, basting every half hour with the pan juices. If it gets too brown, cover loosely with aluminum foil. Remove the turkey from the oven and allow it to rest about 15 minutes before carving. To carve, first cut off the drumsticks and wings, then slice the breasts and thighs on the bias in thin slices.

Remove the stuffing to a serving dish, and pass separately.

MAKE-AHEAD NOTE

The stuffing can be refrigerated up to 2 days. (Once the turkey has been stuffed, it must be cooked immediately.)

A frozen 14- to 16-pound turkey will take 2 to 2½ days to defrost in the refrigerator.

Before roasting the turkey, double-check your oven temperature with an oven thermometer.

Stuff just before roasting, to prevent spoilage.

ROASTED DUCK

MAKES 2 SERVINGS

There is nothing like roasted duck when it's done right: dark, crisp-skinned, and juicy. French cuisine traditionally pairs it with a rich sauce, but I find it so succulent and flavorful that none is needed. (If you do want a sauce, use the green peppercorn sauce on page 202.) A duck makes a perfect dinner for two and preparation is almost as easy as roasting a chicken. Be sure to maintain the original high heat throughout the cooking time. Rub the skin with orange juice, for caramelization.

> SERVE WITH:
>
> VEGETABLE PUREES (SEE PAGES 133–134)
> WILD RICE WITH PINE NUTS (PAGE 119)
> CURRIED COUSCOUS (PAGE 117)
> THE BEST CREAMED SPINACH (PAGE 132)
> GREEN AND YELLOW SQUASH RIBBONS (PAGE 128)
> INDIVIDUAL TIANS OF SUMMER VEGETABLES (PAGE 130)
> APRICOT AND PRUNE SAUCE (SEE PAGE 216)

Keep draining off the fat during cooking: put a bowl in the sink and pour the fat into it. (If the duck slips, it will end up in the sink, not on the floor.)

1 duck, about 5 pounds, gizzard, neck, and wings removed (may be frozen and used for Duck Stock)

Kosher salt
Cracked black pepper
Juice of ½ orange

Preheat the oven to 450°F.

Remove any excess fat from the duck. Season inside and out with salt and pepper and squeeze the orange juice over the breast and legs. Tie the legs together with kitchen twine.

Place the duck, breast-side up, in a baking pan large enough to hold it snugly (13 by 9 by 2 inches works well) and roast for 15 minutes. Drain off the rendered fat and turn the duck on its side. Roast 15 minutes, drain again, turn the duck onto its other side, and roast 10 minutes longer. Drain the fat, turn breast-side up, and roast 35 minutes. Remove from the pan and allow to rest 10 minutes before carving.

To carve, with a sharp knife, cut off the 2 legs where they join the body (they should come off easily). Then cut down the length of the breastbone and carve the meat away from the bone, on the bias, into 5 or 6 slices.

PAN-ROASTING POULTRY

Squab and chicken pieces lend themselves well to pan-roasting. When poultry is seared in a pan and then cooked over medium-high heat until done, it is crisp outside and moist within. The dishes that follow could certainly be cooked in the oven as well, but they are easier to do on the stove top, and you will be pleased with the results.

METHOD

- Cut poultry into serving pieces.
- Heat a bit of oil in a skillet until nearly smoking.
- Season the poultry pieces and sear skin-side down 3 to 4 minutes; turn and cook legs and thighs 3 to 4 minutes more and breasts 5 minutes more.
- Let rest, preferably on a rack over a platter (so they don't sit in their own juices and lose their crisp sear), 3 to 4 minutes before serving. Cover lightly with aluminum foil, if desired.

When done, squab should be slightly firm to the touch, with rosy flesh. Chicken should be cooked through but still juicy. To test for doneness, make a small incision on the underside after the meat has rested. If necessary, put it back in the oven for a few seconds.

PAN-ROASTED SQUAB WITH WILD MUSHROOM RISOTTO

MAKES 6 MAIN-COURSE SERVINGS

ORDER OF PREPARATION

- Slice the mushrooms.
- Simmer the mushrooms and stock.
- Start the risotto. When all the stock has been added and you reduce the heat to low, begin cooking the squab.

*T*his is a hearty dish for the fall and winter and a perfect eat-in-front-of-the-fireplace meal. Mushroom-steeped broth gives this risotto an intense mushroom flavor that combines well with the savory, golden-brown squab.

The squab are pan-cooked in just a little oil and nothing is added to overpower their delicate taste or compete with the flavor of the mushroom risotto. To give the risotto a more intense poultry taste, pour off as much grease as possible from the squab pan juices, deglaze the pan with ¼ cup of Chicken Stock, and stir into the risotto.

> **SERVE WITH:**
>
> STEAMED OR BLANCHED ASPARAGUS
> GREEN AND YELLOW SQUASH RIBBONS (PAGE 128)
>
> **SERVE RISOTTO WITH:**
>
> SIMPLE ROASTED CHICKEN (PAGE 204)
> ROASTED DUCK (PAGE 210)
> SEARED AND ROASTED DUCK BREASTS WITH GREEN-PEPPERCORN SAUCE (PAGE 202)
> PAN-SEARED SWORDFISH (SEE PAGE 168), INSTEAD OF ROSEMARY POLENTA

FOR THE RISOTTO

For risotto, substitute Roasted Garlic Mashed Potatoes (page 133), Pasta with Wild Mushrooms (page 110), or Wild Rice with Pine Nuts (page 119).

3¾ cups Chicken Stock (page 72), Vegetable Stock (page 72), or low-salt canned broth, plus a little extra, if needed

1 ounce dry imported mushrooms (optional)

12 shiitake mushrooms, caps only, sliced thin

3 tablespoons butter

1¼ cups Arborio rice

4 ounces oyster or other wild mushrooms, sliced thin (about 3 cups)

Kosher salt and freshly ground black pepper

If necessary, substitute domestic for wild mushrooms.

In a medium saucepan, heat the chicken stock and the dry mushrooms, if using, over medium heat until the stock is simmering and the mushrooms are soft. Add the sliced shiitake mushrooms and simmer just until they are soft, 4 to 5 minutes. Reduce the heat to low and keep the broth at a low simmer.

In a heavy medium saucepan, melt 2 tablespoons of the butter over medium-high heat and sauté the rice for 1 minute. Add ¼ cup of the simmering mushroom broth and mushrooms to the rice, stirring until it is incorporated. Continue stirring and adding broth $\frac{1}{4}$ cup at a time until about half the broth and mushrooms have been incorporated. Keep the rice at a gentle simmer.

Add the remaining liquid $\frac{1}{2}$ cup at a time, stirring until most has been incorporated before adding more. When all the broth and mushrooms have been added, reduce the heat to low and simmer 5 minutes.

Taste the rice for doneness. It should have some bite, but not be too hard. If it is not done al dente, stir in additional stock, as needed. Stir in the remaining tablespoon of butter and season with salt and pepper.

FOR THE SQUAB

1 tablespoon pure olive oil
6 squab, 1$\frac{1}{4}$ pounds each, deboned
    and cut into serving portions

Kosher salt and freshly ground black
    pepper

In a large skillet, heat the olive oil over high heat until almost smoking. Season the squab pieces with salt and pepper and place in the pan skin-side down. Sear until golden brown, 3 to 4 minutes, and turn. Cook the legs an additional 3 to 4 minutes and the breasts an additional 5 minutes, and remove from the pan. The squab will be rare to medium-rare; cook slightly longer for medium. Allow the squab to rest at room temperature 3 to 4 minutes before serving.

TO SERVE

Drizzle risotto with Chive Oil (page 6) or Red Wine Chicken Sauce (page 35).

Stir the risotto and divide among 6 warm plates. Arrange the squab around the risotto.

MAKE-AHEAD NOTES

☙ The sliced mushrooms can be refrigerated up to 1 day.

☙ The seared squab can be kept at room temperature up to 45 minutes; finish cooking it when the risotto cooks over low heat.

To cut into serving portions, run a sharp knife down each side of the breastbone, as close to the bone as possible. Cut around each breast until it comes free. Run the knife along the fat that separates the joints, to bring each leg-thigh joint into clear view. Cut at the joint and remove each leg and thigh.

COQ AU RIESLING WITH SPAETZLE

MAKES 6 SERVINGS

ORDER OF PREPARATION

- Marinate the hens.
- Blanch and shock the vegetables.
- Brown the hens and cook with the vegetables and bacon.
- While the hens cook, make the spaetzle.
- Reduce the pan juices.

*T*his is an elegant spin-off of the classic coq au vin, made with Cornish hens. Carrots, mushrooms, and seared chicken give the dish a lot of appetizing autumn oranges and browns, and you really can taste the vegetable juices, tarragon, and wine in the full-flavored sauce. The hens are marinated for several hours in Riesling and herbs, which both flavors and tenderizes them.

SERVE SPAETZLE WITH:

PAN-ROASTED SQUAB (PAGE 212)
SEARED AND ROASTED CHICKEN OR DUCK BREASTS (SEE PAGES 200, 202)

FOR THE CORNISH HENS AND VEGETABLES

For hens, substitute any poultry.

For turnips, substitute zucchini. No substitutions for the carrots, mushrooms, and onions! Omit the bacon, if you prefer.

4 Cornish hens, about 1¼ pounds each, cut into 6 pieces each (2 legs, 2 thighs, 2 breasts)

Kosher salt and freshly ground black pepper

¼ cup coarsely chopped shallots

4 sprigs fresh thyme

1 cup Riesling wine

16 white pearl onions

4 medium carrots, cut into ½-inch cubes

3 medium turnips, peeled and cut into ½-inch cubes

2 tablespoons olive oil

10 large white mushroom caps, cut into ½-inch cubes

6 thick slices bacon, cut into ¼-inch cubes, sautéed until brown and crisp, and drained on paper towels

1¼ cups Chicken Stock (page 72) or low-salt canned chicken broth

At least 12 hours before cooking, season the hen pieces with salt and pepper. Place them in a bowl, add the shallots and thyme, and mix well. Add the wine, cover, and refrigerate for 12 hours.

Bring a large pot three-quarters full of salted water to a boil over high heat. Blanch the onions 5 minutes, drain, and shock in ice water. Blanch the carrots and the turnips the same way.

Preheat the oven to 200°F.

Remove the hen pieces from the marinade; strain and reserve the marinade. In a skillet large enough to hold all the pieces in 1 layer or in 2 pans, if necessary, heat the olive oil over medium heat until smoking. Season the hen pieces with salt and pepper, place them in the pan skin-side down, and brown on all sides, about 5 minutes. Add the onions, carrots, turnips, mushrooms, and bacon. Cook, stirring, about 3 minutes; cover and cook another 8 to 10 minutes.

Remove the hen pieces and keep warm on a covered plate or in the oven. Discard the fat from the skillet, leaving the vegetables and bacon. Add the reserved marinade and the chicken stock and cook over high heat until reduced to about 1 cup. Keep warm.

FOR THE SPAETZLE

For spaetzle, substitute any noodles.

3 large eggs	$\frac{1}{2}$ teaspoon kosher salt
3 large egg yolks	$\frac{1}{4}$ teaspoon white pepper
$1\frac{1}{2}$ cups water	$\frac{1}{4}$ teaspoon ground or freshly grated
$2\frac{1}{4}$ cups all-purpose flour, plus extra,	nutmeg
if needed	2 tablespoons olive oil

When you make spaetzle, you may need 2 table-spoons or so extra flour, depending on the type of flour and the size of the eggs. Shock the spaetzle quickly in ice water—they will turn mushy if they are kept in water even a few seconds too long.

In a mixing bowl, whisk together the eggs, egg yolks, and water. Using a rubber spatula, blend in the flour and seasonings. The mixture should be as thick as pancake batter.

In a large pot, bring 4 quarts of lightly salted water to a boil over high heat. Pour the spaetzle mixture into a colander over the boiling water, pressing the mixture through the holes with a rubber spatula. Stir once to distribute it evenly in the water. Cook 1 minute, or until the spaetzle are firm; remove with a large slotted spoon into a bowl of ice water, and immediately remove from the ice water. Drain and toss lightly with olive oil.

TO SERVE

$1\frac{1}{2}$ tablespoons minced fresh tarragon

Mound the spaetzle in the center of a large serving platter. Return the seared Cornish hen pieces to the reduced broth and add the tarragon. Bring to a boil over medium heat and immediately arrange around the spaetzle and serve.

MAKE-AHEAD NOTES

ॐ The Cornish hens in their marinade can be refrigerated up to 12 hours.

ॐ The blanched and shocked vegetables can be refrigerated up to 1 day.

ॐ The cooked spaetzle can be tossed with a little oil, covered with plastic wrap, and refrigerated up to 1 day; reheat over medium heat in a bit of butter or olive oil and stock.

TENDERLOIN OF PORK WITH APRICOTS AND PRUNES

MAKES 4 SERVINGS

ORDER OF PREPARATION

- Macerate the dried fruit in the bourbon.
- Sear and roast the pork loins.
- While the meat is resting, prepare the apricot and prune sauce.

*R*oasted pork served with prunes and apricots is a classic French combination because the savory and sweet flavors play off one another so well. The roast has a golden-brown crust and pale, juicy meat, and the apricot and prune sauce is dark and fruit-flavored. This is one of my favorite pan sauces. It is easy to make, flavorful, and uncomplicated. All you do is add the fruit, deglaze the pan, and then add some stock and spices. Best of all, it can be made quickly, while the meat rests before being sliced.

> SERVE APRICOT AND PRUNE SAUCE WITH:
>
> **ROASTED DUCK (PAGE 210)**

FOR THE PORK

2 pork tenderloins, ¾ to 1 pound each, silver outer membrane removed

Kosher salt and freshly ground black pepper
3 tablespoons virgin or pure olive oil

Tenderloins of pork (as well as beef) are covered by a tough silvery membrane; to remove it, insert the point of a sharp knife under the membrane and cut away from you, angling the knife toward the membrane slightly to avoid cutting off too much meat.

Preheat the oven to 400°F. Season the pork with salt and pepper.

In a large skillet or sauté pan, heat the oil over high heat until smoking and sear the tenderloins on all sides until golden brown. Place in the oven in the skillet, or in a small baking pan, if the skillet is not ovenproof, and roast 15 to 20 minutes, until a meat thermometer inserted into the tenderloins reads 155°F.; it will rise another 5 degrees as the meat rests. Remove from the oven and allow to rest 10 minutes, reserving any juices that accumulate around the meat.

FOR THE APRICOT AND PRUNE SAUCE

12 pitted prunes, thinly julienned
10 dried apricots, thinly julienned
¼ cup bourbon whiskey, such as Jack Daniel's
1 cup Chicken Stock (page 72), Vegetable Stock (page 72), or low-salt canned broth
1 cup Veal Stock (page 74)
½-inch-long piece of lemon peel, julienned
1½ tablespoons butter
Few drops of fresh lemon juice
Kosher salt and freshly ground black pepper

In a small bowl, soak the dried fruit in the bourbon for 25 minutes. Drain, reserving 1 to 2 tablespoons of the liquid.

Return the pan in which you seared the meat to medium-high heat and add the prunes, apricots, and reserved bourbon. Bring to a boil and allow to boil 30 seconds while you deglaze the pan, scraping up any brown bits from the bottom of the pan. Add the stocks, bring to a boil, and add the lemon peel. Reduce the heat to medium and simmer until slightly thickened, about 8 minutes. Stir in the butter and lemon juice and season with salt and pepper.

TO SERVE

Slice the pork about ½ inch thick and arrange on 4 warmed serving plates. Spoon the sauce over the meat.

SADDLE OF LAMB WITH RATATOUILLE AND BASIL OIL

MAKES 4 SERVINGS

ORDER OF PREPARATION

- Prepare the Ratatouille.
- Prepare the lamb sauce and keep warm.
- Prepare the Basil Oil.
- Sear and roast the lamb.

*A*fter making saddle of lamb so many times at work, I have become a real fan of this tender cut, which cooks quickly and is full of rich flavor. It is easy to sear and slice thin and it makes a beautiful presentation. To make the full-flavored sauce, sauté some aromatic vegetables and herbs, add lamb stock, and reduce until creamy. Lamb stock is required in this dish—no substitutes—but it is simple to make and it freezes well.

The juicy lamb has a seared golden-brown crust and is pink in the middle. It is sliced and arranged over thick crimson Ratatouille, which has a fresh herb and tomato flavor. The Basil Oil framing the plate is an intense, beautiful green.

FOR THE LAMB SAUCE

For lamb sauce, substitute Roasted Garlic–Black Olive Oil (page 8) combined with a little basil or rosemary oil.

2 tablespoons olive oil	1 sprig fresh thyme
½ cup thinly sliced onion	1 bay leaf
½ cup thinly sliced carrot	6 parsley stems
3 tablespoons thinly sliced wild mushroom stems or 6 medium domestic mushrooms, thinly sliced	1 tablespoon black peppercorns
	6 cups lamb stock (see page 74)
2 cloves garlic, peeled and sliced thin	Kosher salt and freshly ground black pepper

Spoon some sauce on a plate; run your finger through it: if its track remains for a moment it's done; if it tastes weak, reduce it a bit more.

In a large skillet, heat the olive oil over medium-high heat until just smoking. Add the onion, carrot, mushroom stems, and garlic, and sauté for 5 minutes, or until barely tender. Add the herbs, peppercorns, and lamb stock, bring to a boil, and cook until reduced by about half. Taste and adjust the seasonings. Remove the bay leaf.

FOR THE LAMB

1 tablespoon pure olive oil	1 trimmed saddle of lamb, about 3 pounds, cut into 4 equal pieces

Preheat the oven to 450° F.

In a large ovenproof skillet, heat the oil over high heat until just smoking and sear the lamb on all sides. Transfer the pan to the oven and roast, meaty-side up, 5 minutes for rare, 6 to 7 minutes for medium, or 8 minutes for well done. Allow to rest 5 minutes before carving.

For Basil Oil, substitute Rosemary Oil (page 7).

For an elegant presentation, mold the Ratatouille in a 5-inch ring and arrange the sliced lamb on top.

2 cups Ratatouille (page 142)
3 cups lamb sauce

4 tablespoons Basil Oil (page 5)

Mound the ratatouille in the center of 4 serving plates. Slice the lamb thin and fan it over the ratatouille. Spoon 3 to 4 tablespoons of sauce around the lamb and drizzle about 1 tablespoon of basil oil around that.

MAKE-AHEAD NOTES

ふ The lamb sauce can be refrigerated up to 1 week or frozen; reheat over medium heat, skimming, if necessary.

ふ The Ratatouille can be refrigerated up to 3 days; reheat in a 275°F. oven or over low heat, or microwave.

ふ The Basil Oil can be refrigerated up to 2 days.

DOUBLE-CUT LAMB CHOPS WITH CAPONATA POLENTA AND CRISPY RED ONIONS

MAKES 4 SERVINGS

ORDER OF PREPARATION

- Prepare the Caponata.
- Prepare the Roasted Garlic–Black Olive Oil.
- Prepare the crispy onions.
- Prepare the polenta.
- Sear and roast the lamb.
- While the lamb is roasting, combine the polenta and Caponata.

I prepared this dish for a few hundred enthusiastic diners on the Queen Elizabeth II, *as part of a chefs' cruise. There were several other chefs aboard, and every night, one of us presented a spectacular dinner. As my contribution, these lamb chops were set alongside a colorful mixture of Caponata and creamy polenta. A crown of crisp thin onion slices added height and crunch.*

This recipe shows how versatile polenta can be. Caponata is only one great stir-in; try adding Niçoise olives, spices, fresh herbs, or roasted tomatoes.

To get 8 double-cut chops, you'll need 2 full racks; have your butcher scrape the bones clean ("french") and cut the chops. You can also cook this as whole racks.

> **SERVE THE LAMB WITH:**
>
> **RATATOUILLE (PAGE 142)**
> **CONFIT BAYALDI (PAGE 138)**
> **EGGPLANT PROVENÇAL IN ROASTED TOMATOES (PAGE 136)**
> **ROASTED GARLIC MASHED POTATOES (PAGE 132)**
>
> **SERVE CRISPY ONIONS:**
>
> **OVER ANY SEARED OR ROASTED MEAT, POULTRY, OR FISH**

FOR THE CRISPY RED ONIONS

1 large red onion, peeled and very thinly sliced (use a mandoline or sharp knife)

Flour for dredging (preferably Wondra)

Vegetable oil for frying

Kosher salt and freshly ground black pepper

Dredge the onion slices in flour. In a large heavy skillet, heat 2 inches of oil over medium-high heat until shimmering. Add the onion and fry until light golden brown. Drain on paper towels and season with salt and pepper. Reserve, keeping warm.

FOR THE LAMB

2 racks of lamb, frenched, cut into 8 double-chop portions

Kosher salt and freshly ground black pepper

1 tablespoon pure olive oil

Preheat the oven to 450° F. Season the lamb with salt and pepper.

Heat the oil in a large skillet over high heat and sear the chops for 1 minute on each side.

Cover the bones with aluminum foil to prevent burning. Place the skillet with the lamb in the oven for 3 to 4 minutes, turn the chops, and cook another 4 to 5 minutes for medium-rare. Remove from the oven and allow to rest 5 to 10 minutes before serving.

TO SERVE

Instead of combining, serve the Caponata and polenta side by side or with the Caponata over the polenta.

2 cups cooked polenta (see page 120)
¾ cup hot Caponata (page 140)
Kosher salt and freshly ground black pepper

½ cup Roasted Garlic–Black Olive Oil (page 8)
Fresh tarragon or thyme, for garnish

Combine the polenta and caponata, taste, and reseason, if necessary. Divide the mixture among 4 plates, place a double lamb chop beside the polenta, and top with the crispy onions. Drizzle with the roasted garlic–black olive oil and garnish with the herbs.

MAKE-AHEAD NOTES

∾ The Caponata can be refrigerated up to 3 days.

∾ The Roasted Garlic–Black Olive Oil can be refrigerated up to 2 days.

∾ The crispy onions can be kept at room temperature up to 1 day; reheat at 250° F.

∾ The polenta can be kept in a covered bowl on a warm part of your stove for about 1 hour.

∾ The seared lamb can be kept at room temperature up to 1 hour before roasting.

To cook a whole rack of lamb:
∾ sear in hot oil over high heat
∾ roast fat-side down 12 minutes
∾ turn and roast 5 minutes, or to desired doneness
∾ let rest, preferably on a rack over a platter (so it doesn't sit in its own juices and lose its crisp sear), 5 to 10 minutes, before serving. Cover lightly with aluminum foil, if desired

PAN-ROASTING MEATS

Chops and similar small cuts of pork, lamb, and veal are very easy to cook in a pan on top of the stove. Like pan-seared poultry, these meats also could be done by the sear-and-roast method, but stove-top cooking is simpler and works just as well. After the meat is quickly cooked, it can be combined with all sorts of grain or vegetable dishes for interesting main courses.

Cooking time for boneless chops will be a minute or two less than for bone-in chops.

METHOD

❧ Cook the seasoned chops in hot oil over medium heat, turning once, until done.

❧ Let rest, preferably on a rack over a platter (so they don't sit in their own juices and lose their crisp sear), 4 to 5 minutes. Cover lightly with aluminum foil, if desired.

❧ Pour off any accumulated juices and use for sauce.

LAMB LOIN CHOPS WITH ROASTED FENNEL, TOMATOES, AND OLIVES

MAKES 4 SERVINGS

ORDER OF PREPARATION

- Roast the garlic.
- Sauté and roast the vegetables.
- While the vegetables are roasting, cook the lamb chops and allow to rest.

This is an easy dish to put together not long before serving; the colorful vegetables roast in the oven and when they are almost done, lamb chops are quickly seared on top of the stove.

When you take these fragrant roasted vegetables out of the oven, they are so glossy and beautiful, you will want to bring the skillet straight to the table. Serve the chops and vegetables with Roasted Garlic Mashed Potatoes (page 132) and a drizzle of Basil Oil, Roasted Garlic–Black Olive Oil, or Rosemary Oil. This is a warming meal for fall or winter.

SERVE ROASTED VEGETABLES WITH:

SIMPLE ROASTED CHICKEN (PAGE 204)
SADDLE OF LAMB (SEE PAGE 218)
RACK OF LAMB (SEE PAGE 220)
ROASTED VEAL CHOPS (SEE PAGE 224)
HERB-ROASTED HALIBUT (SEE PAGE 154)
ROASTED COD (SEE PAGE 173)
SEARED AND ROASTED TUNA OR SWORDFISH (SEE PAGE 151)

FOR THE ROASTED VEGETABLES

For roasted vegetables, substitute Ratatouille (page 142), Confit Bayaldi (page 138), caponata polenta (see page 220).

Kosher salt

3 medium bulbs fennel, quartered and cored, bruised outside pieces discarded

1 tablespoon butter

1 tablespoon extra-virgin olive oil

2 medium-size tomatoes, quartered, cored, and seeded; then cut in half

4 cloves Oven-Roasted Garlic (page 37)

16 Niçoise olives, pitted

1 tablespoon Lemon Confit (page 38), optional, or lemon zest

¾ cup Vegetable Stock (page 72) or low-salt canned vegetable broth

Preheat the oven to 350° F.

Fill a medium pot with salted water and bring to a boil over high heat. Blanch the fennel until just tender, 3 to 4 minutes, drain, and rinse under cold running water. Drain well.

In a large ovenproof skillet, heat the butter and oil over medium-high heat until the butter is melted. Sauté the fennel until golden brown, about 3 minutes. Add the tomatoes, garlic, olives, and lemon confit and pour in the stock. Place in the oven until the vegetables are soft and roasted, about 45 minutes. Season with salt and pepper.

FOR THE LAMB CHOPS

8 lamb loin chops, 1 inch thick

Kosher salt and freshly ground black pepper

1 teaspoon virgin or pure olive oil

Season the chops on both sides with salt and pepper. In a large skillet, heat the oil over high heat until just smoking. Add the chops, reduce the heat to medium, and cook about 4 minutes. Turn and cook until cooked through, another 1 to 2 minutes. Remove from the pan and allow to rest 4 to 5 minutes. Divide among 4 serving plates and spoon the roasted vegetables alongside.

MAKE-AHEAD NOTE

↜ The sautéed and roasted vegetables can be refrigerated up to 3 days (but they will be best if done just before serving).

PAN-ROASTED VEAL CHOPS WITH CARAMELIZED ONION SAUCE

MAKES 4 SERVINGS

ORDER OF PREPARATION

- Prepare the onion sauce.
- Cook the veal and allow it to rest.
- While the veal is resting, add the veal juices to the onion sauce.

*T*he chops used in this recipe are boneless, which speeds up the cooking time somewhat. They are nicely seared to a deep brown and served under a sauce that is rich in flavor and slightly sweet and sour. If you like this sauce as much as I do, try the Caramelized Onion Tarts (page 144).

This is one dish that doesn't work well if the meat is seared ahead, because the boneless chops are too thin and would overcook.

FOR THE CARAMELIZED ONION SAUCE

If made with Veal Stock, the sauce will have more body; if made with chicken or vegetable stock, it will be lighter.

2 tablespoons extra-virgin olive oil, plus 2 teaspoons, if needed
2 medium-size red onions, very thinly sliced
1½ tablespoons sugar
½ cup red wine
1 tablespoon red wine vinegar (or substitute sherry vinegar)
1½ cups Veal Stock (page 74), Vegetable Stock (page 72) or Chicken Stock (page 72), or low-salt canned broth

1½ tablespoons cold butter, cut in pieces
1 teaspoon sherry vinegar
Kosher salt and freshly ground black pepper

In a large sauté pan, heat the oil over medium-high heat until shimmering. Add the onion slices, sprinkle with the sugar, and cook until the onions caramelize, 10 to 12 minutes. Stir occasionally at first, then more frequently, once the onions begin to brown. Add 1 to 2 teaspoons olive oil, if needed, to moisten the mixture.

Raise the heat to high and add the wine and vinegar. Bring to a boil and boil for 1 minute. Add the stock, reduce the heat to medium, and simmer 15 minutes. Swirl in the butter until incorporated, add the sherry vinegar, and cook 30 seconds. Season to taste with salt and pepper.

FOR THE VEAL

4 boneless veal loin chops, ¾ to 1 inch thick

Kosher salt and freshly ground black pepper

1 tablespoon pure olive oil

Season the veal on both sides with salt and pepper. In a large sauté pan, heat the oil over medium-high heat until smoking. Add the veal and cook about 4 minutes. Turn and cook until done, 1 to 2 minutes. Let the chops rest 5 minutes before serving.

TO SERVE

For the onion sauce, substitute Red Wine Chicken Sauce (page 35), a drizzle of herbal oil, such as Chive Oil (page 6).

Stir the veal pan juices and any juices that have accumulated around the chops into the caramelized onion sauce. Divide the chops among 4 plates and spoon the sauce over them.

MAKE-AHEAD NOTE

☙ The onion sauce can be refrigerated up to 3 days; reheat over medium heat.

PAN-ROASTED PORK LOIN CHOPS AND GINGER–ORANGE SAUCE WITH CANDIED GINGER

MAKES 4 SERVINGS

ORDER OF PREPARATION

- Prepare the Ginger–Orange Sauce.
- Cook the pork chops.

Pork's accommodating nature pairs well with many fruit-based accompaniments—classic French cuisine makes use of many such combinations. This rich orange sauce is sweet and spicy, with chunks of candied ginger, adding a more adventurous note. It provides a delicious complement to succulent seared chops, and the whole dish cooks in minutes if you've made the sauce ahead of time.

SERVE WITH:

SIMPLE BRAISED LENTILS (PAGE 118)
PUMPKIN RISOTTO (PAGE 116)
ROSEMARY POLENTA (PAGE 122)
CAPONATA POLENTA (SEE PAGE 220)
ROASTED GARLIC MASHED POTATOES (PAGE 133)

For Ginger–Orange Sauce, substitute cranberry syrup (see page 206), Spiced Plum Sauce (page 32), or Caramelized Pear Sauce (page 33).

4 center-cut pork loin chops, ¾ to 1 inch thick
Kosher salt and freshly ground black pepper

2 teaspoons pure or virgin olive oil
½ to ⅔ cup Ginger–Orange Sauce with Candied Ginger (page 30)

Season the chops with salt and pepper. In a large sauté pan or skillet, heat the oil over medium-high heat until almost smoking. Add the chops, reduce the heat to medium, and cook about 4 minutes. Turn and cook until done, 1 to 2 minutes.

To serve, divide among 4 serving plates and spoon the ginger–orange sauce over each serving.

MAKE-AHEAD NOTES

❧ The candied ginger can be refrigerated up to 10 days.

❧ The Ginger–Orange Sauce can be refrigerated up to 1 week.

❧ The seared pork chops can be placed on a baking sheet and kept at room temperature up to 1 hour, and then finished in a 400° F. oven (but they are much better pan-seared just before serving).

PAN-ROASTED MEDALLIONS OF BEEF

MAKES 6 TO 8 SERVINGS

Medallions of beef make an elegant and festive centerpiece to an important meal and are very easy to prepare. Pork or veal medallions cut from the loin can be treated the same way. If you want to gild the lily a bit, add a drizzle of Port Wine Sauce (page 31) made with Veal Stock.

> **SERVE WITH:**
>
> THE BEST CREAMED SPINACH
> (PAGE 132)
> EGGPLANT PROVENÇAL IN
> ROASTED TOMATOES
> (PAGE 136)
> PUREED VEGETABLES (SEE
> PAGES 133–134)

3 pounds beef tenderloin, cut into 6 to 8 medallions, about 1½ inches thick

Kosher salt and freshly ground black pepper
3 tablespoons virgin olive oil

Season the meat on both sides with salt and pepper.

In a large skillet or sauté pan over high heat, heat the oil until smoking. Add the medallions and sear on all sides. Cook 3 to 4 minutes on one side, then turn over and cook on the other side until medium-rare, 3 to 4 minutes more.

Remove from heat and let rest 5 minutes before serving.

Some cuts of meat, such as lamb shanks, veal shoulder, breast, and shank, and oxtails, are tough and gelatinous, yet full of flavor. Long, slow cooking in a flavored liquid tenderizes them and melts away their fat. Braising can be done in the oven or on the stove, and the braising liquid, usually slightly thickened, can be used to sauce the finished dish.

METHOD

- Sear the seasoned meat in hot oil over high heat until golden brown on all sides.
- Add liquid and cut vegetables and bring to a boil.
- Cook in a hot oven, turning, until very tender.
- Skim fat from the braising liquid and reserve liquid for the sauce.

BRAISED LAMB SHANKS WITH WHITE BEANS AND ROSEMARY

MAKES 4 SERVINGS

ORDER OF PREPARATION

- Roast the garlic.
- Braise the lamb.
- While the lamb cooks, simmer the beans.
- After the lamb is done, prepare the sauce.

I *think of this full-flavored ragout of tender lamb as a perfect dish for winter. Its combination of rosemary and white beans with lamb is classic French. Recipes like this, utilizing less expensive cuts of meat, are very popular in French country cooking.*

The liquid that the meat has cooked in becomes lamb stock. Any extra may be degreased, frozen, and used for the next batch of lamb shanks or in recipes calling for lamb stock.

FOR THE LAMB

4 lamb shanks, 1 to 1¼ pounds each
Kosher salt and freshly ground black pepper
1 tablespoon virgin or pure olive oil
4 cups Vegetable Stock (page 72), Chicken Stock (page 72), or low-salt canned broth
2 cups water
3 sprigs rosemary

1 head garlic, halved crosswise
2 stalks celery, cut into medium dice
2 medium carrots, peeled and cut into medium dice
1 small onion, cut into medium dice
Up to 1 cup small-diced mushroom stems (optional)
1 teaspoon black peppercorns
1 bay leaf

Preheat the oven to 425°F. Season the lamb shanks with salt and pepper.

In a large, high-sided skillet or pot, heat the olive oil over high heat until smoking and sear the lamb until golden brown on all sides. Add all the remaining ingredients, bring to a boil, and place in the oven. Braise, turning the shanks every half hour, until the meat is very tender but still on the bone, about 2 hours.

Transfer the shanks to a warm platter and keep warm. Discard the bay leaf. Skim the grease from the braising liquid and reserve 3 cups for the sauce; cool and refrigerate or freeze the remainder.

FOR THE WHITE BEAN SAUCE

For white beans, substitute flageolets or a 19-ounce can of cooked beans.

1 cup dried white beans
3 cups braising liquid (above)
2 medium-size tomatoes, quartered, seeded, and cut into ½-inch dice

6 cloves Oven-Roasted Garlic (page 37)
1 sprig rosemary
Kosher salt and freshly ground black pepper

You can cook dried beans without presoaking, although there may be some variation in cooking time, as older beans will take longer to cook than those from the current year's crop.

Combine the dried beans with water to cover by an inch in a medium saucepan. Bring to a boil over high heat, then reduce the heat to medium and simmer for 45 minutes, or until tender. Drain.

In a medium saucepan, combine the braising liquid, tomatoes, beans, garlic, and rosemary and simmer over medium-high heat until slightly thickened, about 15 minutes. (The beans will thicken the sauce.) Season with salt and pepper.

TO SERVE

Place each lamb shank in a warm shallow bowl, and ladle the sauce around it.

MAKE-AHEAD NOTES

ᴥ The roasted garlic can be refrigerated up to 2 weeks.

ᴥ The braised lamb shanks can be refrigerated up to 2 days. (Remove the meat from the liquid, strain the liquid, cool it at room temperature, and pour it back over the meat.)

ᴥ The cooked beans can be refrigerated up to 1 day.

BLANQUETTE DE VEAU

ORDER OF
PREPARATION

- Blanch the pearl onions and the fresh peas.
- Sauté the mushrooms and pearl onions.
- Prepare the blanquette.

V*ery pretty with mushrooms, pearl onions, and carrots, my updated version of this classic example of* cuisine bonne femme *allows the veal flavor to come through. Its cream sauce is lightened by the cooking liquid and a touch of lemon, without the traditional egg yolks. Serve over rice or fresh pasta, to soak up the delicious sauce.*

Unlike other elegant veal dishes, this one uses inexpensive cuts of meat, but braising ensures that it will be tender. As the cooking liquid is combined with Veal Stock, the pan is deglazed to incorporate all the tasty bits of meat stuck to the bottom.

FOR THE MUSHROOMS

Kosher salt

15 pearl onions, peeled

1 tablespoon butter

1 tablespoon pure olive oil

15 medium domestic or wild mushrooms, quartered

Freshly ground black pepper

In a medium saucepan, bring salted water to a boil over high heat. Add the onions and blanch until tender, about 3 minutes; drain.

In a large skillet, heat the butter and oil over high heat until bubbling. Sauté the mushrooms and pearl onions until golden brown, 3 to 4 minutes. Season with salt and pepper.

FOR THE VEAL

Omit the peas if you choose, but don't substitute another vegetable.

2 to 2½ pounds veal stew meat (shoulder, breast, or shank), trimmed and cut into 1-inch cubes

Kosher salt and freshly ground black pepper

2 tablespoons pure olive oil

3 cups Veal Stock (page 74), or 1½ cups Veal Stock and 1½ cups Vegetable Stock (page 72) or Chicken Stock (page 72), or low-salt canned broth

1 stalk celery, cut into medium dice

4 medium carrots, peeled: 1 cut into medium dice, 3 cut into ¼-inch slices

½ medium onion, cut into 2 equal pieces

1 bay leaf

½ teaspoon whole black peppercorns

¼ teaspoon whole allspice berries

1 cup heavy cream

1 cup frozen tiny peas, thawed, or fresh peas blanched in salted water for 3 minutes

Small piece lemon rind (about 1 by 2 inches), thinly julienned

Few drops of fresh lemon juice

Season the veal pieces on all sides with salt and pepper. In a medium to large skillet, heat 1 tablespoon of the oil over high heat until smoking. Add about half the veal in a single layer and sear until golden brown on both sides. Remove the meat from the pan and repeat with the remaining oil and veal. Return the first batch of veal to the pan, add the stock, and bring to a boil, stirring to loosen the browned bits on the bottom of the pan and incorporate them into the stock.

Add the celery, diced carrot, onion, bay leaf, peppercorns, and allspice and bring to a boil. Reduce the heat to medium, cover, and simmer until the meat is very tender, 1 to $1\frac{1}{4}$ hours.

Don't be afraid to boil the cream; it is necessary for a properly thickened sauce.

Remove the veal to a plate. Strain the cooking liquid through a fine strainer, pour it back into the pan, and bring it to a boil over high heat. Reduce the heat to medium-high and boil gently 10 minutes. Add the sliced carrots and continue boiling 10 minutes more, until about 1 cup liquid remains. Add the cream and boil gently for 2 minutes. Add the veal, mushroom mixture, peas, and lemon rind and heat through.

Season the blanquette with salt and pepper and add the lemon juice.

MAKE-AHEAD NOTES

The blanched pearl onions and fresh peas can be refrigerated up to 1 day.

The blanquette can be refrigerated up to 3 days; reheat over medium heat.

BRAISED OXTAIL STEW

MAKES 4 TO 5 SERVINGS

ORDER OF PREPARATION

- Braise the oxtails.
- Prepare the vegetable garnish.
- Heat the meat and vegetables together.

*O*xtails *(really beef or veal tails) don't have a lot of meat, but what is there is delicious and well worth picking off the bones. In this example of rustic French cooking, the oxtails are dark and moist and the braising liquid is richly flavored.*

> **SERVE WITH:**
> ....
> **ROSEMARY POLENTA (PAGE 122)**
> **ANY PASTA**

FOR THE OXTAILS

5 pounds oxtails

Kosher salt and freshly ground black pepper

2 tablespoons pure olive oil

4 cups beef stock (see Veal Stock, page 74) or low-salt canned beef broth

2 cups red wine

4 medium carrots, peeled and cut into medium dice

10 domestic mushrooms

1 medium onion, cut into medium dice

1 bay leaf

6 to 8 sprigs thyme

Preheat the oven to 375°F. Sprinkle the oxtails with salt and pepper.

In a large ovenproof saucepan or casserole, heat the oil over medium-high heat until just smoking and sear the oxtails on all sides. Remove the meat and add the stock, wine, carrots, mushrooms, onion, bay leaf, and thyme. Raise the heat to high and bring to a boil, stirring and scraping the bottom of the pan to deglaze. When the liquid begins to boil, return the oxtails to the saucepan.

Cook in the oven until tender, 2 to 2½ hours.

Remove the oxtails to a platter and keep warm, covered with foil. There should be about 4 cups of braising liquid left. Skim as much fat as possible from the top and place the pan over high heat. Bring to a boil and reduce by one third. Keep warm.

FOR THE VEGETABLE GARNISH

For cipollini, substitute pearl onions.

4 medium carrots, peeled and cut into ¼-inch rounds

Kosher salt

2 tablespoons virgin olive oil

8 ounces cipollini onions, peeled

12 shiitake mushrooms (about 8 ounces), caps only

Freshly ground black pepper

Blanch the carrots in a large pot of boiling salted water until just tender, 3 to 4 minutes, and shock in a bowl of ice water.

In a medium skillet, heat the oil over medium heat until shimmering. Add the onions and sauté until golden brown. Add the mushrooms and carrots and continue to cook until the onions and mushrooms are tender, about 5 minutes longer. Season with salt and pepper.

TO SERVE

Return the meat and the vegetable garnish to the pan the meat was braised in and heat through over medium-high heat. Taste and season with salt and pepper. Arrange the meat and vegetables on serving plates.

MAKE-AHEAD NOTES

❧ The vegetable garnish can be refrigerated up to 3 days.

❧ The stew can be refrigerated up to 3 days; rewarm over medium heat.

CHAPTER 8

DESSERTS

Although dessert preparation certainly figured prominently in my professional training, I really learned about desserts *after* graduation, when I started my first job and much to my surprise was named pastry chef! The "recipes" the chef handed me were only lists of ingredients, without any methods of preparation or even clues to which ingredients belonged with each other. I completely immersed myself in the techniques of matching ingredients properly and measuring with precision; careful handling of chocolate and butter; and preparation of pastries, syrups, and crème anglaise. Before long, I came to understand the importance of preserving the fresh, true flavors of fine ingredients. I made many classic French desserts, but I also got plenty of practice in making dishes that were fun to do and imaginative.

In the years since, I have continued to be guided by that combination of tradition and fun—as was my selection of desserts for this book. The chocolate mousses, clafouti, *financier,* tarte Tatin, and maca-roons will be familiar to lovers of classic French food. Desserts like maple–cinnamon bread pudding and Butter-Pecan Cookies are younger and more American in spirit, but still are firmly based on the French respect for fine ingredients and pure flavors.

Like the other foods in this book, all my desserts stay true to their flavors: Eggnog Cheesecake is rich, sweet, and eggy; chocolate mousse will hit you with a sensuous jolt of taste and aroma; the fruit pies are pure essence of fruit—and not much else. These are not fussy desserts that call for great feats of magic on the part of the cook; all they require are the best pure ingredients: good chocolate, real vanilla extract, butter (not margarine!), and ripe, juicy fruit.

For me, dining is incomplete without dessert. Whether it is some simple cookies or a chocolate layer cake, dessert sends the message: "Sit back, relax, enjoy something sweet, and think about how delicious this meal has been." It always surprises me when people who have made everything else from scratch serve a purchased dessert. All the recipes you'll find in this chapter are so easy to make you won't have to choose between making the meal or making the dessert. And although I have simplified many of the prepara-tions, I haven't detracted from their elegance and richness, because desserts should be special—and fun.

Often made in one bowl, mousses, clafoutis, and pudding cakes taste sophisticated, but are so easy. And because they are served in individual portions, they make an elegant presentation and look like you have taken a lot more time than you really have.

PEAR CLAFOUTI

MAKES 8 SERVINGS

Clafouti, a French pudding cake, is the simplest of desserts, combining custard and fruit. You can bake the clafouti in a large pan or individual ramekins, and even pour it into a tart shell. The custard will puff up in the oven and fall again about 5 minutes after it is done.

The classic clafouti is made with cherries, but the recipe works well with almost any fresh fruit. Just slice the fruits thin so they won't fall to the bottom.

Proportions for the custard are 1 egg to ⅓ cup of cream. To make individual clafoutis, omit the flour. Pour the batter into eight 4½-ounce ramekins and bake 20 to 25 minutes at 375° F.

1 tablespoon unsalted butter
⅓ cup plus 1 tablespoon sugar
4 medium Bartlett or Anjou pears
3 large eggs
1 vanilla bean or 2 teaspoons extract

6 tablespoons sifted all-purpose flour
1½ cups heavy cream
1 teaspoon ground cinnamon
1 tablespoon Poire William or other
    pear brandy (optional)

Preheat the oven to 375° F. Grease a 10½-inch-round, 4½-inch-deep Pyrex baking dish with the butter and sprinkle with 1 tablespoon of the sugar.

Peel, quarter, and core the pears and slice very thin. Arrange the pears on the bottom of the dish. In a mixing bowl, beat the eggs until fluffy. Slit the vanilla bean lengthwise and scrape the seeds into the bowl. Add the remaining sugar, flour, cream, cinnamon, and Poire William, if using, and whisk together well. Set aside to rest at room temperature 10 minutes.

Pour the batter over the pears and bake until the custard is golden, puffy, and firm, about 40 minutes. Serve warm or at room temperature.

MAKE-AHEAD NOTES

❧ You may slice the fruit and prepare the batter and refrigerate them separately up to 5 hours in advance.

❧ The baked clafouti can be kept at room temperature for several hours.

WHITE CHOCOLATE MOUSSE

MAKES 10 TO 12 SERVINGS

ORDER OF PREPARATION

- Prepare the Italian meringue; cool.
- While the meringue is cooling, melt the chocolate, and whip the cream.
- Combine the mousse ingredients and chill.

*W*hen you want a delicate dessert with lovely, subtle chocolate flavor, this is the one to choose. Since white chocolate is sweeter than dark, this mousse is a bit sweeter than the Bittersweet Chocolate Mousse that follows, but a touch of lemon helps give it balance. It is softer, too, and super-light, thanks to the Italian meringue.

Italian meringue is made by beating boiling sugar syrup into egg whites. It gives desserts a delightfully light texture and can be used in cakes and fudge, as well as mousses.

FOR THE ITALIAN MERINGUE

½ cup egg whites (about 4 large whites), at room temperature	½ cup water
	½ cup sugar
1 tablespoon grated lemon zest	

Beat the egg whites in the bowl of an electric mixer, using the whisk attachment at medium-high speed (or use a hand-held mixer). When they are frothy, reduce the speed to medium and continue beating until they stand in soft peaks. Add the lemon zest and beat on high until they form stiff peaks.

Because the meringue stabilizes the mousse, no gelatin is added.

Meanwhile, in a small pot over high heat, bring the water and sugar to a boil without stirring. When the sugar syrup reaches 239° F. (the soft-ball stage), which should take 90 seconds, slowly drizzle it into the beaten whites, beating continuously, until the meringue is shiny and stiff, 3 to 4 minutes. Reduce the mixer speed to medium and continue beating until the mixer bowl feels cool to the touch. Set aside in the bowl.

FOR THE MOUSSE

½ pound white chocolate	Few drops of lemon juice
2 cups heavy cream	

In the top of a double boiler set over barely simmering water, melt the chocolate until just warm but not hot. Keep warm over the hot water, with the heat turned off. Alternatively, melt a few chunks at a time in a microwave.

In a large mixing bowl, beat the cream to soft peaks. With an electric mixer on low speed (or a hand-held mixer), slowly drizzle the warm melted chocolate into the Italian meringue. Pour the mixture into a larger bowl and whisk in half the whipped cream. Fold in three quarters of the remaining whipped cream. Then fold in the lemon juice along with the remaining whipped cream.

TO SERVE

Pour into serving glasses or bowls and refrigerate for at least 4 hours before serving.

MAKE-AHEAD NOTE

ༀ The mousse can be refrigerated up to 3 days.

Tips for making Italian meringue:

ༀ The egg whites must be at room temperature, with no trace of yolk.

ༀ The beaters (or whisk) and bowl must be clean and dry.

ༀ Timing is important. Whites and sugar should be ready at the same time.

ༀ If the sugar comes to a boil before the whites are completely beaten, add a bit of cold water and reduce the heat to low or medium while you finish beating the whites.

BITTERSWEET CHOCOLATE MOUSSE

MAKES 8 TO 10 SERVINGS

ORDER OF PREPARATION

- Melt the chocolate.
- Whip the cream and refrigerate.
- Prepare the egg and sugar mixture.
- Combine the mousse ingredients and chill.

This may be the best chocolate mousse you will ever taste! Chef Dennis Foy introduced me to it when I worked at his restaurant, The Tarragon Tree, and I have never found a better recipe. Unlike many mousses I have tasted, this one is just sweet enough and not at all cloying. It reminds me of European chocolates, which are more deeply flavored and less sweet than those we have here. It is also dense enough to double as a cake filling; see Simple Chocolate Cake, page 246.

4 ounces unsweetened chocolate	¼ cup water
4 ounces semisweet chocolate	¼ cup Cognac or dark rum (optional)
3 cups heavy cream	1 tablespoon butter, cut into small
4 large egg yolks	pieces, at room temperature
½ cup sugar	

Boil the sugar and water mixture for 90 seconds, but no more. The syrup should form a string when a wooden spoon dipped into it is lifted out.

In the top of a double boiler over barely simmering water, melt the unsweetened and semisweet chocolates together. The chocolate should be just warm.

In the bowl of an electric mixer, using the whisk attachment (or with a hand-held mixer), whip the cream at high speed until it forms soft peaks; chill.

In the bowl of an electric mixer, using the whisk attachment, beat the yolks at high speed until thick and lemon colored. While the yolks are beating, combine the sugar and water in a small pot and bring to a boil over high heat. Boil exactly 90 seconds without stirring. Slowly pour the sugar mixture into the egg yolks, continuing to beat. Add the optional Cognac.

Replace the whisk with the paddle attachment, reduce the speed to medium-low, and slowly add the chocolate mixture. Beat 4 to 5 minutes, scraping the bottom of the bowl once or twice, until both the mixture and the bowl feel warm but not hot. Add the butter piece by piece and mix well.

Cool down the chocolate—egg yolk mixture so that it is just barely warm to the touch before you whisk in the whipped cream.

Pour the chocolate mixture into a large bowl and whisk in half the whipped cream. With a spatula, gently fold in the remaining whipped cream.

Pour the mousse into 8 to 10 serving glasses or bowls and refrigerate at least 3 hours, or up to 3 days.

MAKE-AHEAD NOTE

∾ The mousse can be refrigerated up to 3 days.

WARM ORANGE–LIME PUDDING CAKES

MAKES 6 SERVINGS

*D*uring baking, the batter for this old-fashioned dessert separates into 2 layers: the bottom becomes a citrus pudding and the top, a fluffy sponge cake. They reheat remarkably well in the microwave—the sponge remains just as light as when originally made.

For a slightly tart flavor, use all lemon juice.

¼ cup flour
Pinch of kosher salt
Juice of 3 limes (about ¼ cup)
Juice of 1 orange (about ⅓ cup)
½ cup sugar

2 tablespoons butter, at room temperature
2 large eggs, separated, at room temperature
1 cup light cream, scalded

Preheat the oven to 325°F.

Combine the flour and salt and reserve. Combine the lime and orange juices in a small bowl (there should be about ½ cup).

Whisking most of the beaten egg whites into the batter keeps the batter light; the remaining whites are then gently folded in. Serve the golden-brown cakes without unmolding.

In the bowl of an electric mixer, using the whisk attachment, or in a large mixing bowl, using a hand-held electric mixer, cream the sugar and butter together at high speed until light and fluffy. Reduce the speed to medium and add the egg yolks one at a time, making sure each is incorporated before adding the next. Mixing at low speed, add the flour mixture alternately with the scalded cream, then add the juice.

In another bowl, using the whisk attachment, or in a large mixing bowl, using a hand-held electric mixer, beat the egg whites at high speed until stiff. Whisk two thirds of the whites into the yolk mixture, then gently fold in the remaining third, incorporating well (this keeps the batter light).

For a single large cake, bake the batter in a 9-inch Pyrex baking dish for 45 to 55 minutes at 325°F.

Set six 6-ounce ramekins in a roasting pan and ladle the batter into the cups, stirring often to get a good mix of froth and batter in each ladleful. Pour hot water into the roaster to come almost halfway up the sides of the cups. Bake until the cakes are golden brown and a knife inserted in the top comes out clean, 25 to 30 minutes. Transfer the ramekins to a rack to cool. Serve at room temperature without unmolding.

MAKE-AHEAD NOTE

❧ You can refrigerate the baked and cooled pudding cakes up to 2 days; microwave 15 to 20 seconds for 1 cake; 20 to 25 seconds for 2 cakes.

MAPLE–CINNAMON BREAD PUDDING WITH VANILLA CREAM

MAKES 12 SERVINGS

ORDER OF PREPARATION

- Prepare the bread pudding.
- While the pudding is baking, prepare the vanilla cream.

*W*ith its base of golden-brown crusted, egg-soaked bread, this is like French toast for dessert. It comes out of the oven in a fragrant haze of maple and cinnamon. The vanilla cream accompaniment is a rich crème anglaise, a classic

SERVE VANILLA CREAM WITH:

SIMPLE CHOCOLATE CAKE (PAGE 246)
WHITE CHOCOLATE PECAN CAKE (PAGE 250), INSTEAD OF THE ORANGE CRÈME ANGLAISE

French dessert sauce that is made by stirring egg yolks, cream, and sugar over low heat until thick. This recipe makes about 2½ cups of vanilla cream.

FOR THE BREAD PUDDING

For day-old bread, substitute fresh bread that has been dried slightly in a 200° F. oven.

Butter for greasing the pan
5 large eggs
2½ cups heavy cream
1 cup maple syrup
1½ teaspoons ground cinnamon, plus extra for dusting

1 teaspoon vanilla extract
5 cups day-old Italian or French bread, cut into 1-inch squares
¾ cup medium-coarsely chopped pecans

Preheat the oven to 350° F. Lightly butter a 13 by 9 by 2-inch baking pan.

In a large mixing bowl, beat the eggs with the cream, syrup, cinnamon, and vanilla. Add the bread squares and stir until they have absorbed the liquid. Stir in the chopped pecans. Pour into the prepared pan, smooth the top, and sprinkle with more cinnamon. Bake until golden brown and firm, with no wiggly spots, 35 to 40 minutes.

FOR THE VANILLA CREAM

Substitute vanilla ice cream for the vanilla cream.

4 large egg yolks
⅓ cup sugar

2 cups heavy cream
1 vanilla bean, split

In a mixing bowl, beat the egg yolks and sugar together until pale yellow.

In a medium saucepan, combine the cream and the vanilla bean and bring to a boil over medium heat.

Pour about ½ cup of the cream into the yolks and whisk to combine. Pour the mixture back into the remaining cream and cook over low to medium heat, stirring constantly, until it coats a spoon. Do not allow it to boil. Remove from the heat and strain through a fine strainer.

TO SERVE

Cool the bread pudding to room temperature and serve in squares, surrounded by spoonfuls of the vanilla cream.

MAKE-AHEAD NOTES

๛ The bread pudding can be refrigerated up to 6 days; microwave to reheat.

๛ The vanilla cream can be refrigerated up to 4 days.

Tips for preparing vanilla cream:

๛ Warm the yolks by stirring in a bit of the hot cream.

๛ Cook gently over low to medium heat; do not boil.

๛ For vanilla ice cream, freeze cooled vanilla cream in an ice-cream machine, following the manufacturer's instructions.

Everyone has sweet memories of exceptional cakes—those served for birthdays, sweet sixteens, or graduations long ago. I think that is why any cake is welcomed as a special dessert, making the meal an occasion. Baking a cake shows your guests that you have made some effort—even when the process is actually quite easy.

The cakes in this chapter are inspired by French classics, but their methods of preparation are pared down and simplified to fit into a real-life cooking schedule. For flawless results follow the directions carefully and always measure accurately.

A baking sheet on the oven rack under the cake pans will catch spills and keep your oven clean.

For the best cakes, use the best ingredients:

- good-quality chocolate
- real vanilla extract
- butter (not margarine)
- ripe, juicy fruit

PRUNE STREUSEL CAKE

MAKES 8 TO 10 SERVINGS

ORDER OF PREPARATION
- Soften the prunes.
- While the prunes are softening, prepare the streusel.
- Prepare the batter and assemble the cake.

A *light, buttery cake layered with rich, orange-steeped prunes and topped with crunchy streusel, this reminds me of the prune Danish of my childhood Sunday mornings. Because it is so unpretentious, it is lovely with breakfast or as a coffee cake, but it works equally well as dessert after a homey dinner. I sometimes like to make this with a combination of prunes and apricots.*

FOR THE PRUNES

To prepare in a microwave, combine prunes and orange juice, cover and microwave on high 1 minute; let stand 2 to 3 minutes.

1¼ cups orange juice, fresh or good-quality purchased

12 ounces pitted prunes

In a small saucepan, bring the orange juice to a boil over high heat. Pour over the prunes and let sit 1½ hours at room temperature. Drain, discarding any remaining juice, and cut the prunes in half.

FOR THE STREUSEL

½ cup sugar

½ teaspoon cinnamon

¾ cup all-purpose flour

1 stick (4 ounces) cold butter, cut into
8 pieces

In the bowl of an electric mixer, using the paddle attachment, combine the sugar, cinnamon, and flour on low speed. Increase the speed to medium and add the butter piece by piece, mixing until the topping is coarse and crumbly.

FOR THE CAKE

For almond extract, substitute vanilla extract.

For buttermilk, substitute ⅔ cup plain yogurt combined with ⅓ cup milk.

3 sticks (12 ounces) butter, at room temperature, plus extra for greasing the pan

1 cup sugar

4 large egg yolks

¾ cup buttermilk

1¼ teaspoons almond extract

2½ cups flour

1 tablespoon baking powder

Pinch of kosher salt

Preheat the oven to 375° F. Lightly butter a 10 by 7½ by 2-inch baking pan.

In the bowl of an electric mixer, using the whisk attachment (or using a hand-held mixer), cream the butter and sugar at high speed until light and fluffy. Add the yolks one at a time, making sure each is incorporated before adding the next. Add the buttermilk and almond extract and blend.

In another bowl, combine the flour, baking powder, and salt. Add to the batter and mix well.

Spread half the batter in the prepared pan. Scatter with half the prunes. Repeat with the remaining batter and prunes. Sprinkle with the streusel. Bake until golden brown and slightly firm to the touch in the center, about 1 hour.

MAKE-AHEAD NOTES

ॐ The streusel can be refrigerated up to 12 days.

ॐ The finished cake can be refrigerated up to 3 days; reheat before serving in a 300° F. oven for 3 to 4 minutes.

SIMPLE CHOCOLATE CAKE

MAKES TWO 9- OR 10-INCH CAKES, EACH SERVING 10 TO 12

ORDER OF
PREPARATION
• Bake the cakes and let
cool.
• While the cakes are
baking and cooling,
toast the almonds and
prepare the ganache.

This is a moist, multipurpose cake coated with a ganache, a rich, liquid mixture of melted chocolate and heavy cream. Depending on its temperature, ganache will act like a smooth, rich glaze or a thick, spreadable frosting, making it a most versatile embellishment for any kind of cake. As with all chocolate desserts, use the best-quality chocolate you can find—it really makes a difference. A scoop of vanilla ice cream is the perfect accompaniment.

This recipe makes two 9- or 10-inch cakes. You can serve one cake and freeze the other for another time, or layer the two cakes for a classic dessert presentation. Or, spread the bottom layer with 3 cups of chocolate mousse (see page 240), cover with the second layer, and frost with ganache.

FOR THE CAKE

1 teaspoon baking soda	1 teaspoon vanilla extract
1/3 cup sour cream	2 cups sugar
Butter or vegetable oil spray for greasing, if not using nonstick pans	4 large egg yolks
3 ounces unsweetened chocolate, finely chopped	2 cups minus 2 tablespoons all-purpose flour
1 stick (4 ounces) butter	1 teaspoon baking powder
1 cup boiling water	2 large egg whites

Preheat the oven to 350° F. In a mixing bowl, mix together the baking soda and sour cream with a wooden spoon and let sit for 5 minutes. Grease two 9- or 10-inch cake pans, or use nonstick pans.

Place the chocolate and butter in a medium bowl and pour the boiling water over them. Whisk in the vanilla and sugar, then whisk in the yolks one at a time. Add the sour cream mixture and blend. Combine the flour and baking powder and add to the chocolate mixture, mixing just until combined.

In the bowl of an electric mixer, using the whisk attachment, or using a hand-held electric mixer, beat the egg whites at high speed to soft peaks. Fold them into the chocolate mixture.

Pour the batter into the prepared pans and bake until lightly springy, about 30 minutes. Let cool 10 minutes in the pans, then invert onto racks and cool to room temperature.

8 ounces semisweet chocolate, broken   1 cup heavy cream
    up into small pieces

In a small bowl set over a pot of simmering water, heat the chocolate and cream together, stirring, until smooth and combined. Keep it warm over the water or on a warm part of your stove top until ready to use.

TO FINISH THE CAKE

¾ cup thin-sliced almonds, toasted in
    a 400° F. oven until light golden,
    3 to 5 minutes (optional)

When the cakes are well cooled, pour the ganache over the top and let it run down the sides. Smooth it with a spatula, filling in any gaps. Sprinkle with the optional almonds.

For a 2-layer cake, cool one third of the ganache in a small bowl at room temperature, set in a larger bowl of ice cubes, or in the refrigerator, until somewhat stiff. Keep the remaining ganache warm in a bowl set over water that has been brought to a simmer and removed from the heat. Cut a thin slice off the top of each layer with a serrated knife, leaving a flat surface. Spread the stiffened ganache over one layer and cover with the second. Pour the warm ganache over the top.

MAKE-AHEAD NOTES

☙ The cooled cake layers can be refrigerated up to 3 days or frozen up to 1 month.

☙ Toasted almonds can be refrigerated up to 1 week.

☙ The ganache can be refrigerated up to 3 weeks. Before using, let it come to room temperature, or microwave it briefly, then stir to smooth it out.

To make cupcakes:

☙ Use half the batter to make 6 to 8 cupcakes.

☙ Bake 15 to 20 minutes at 350° F.

☙ Frost with half the ganache, chilled to a spreadable consistency.

PLUM *FINANCIER* WITH CINNAMON–PLUM SAUCE

MAKES 6 SERVINGS

ORDER OF PREPARATION

- Prepare the brown butter.
- Prepare the cake batter and refrigerate.
- Prepare the plum sauce.
- Bake the cakes.

The financier *is a classic French cake, made with almond flour and egg whites, that can be baked in large or small versions. Traditionally, these cakes were baked in small rectangular molds to resemble gold bricks, hence the name* financier. *Thin, with a chewy texture and nutty sweetness, these cakes are here surrounded by a tart, fruity plum sauce that accents their flavor and provides beautiful purple color. Their assembly is not complicated, but the batter must be made 2 to 3 hours in advance of baking so it can thicken before being spooned into the molds.*

FOR THE BROWN BUTTER

$1\frac{1}{2}$ sticks (6 ounces) butter

In a small saucepan, melt the butter over medium-high heat. Continue to cook the butter until it becomes lightly golden brown and gives off a nutty aroma, 6 to 7 minutes.

FOR THE CAKE

For plums, substitute about 1 cup raspberries, blueberries, pitted cherries, apples, peaches, or nectarines.

If you grind almonds in the food processor, be careful not to overprocess, or they will become nut butter.

$\frac{1}{2}$ cup all-purpose flour

$\frac{1}{2}$ cup almond flour (available in specialty food shops) or very finely ground almonds

$1\frac{1}{4}$ cups confectioners' sugar

6 ounces melted brown butter (above)

5 large egg whites

Butter, for greasing the flan rings

2 large or 3 medium-size ripe plums, cut into 15 thin slices

Confectioners' sugar, for sprinkling

Combine the flours and sugar in a large mixing bowl and mix in the brown butter. Mix in the egg whites and stir until just combined; do not overmix. Refrigerate 2 to 3 hours.

Preheat the oven to 350° F. Line a baking sheet with parchment paper. Butter six 3- to 4-inch round flan rings and place them on the baking sheet. Spoon in the batter to half-fill each ring and arrange 5 plum slices in a fan shape on top. Bake until golden brown and firm to the touch, about 30 minutes. Remove the rings and sprinkle the cakes with confectioners' sugar.

*Substitute 1¹/₂ cups rasp-
berries, blueberries, or
pitted cherries for the
plums in the sauce.*

3 medium-size ripe plums, pitted and
    cut into medium dice
1 cinnamon stick
3 tablespoons sugar

Few drops of fresh lemon juice
    (optional)

In a medium saucepan, combine the plums, cinnamon stick, sugar, and 1 cup
water and bring to a boil over medium heat. Reduce the heat to medium-low
and boil gently until slightly thickened and syrupy, about 15 minutes.
Remove the cinnamon stick, transfer the syrup to a food processor, and
process until thick and smooth. Pour it into a small bowl and add optional
lemon juice to taste.

TO SERVE

Divide the warm *financiers* among 6 plates and drizzle the plum sauce around
each cake.

MAKE-AHEAD NOTES

❧ The cake batter should be refrigerated 2 to 3 hours before baking.

❧ The plum sauce can be refrigerated up to 5 days or frozen up to 1 month.

❧ The brown butter can be refrigerated up to 10 days. When ready to use,
remelt over medium heat or in the microwave.

❧ The finished cakes can be refrigerated up to 3 days. Reheat in a 300°F.
oven for 5 minutes.

Flan rings are stainless-steel rings about ³/₄ inch high, available at
kitchen supply stores.

❧ Substitute large tuna cans, with top and bottom removed.

❧ Use 8- or 9-inch flan rings to make large tarts.

WHITE CHOCOLATE PECAN CAKE WITH ORANGE CRÈME ANGLAISE

MAKES ONE 9-INCH CAKE, SERVING 8 TO 10

ORDER OF PREPARATION

- Bake the cake.
- Prepare and cool the orange crème anglaise.
- Sprinkle the cake with optional confectioners' sugar, slice, and top with the orange crème anglaise.

*T*his cake sounds rich and a bit complicated, but don't be deceived. It is light and somewhat chewy under a brittle crust—perfect with afternoon tea or morning coffee. The orange flavor combines well with the white chocolate and the hint of nuttiness contributed by the pecans. It is simple to make, with all the ingredients mixed in one bowl.

> **INSTEAD OF CRÈME ANGLAISE, SERVE WITH:**
>
> **ICE CREAM**
> **FRESH FRUIT**
>
> **SERVE ORANGE CRÈME ANGLAISE WITH:**
>
> **SIMPLE CHOCOLATE CAKE (PAGE 246)**

Thick, slightly tart buttermilk gives the cake a smooth, fine texture and also interacts with the baking soda to make the cake rise. Don't substitute all-purpose flour for cake flour; it will give a less tender cake. Crème anglaise, a classic dessert sauce, here is flavored with orange juice and zest to echo the cake's subtle orange flavor.

For tips on melting chocolate, see page 240.

FOR THE CAKE

For pecans, substitute almonds.

1 stick (4 ounces) butter, at room temperature, plus a little for greasing the pan

4 ounces white chocolate

1 cup sugar

2 eggs

1¼ cups cake flour

½ teaspoon baking soda

½ cup buttermilk

1 teaspoon vanilla extract

½ cup (about 2 ounces) finely ground pecans

1 teaspoon grated orange zest

Preheat the oven to 325° F. Lightly butter a 9-inch nonstick baking pan. Place a baking sheet on the lowest oven rack.

In the top of a double boiler, melt the chocolate over just-simmering water. It should be warm, but not hot. Allow it to cool slightly at room temperature.

In the bowl of an electric mixer, cream together the butter and sugar, using the paddle attachment at medium speed (or use a hand-held mixer). Add the eggs one at a time, making sure each is incorporated before adding the next. In 2 separate bowls, combine the flour and baking soda, and the buttermilk and vanilla. Add the 2 mixtures to the creamed mixture alternately. Add the melted chocolate, pecans, and zest and blend thoroughly.

Pour the batter into the prepared pan, place it on the rack above the baking sheet, and bake until the cake is light golden brown and a toothpick inserted comes out dry, about 40 minutes. Cool it in the pan for 5 minutes; then invert onto a cake rack to finish cooling.

FOR THE ORANGE CRÈME ANGLAISE

When you prepare the crème anglaise, whisk a little of the cream–juice mixture into the egg mixture first, to warm the eggs so they don't scramble.

2 large egg yolks	¾ teaspoon grated orange zest
1½ tablespoons sugar	½ cup heavy cream
1½ cups orange juice, fresh or good-quality purchased	½ cup whole milk
	1 vanilla bean, split

In a small bowl, whisk together the egg yolks and sugar, and set aside.

In a small saucepan over high heat, reduce the juice and zest until thick, bubbly, and syrupy, about 10 to 12 minutes.

Meanwhile, in a small, heavy saucepan, scald the cream and milk with the vanilla bean over high heat. Add them to the reduced juice and stir to combine. Whisk a little of the cream–juice mixture into the reserved egg mixture and then pour back into the pan of cream. Cook over low heat, stirring with a wooden spoon until the mixture coats the back of the spoon, about 1 minute. Do not allow the mixture to boil. Strain through a fine sieve into a bowl set into a larger bowl of ice cubes and cool completely; then refrigerate.

TO SERVE

Confectioners' sugar (optional)

Sprinkle confectioners' sugar over the top of the cake, if desired, and slice. Spoon about 2 tablespoons of crème anglaise over each slice of cake.

MAKE-AHEAD NOTES

☙ Orange crème anglaise can be refrigerated up to 4 days.

☙ The cake can be refrigerated up to 3 days.

EGGNOG CHEESECAKE

MAKES 12 TO 16 SERVINGS

The match of eggnog and cheesecake was made in heaven for this cake, fragrant with cinnamon and nutmeg. In addition to its surprising taste, eggnog provides an unexpected lightness of texture that cuts through cheesecake's traditional richness.

I've provided a recipe for homemade eggnog, which can be enjoyed on its own and multiplied up to serve a crowd. (For extra spirit, to each 2 cups, add a little good-quality dark rum or brandy.) However, the results will still be pleasing if you use a good purchased eggnog.

FOR THE EGGNOG

3 large egg yolks	¼ teaspoon cinnamon
½ cup sugar	½ teaspoon grated nutmeg
¼ teaspoon ground allspice	1 pint heavy cream

Beat the yolks and sugar in an electric mixer, using the whisk attachment, until pale. Add the allspice, cinnamon, and nutmeg. Slowly beat in the heavy cream.

FOR THE CAKE

To make graham cracker crumbs, place 1 or more graham crackers in a resealable plastic bag and crush with a rolling pin or heavy pan.

Softened butter, for greasing the pan	½ cup heavy cream
2 to 3 tablespoons graham cracker crumbs	1½ cups eggnog
1½ pounds cream cheese, at room temperature	1 teaspoon vanilla extract
	1 teaspoon ground cinnamon
¾ cup sugar	¾ teaspoon grated nutmeg
4 large eggs	2½ tablespoons dark rum or brandy (optional)

Preheat the oven to 325° F. Lightly butter the bottom and sides of a 9- or 10-inch round cake pan. Place a circle of parchment in the bottom of the pan (use the pan as a pattern to trace the circle), butter the parchment, and sprinkle the bottom and sides with the graham cracker crumbs.

In the bowl of an electric mixer, using the paddle attachment (or use a hand-held mixer), beat the cream cheese on medium speed for 5 minutes, scraping the bowl occasionally with a rubber spatula. The cheese must be smooth and creamy, because any lumps will not melt during baking. Add the sugar and beat another 2 to 3 minutes, scraping. Add the eggs one at a time, incorporating each before adding the next.

If using a standing mixer, replace the paddle with the whisk attachment, reduce the speed to low, and add the cream, eggnog, vanilla, spices, and optional rum. Beat until thoroughly mixed, and scrape the bowl one last time.

Pour the mixture into the prepared pan, place in a larger roasting pan, and fill with hot water to reach halfway up the sides of the smaller pan. Bake until set, about 1 hour; then turn off the heat and leave the cake in the oven 1 hour longer. Remove from the water bath and cool to room temperature on a rack. Refrigerate 6 to 8 hours or overnight.

MAKE-AHEAD NOTE

➷ After its initial refrigeration, the cake can be refrigerated up to 5 days or frozen up to 1 month.

To remove the chilled cake from the pan:

➷ dip the pan into hot water

➷ turn the cake out onto a rack

➷ cover the cake with a plate and flip it back over onto the plate

If the cake does not come out of the pan easily:

➷ turn your stove burner (gas or electric) to very low and run the pan back and forth over the heat just to loosen the bottom

➷ then invert as above

I think pies and tarts show off sweet, ripe fruits to their greatest advantage. While the perfect piecrust should be light, flaky, and tender, tart crust (pâte brisée) should be short, dense, and a bit sturdier, to stand up without the support of the tart pan once it has baked. A lemon tart's custardy filling sets up firm and golden, and therefore doesn't need a top crust, while fruit pies, such as apple, rhubarb, or Concord grape, need a pastry covering to enclose the bubbling fruit; experiment with different crusts that look tempting and pretty. Bake all pies and tarts with the oven rack in center position. If the piecrust starts to get too dark, cover it with aluminum foil.

PERFECT FLAKY PIECRUST

MAKES FOUR 9-INCH PIECRUSTS

During my early days as a pastry chef, the perfect piecrust seemed to elude me. When I complained to my grandmother, she offered me her prized recipe, which had served her well over a lifetime of baking. It is always flaky and tender and I've been using it ever since. A touch of vinegar helps prevent the formation of gluten, which toughens piecrust. This recipe makes four 9-inch crusts; extras freeze beautifully.

4 cups all-purpose flour
2 teaspoons sugar
1 teaspoon kosher salt
1¾ cups plus 2 tablespoons solid
    vegetable shortening

1 large egg
1 tablespoon cider vinegar
1 tablespoon white vinegar
1 tablespoon water

Place the flour, sugar, and salt in a medium mixing bowl. Add the shortening and mix with a fork or pastry cutter until crumbly.

Combine the egg, vinegars, and water, add to the flour mixture, and mix until the flour is moistened. Divide into 4 portions, shaping each into a disc. Wrap each in plastic and refrigerate at least 30 minutes and up to 1 week.

MAKE-AHEAD NOTE

~ The crust can be refrigerated up to 1 week or frozen up to 1 month; defrost overnight in the refrigerator before rolling.

STRAWBERRY RHUBARB PIE

*D*elicate-pink rhubarb sits under a golden lattice crust in this slightly sweet and slightly tart old-fashioned pie. Rhubarb freezes well, so buy extra in the summer and save it in the freezer for a welcome and unexpected winter treat.

ORDER OF PREPARATION

- Prepare, roll out, and chill the piecrust.
- While the crust is chilling, slice the fruit and combine with the flour, spices, and orange zest.
- Pour the fruit into the crust and top with a lattice crust.

2 Perfect Flaky Piecrusts (page 254), thawed, if frozen
3½ cups rhubarb in ½-inch pieces (1 pound)
1¾ cups stemmed and halved strawberries (1 pint)

½ cup sugar
¼ cup flour
½ teaspoon cinnamon
½ teaspoon grated orange zest
2 tablespoons heavy cream

Preheat the oven to 375°F. Roll out 1 piecrust and fit into a 9-inch pie tin, leaving a 1-inch overhang. Refrigerate 15 minutes. Roll out the other crust about ⅛ inch thick and cut into 1-inch-wide strips. Place the strips on parchment or waxed paper and refrigerate 15 minutes.

In a mixing bowl, toss the rhubarb, strawberries, sugar, flour, cinnamon, and orange zest. Pour into the chilled pie shell. Weave the dough strips into a lattice pattern to cover the top, turn up the overhanging dough, and crimp the edges. Brush the edges and lattice with the cream. Bake 30 minutes; then reduce the oven temperature to 350°F. and continue baking until the crust is golden brown and the filling is bubbly, 20 to 30 minutes.

Place a cookie sheet under baking pies to catch juices that bubble over.

MAKE-AHEAD NOTES

- The piecrust can be refrigerated up to 1 week or frozen up to 1 month.
- The sliced fruit can be refrigerated up to 1 day.
- The finished pie can be refrigerated up to 2 days.

MY MOM'S CINNAMON APPLE PIE

MAKES 6 TO 8 SERVINGS

ORDER OF PREPARATION

- Prepare the piecrust.
- Slice the apples and combine with the flour, spices, and raisins.
- Roll out the crust and spoon in the apple mixture; cover with top crust and bake.

*T*he pure apple taste of this pie is enhanced by the fragrance of cinnamon and nutmeg. Very little sugar is added to the apples, but the sugar glaze on the top crust adds a bit of sweetness, as well as an elegant look. A combination of 3 apple varieties gives the pie an especially lush, fruity flavor and an interesting texture.

My mother was inspired to make this pie when she attended cooking classes, and it always has been a favorite at our holiday dinners.

2 Perfect Flaky Piecrusts (page 254), defrosted, if frozen

7 medium apples, peeled and sliced ¼ to ½ inch thick (use a combination of Empire, Cortland, and Granny Smith)

1 tablespoon all-purpose flour

2 tablespoons sugar

1 tablespoon plus 1 teaspoon ground cinnamon

1 teaspoon grated nutmeg

½ cup raisins

¼ cup confectioners' sugar

1 tablespoon milk

Preheat the oven to 375°F. Roll out 1 crust to fit into a 9-inch pie tin, allowing a 1-inch overhang, and press it into the tin.

Place the apples in a large bowl. Combine the flour, sugar, cinnamon, and nutmeg and toss with the apples, coating them well. Mix in the raisins and pour the apple mixture into the prepared pie shell.

Roll out the second crust into a circle approximately 9 inches in diameter and fit it over the apples. Bring up the overhanging crust to seal and crimp the edges with your fingers or a fork. Cut 8 slits around the center of the top crust. Bake until golden brown, about 1 hour.

In a small bowl, mix the confectioners' sugar and milk until smooth. When the pie is done, cool at room temperature for 10 minutes, then brush with the sugar glaze. Serve warm or at room temperature.

MAKE-AHEAD NOTES

❧ The piecrust can be refrigerated up to 1 week or frozen up to 1 month.

❧ The finished pie can be refrigerated up to 2 days.

CONCORD GRAPE PIE

MAKES 6 TO 8 SERVINGS

ORDER OF PREPARATION
- Prepare the piecrust.
- Prepare the grape filling.
- Pour the grapes into the crust, cover with the top crust, and bake.

W*e had 2 or 3 grapevines on our property when I was growing up in New Jersey. I loved the ripe grapes, with their sweetness and fruity aroma, and I soon began putting them in pies. This latest version of my original recipe uses red seedless and Concord grapes; combining 2 varieties of grape gives the pie depth and juiciness, each complementing the other's flavor and color. Like a blueberry pie, this is juicy and fragrant with cinnamon. Seeding the Concords takes a little time, but their deep, winy flavor is worth it.*

☙ *Concord grapes are available mainly in September and October.*

2 Perfect Flaky Piecrusts (page 254), thawed, if frozen	1 teaspoon grated orange zest
3¼ cups red seedless grapes (just over 1 pound), about half of them cut in half	¼ cup minus 1 tablespoon all-purpose flour
	¼ cup sugar
3¼ cups seeded Concord grapes (just over 1 pound), about half of them cut in half	Pinch of cinnamon
	Pinch of ground nutmeg
	1 tablespoon butter, in small bits
	1 tablespoon half-and-half

Preheat the oven to 375°F. On a lightly floured surface, roll out 1 crust to fit a 9-inch pie tin, allowing a 1-inch overhang, and press it into the tin. Roll out the second crust and reserve.

In a medium bowl, combine the grapes and orange zest. In a small bowl, combine the flour, sugar, cinnamon, and nutmeg. Add to the grapes and toss to combine.

Pour the grapes into the prepared pie shell and dot with the butter. Cover with the second crust. Bring up the bottom overhang, press the edges together all around, and crimp the edges. Cut 5 or 6 slits or small holes in the top crust and brush with the half-and-half.

Bake until the crust is golden and the fruit is bubbly, 60 to 70 minutes. Allow to cool at room temperature for 30 minutes before serving.

MAKE-AHEAD NOTES

☙ The piecrust can be refrigerated up to 1 week or frozen up to 1 month.

☙ The sliced grapes can be refrigerated up to 1 day.

☙ The finished pie can be refrigerated up to 3 days.

PEACH TARTE TATIN

MAKES 8 SERVINGS

ORDER OF PREPARATION

- Prepare and chill the sweet pâte brisée.
- While the crust is chilling, cook the peaches and place in a cake pan.
- Cover with the crust and bake.

A French classic, tarte Tatin traditionally is made with caramelized apples under a pastry crust, baked in a heavy skillet. It is then inverted, so the fruit is served on top of the crust. Garnish with whipped cream, Crème Fraîche (page 39), or ice cream.

I use a cake pan for this buttery version made with peaches, which give off a pretty, pink syrup as they caramelize. The tarte is really simple—only a crust and peaches—but it makes a perfect summer dessert. For this recipe, pâte brisée is given an extra touch of sugar.

FOR SWEET PÂTE BRISÉE

1¾ cups all-purpose flour
½ teaspoon kosher salt
½ tablespoon sugar

1 stick plus 7 tablespoons butter (7½ ounces), at room temperature
⅓ cup cold water

In the bowl of an electric mixer, using the dough hook on low speed (or use a hand-held mixer), combine the flour, salt, and sugar. Add the butter by chunks, waiting for each to be incorporated before adding the next. When the mixture is the consistency of coarse meal, add the water and mix thoroughly, but do not overmix, which would toughen the dough. The dough will be moist.

Gently shape the dough into a disc, wrap in plastic wrap, and refrigerate at least 4 hours or overnight. When ready to bake, roll the dough into a 9-inch circle, ⅛ inch thick.

FOR THE TARTE TATIN

Substitute 1 teaspoon vanilla extract for the vanilla bean.

6 tablespoons butter, plus extra, if needed, for buttering the pan
¾ cup sugar
1 vanilla bean, split and scraped (optional)

4 medium to large almost-ripe peaches, pitted and quartered

In a large, heavy skillet over medium-high heat, melt the butter, sprinkle the sugar over it, and cook without stirring until the sugar begins to melt. Then stir gently, as the sugar begins to caramelize. Add the optional vanilla bean seeds. When the mixture begins to bubble, add the peaches and simmer until they caramelize, about 20 minutes.

Preheat the oven to 375°F.

Arrange the caramelized peaches skin-side down in a 9-inch cake pan, preferably nonstick. (If you use a regular pan or the traditional heavy skillet, butter it.) Cover with the crust and bake until golden brown, 20 to 25 minutes. Allow to cool at room temperature 5 minutes, then invert onto a rimmed serving plate (the tart will be juicy), tapping gently all around to release the peaches. Serve warm.

MAKE-AHEAD NOTES

❧ The sweet pâte brisée must be chilled 4 hours or overnight; it can be frozen up to 1 month.

❧ The sliced peaches can be refrigerated up to 12 hours.

❧ The baked tarte Tatin can be refrigerated in the baking pan overnight; rewarm in a 200°F. oven, then invert and serve.

LEMON TART WITH WALNUT CRUST

MAKES 10 SERVINGS

ORDER OF
PREPARATION

• Prepare and refrigerate
the walnut crust.
• Bake the crust.
• While the crust is bak-
ing, prepare the filling.
• Bake until set.

*F*rom its smooth, pale yellow filling, you might think this was a classic lemon tart, but the crunchy walnut crust adds a contrasting texture that makes it a much more interesting mouthful. It is tangy, fresh tasting, and not too sweet. The crust is partially prebaked and cooled before the creamy lemon filling is added, and then the tart is baked until golden.

FOR THE WALNUT CRUST

For the walnut crust, substitute Perfect Flaky Piecrust (page 254).

1½ sticks (6 ounces) butter, slightly
    chilled
½ cup confectioners' sugar
1 teaspoon granulated sugar
1 large egg

1¾ cups all-purpose flour
½ cup finely ground toasted walnuts
    (see Basic Preparation Techniques,
    page xv)

In the bowl of an electric mixer, using the paddle attachment, beat together the butter and sugars at high speed until light and fluffy. Add the egg and mix until combined. With the mixer on slow speed, add the flour and combine; then add the walnuts. Mix until the dough comes together. Shape the dough into a smooth oval, wrap in plastic, and refrigerate at least 4 hours or overnight.

If the walnut dough crumbles or breaks, patch with a little extra dough.

When ready to bake the shell, preheat the oven to 400° F. On a lightly floured surface, roll the dough to an ⅛-inch thickness. Arrange it in a lightly oiled 10-inch tart pan or pie tin. Line with foil or parchment paper and weight with beans or pie weights. Bake the crust until light golden brown, 20 to 25 minutes. Cool to room temperature.

FOR THE LEMON FILLING

For lemon juice, substitute orange juice or half orange and half grapefruit juice and reduce the sugar to ¾ cup.

4 large eggs
⅞ cup sugar, plus 1 to 2 tablespoons,
    if needed
½ cup plus 2 tablespoons fresh lemon
    juice (about 2½ lemons)

¼ cup heavy cream
Confectioners' sugar, for sprinkling

In a food processor or electric mixer, beat the eggs at medium-high speed until frothy, about 1 minute (or use a hand-held mixer). Add the sugar and mix until combined. Add the juice and cream and mix until combined. Strain through a fine strainer and pour into the prepared piecrust.

Reduce the oven temperature to 350°F. Bake 15 minutes; then reduce to 325°F. and bake until the filling is just set, 10 to 15 minutes. Cool at room temperature. Serve at room temperature or chilled, topped with a sprinkle of confectioners' sugar.

MAKE-AHEAD NOTES

🦢 The unbaked walnut crust must be refrigerated 4 hours and can be refrigerated up to 10 days, or frozen up to 2 weeks.

🦢 The finished tart can be refrigerated up to 2 days.

Undoubtedly, most people's first attempt at baking, as well as the first dessert they ever tasted, was a cookie. Cookies are among the easiest baked desserts to prepare, but that doesn't mean they can't be full of subtle flavors and textures. These cookie recipes are flavored with butter, nuts, and chocolate and range from not too sweet to just this side of decadent.

    🖎 To ensure that your cookies will be uniform in size, chill the dough for 8 hours or overnight. Then form cookies by using your hands to roll equal portions of dough into even balls.

    🖎 Turn cookie sheets halfway through baking, to ensure even cooking.

    🖎 Cool cookies completely before storing in an airtight container.

MACAROONS

MAKES 20 TO 25 DOUBLE COOKIES

ORDER OF PREPARATION

- Bake the macaroons.
- While the macaroons are baking, prepare the ganache.
- Put the macaroons together with the ganache.

These delightful little cookies, a favorite in French cuisine, are golden and crisp on the outside and light and chewy inside, with the delicate flavor of almonds. Chocolate ganache adds a bit of creamy richness to each bite. They are ethereal and addictive.

Don't be intimidated by the fact that these cookies are made with a pastry bag; they don't require super skill. Just use a plain tip and be sure to pipe out all the cookies the same size, because you will be sandwiching 2 together. You can make them smaller or larger than the 1 inch I suggest, if you prefer.

FOR THE MACAROONS

For chocolate macaroons add 2 to 3 tablespoons sifted unsweetened cocoa powder to the flour–almond mixture.

1 cup confectioners' sugar
½ cup finely ground almonds
2 large egg whites, at room temperature

1 tablespoon granulated sugar
¼ teaspoon vanilla extract
¼ teaspoon almond extract

Preheat the oven to 350° F. Line 2 baking sheets with parchment paper.

Sift the confectioners' sugar into a mixing bowl. Add the ground almonds and combine.

In a separate dry bowl, beat the egg whites until they form soft peaks. Add the granulated sugar and extracts and continue to beat until they form stiff peaks. Sprinkle the sugar–almond mixture into the beaten whites and combine with a rubber spatula until smooth.

Using a pastry bag with a ¼- or ½-inch round tip, pipe 1-inch rounds onto the prepared baking sheets. Let them sit at room temperature until a slight crust forms, about 10 minutes.

The cookies are easiest to bake and remove from the parchment on a day with low humidity.

Bake until golden brown, 10 to 15 minutes, turning the pans once from back to front. When the macaroons are done, run a little cold water under the sheets of parchment, let the cookies sit 1 to 2 minutes, then gently lift them off the paper. Let them cool to room temperature.

TO SERVE

½ cup chocolate ganache
(see page 247)

For classic macaroons take the warm cookies off the parchment paper and put them together without any filling: they will stick to each other.

Spread ½ teaspoon ganache on the flat side of a macaroon and top with the flat side of another macaroon, gently pressing them together. Repeat with the remaining macaroons and ganache.

MAKE-AHEAD NOTES

⁊ The ganache can be refrigerated up to 3 weeks. Before using, let it come to room temperature, or microwave it briefly to bring to room temperature, then stir to smooth it out.

⁊ The finished macaroons, with ganache, can be stored at room temperature in an airtight container up to 1 week.

Using a pastry bag:

⁊ fit the tip into the narrow end of the bag, then fold down the wide end a few inches and fill the bag halfway

⁊ twist the top closed and squeeze the bag once or twice to get the air out and to pack the contents solidly

⁊ hold the bag in one hand and grasp the twisted top with the other. Turn the bag and apply a little pressure, gently squeezing rounds of batter onto the baking sheet

⁊ when you have piped out all the cookies, rinse the bag with hot water

BUTTER-PECAN COOKIES

These firm little cookies melt in your mouth with a rush of intense pecan flavor. They are golden brown and crisp, with a buttery texture and nutty aroma, and are not overly sweet.

For up to ¼ of the pecans, substitute walnuts.

2 sticks (8 ounces) butter, at room
   temperature
½ cup sugar
½ teaspoon vanilla extract
½ teaspoon almond extract
2 cups all-purpose flour

2 cups shelled pecans (8 ounces),
   finely ground in a food processor
2 tablespoons water
Butter for greasing the baking sheets
Confectioners' sugar for dusting

At least 2 hours before baking, cream the butter and sugar in the bowl of an electric mixer, using the paddle attachment at medium speed (or use a hand-held mixer). Add the vanilla and almond extracts. Add the flour and ground nuts alternately in 2 batches and mix until combined, scraping the bottom and sides of the bowl occasionally. Add the water to moisten any dry spots in the dough and mix well. Refrigerate the dough at least 2 hours or as long as overnight.

When ready to bake, preheat the oven to 350° F. Lightly grease 2 baking sheets. Form the dough into 1-inch balls and place 2 inches apart on the baking sheets; do not flatten them. Bake until lightly golden brown, 20 to 25 minutes. Cool on racks, then dust with confectioners' sugar.

MAKE-AHEAD NOTES

☙ Ground nuts can be stored, covered, at room temperature up to 1 day.

☙ The cookie dough must be refrigerated 2 hours and can be refrigerated as long as overnight.

☙ The finished cookies can be stored at room temperature, in an airtight container, up to 10 days.

GROVE STREET BROWNIES

MAKES 12 BROWNIES

*T*hese are the best brownies I know—dense, loaded with chocolate, and crunchy with walnuts. When you bite into one, the rich cake surprises you with unexpected pockets of pure melted chocolate.

The recipe was given to me by the original owners of the Grove Street Cafe in Greenwich Village, who were the first to educate me about culinary schools, when I decided on a career in the food business. In the cafe, they served a small brownie along-side some of their desserts—mousses and such—and before long, people were ordering the desserts just to get the brownies.

1¼ sticks (5 ounces) butter, plus a little for greasing the pan	5 large eggs
1½ cups sugar	½ teaspoon kosher salt
4 tablespoons water	½ teaspoon baking soda
24 ounces semisweet chocolate chips, or solid chocolate, coarsely chopped	1½ cups all-purpose flour
	1 cup coarsely chopped walnuts
	1 teaspoon vanilla

I think these brownies are perfect as is, but you may omit the nuts if you prefer.

Preheat the oven to 350°F. Butter a 13 by 9 by 2-inch baking pan.

In a large saucepan, melt the butter over medium-high heat. Add the sugar and water, and bring to a boil. Remove from the heat and add 12 ounces of the chocolate, stirring until smooth. Whisk in the eggs one at a time, making sure each is incorporated before adding the next. Add the salt, baking soda, and flour and mix gently until incorporated. Stir in the remaining chocolate, the nuts, and the vanilla.

Be careful where you insert the toothpick to test doneness, because you may hit a pocket of molten chocolate and mistake it for unbaked batter.

Pour the batter into the prepared pan and bake until the center feels firm to the touch and a toothpick inserted into the cake comes out dry, 30 to 40 minutes. Cool on a baking rack. When cool, cut into 2½-inch squares.

MAKE-AHEAD NOTE

The brownies can be tightly wrapped and kept at room temperature up to 2 days.

ACKNOWLEDGMENTS

The enthusiasm and commitment of many people have enriched my work and I am especially grateful to them.

My coauthor, Joan Schwartz, found my voice and *ooh*ed and *ahh*ed over my recipes. She cheerfully joined me in hours of reworking recipes and text, faxing and refaxing, and settling for no less than perfection. Her unstinting work and attention to detail helped me craft the book I had long dreamed of writing.

Our agent, Jane Dystel, first saw the possibility of this book and provided the guidance, insight, and tenacity that made it happen.

Pam Krauss, our knowledgeable and talented editor, shared our goals and worked hard to make the book the best it could be.

Geralyn Delaney has been a sparkling, creative publicist and a friend I can always rely on.

Dennis Foy, my friend and mentor, taught me the value of simplicity in food and approach over fifteen years ago. The professional training I received from him has become a natural part of the way I cook and work today.

Drew Nieporent, a good friend through thick and thin and an extraordinary restaurateur, encouraged me to develop and expand my own personal style of cooking. Working with Drew for nearly eight years at Montrachet allowed me to travel all over the world, meet a host of interesting people, and cook for and with chefs I had always admired.

The Montrachet staff under Chris Gesualdi, who succeeded me as chef, added their ideas and finishing touches, and made the kitchen a harmonious place.

I'm blessed with a close and loving family, all of whom I sincerely thank:

My parents, Marion and Phil Ponzek, whose constant love and support have enabled me to do what I most wanted in life.

My grandmother Stephanie Ponczek, who is still copying down new recipes at the age of eighty-three ("I have to try this recipe!"), inspired me to cook and bake for the sheer love of it.

My sister Gail, who has been loving and supportive as long as I can remember, including when she broke the the news to my parents that I had decided to leave engineering school and study cooking. She was there for me through that career transition, and all the years following.

INDEX

CONVERSION CHART

Equivalent Imperial and Metric Measurements

American cooks use standard containers, the 8-ounce cup and a tablespoon that takes exactly 16 level fillings to fill that cup level. Measuring by cup makes it very difficult to give weight equivalents, as a cup of densely packed butter will weigh considerably more than a cup of flour. The easiest way therefore to deal with cup measurements in recipes is to take the amount by volume rather than by weight. Thus the equation reads:
1 cup = 240 ml = 8 fl. oz.   *½ cup = 120 ml = 4 fl. oz.*

It is possible to buy a set of American cup measures in major stores around the world.

In the States, butter is often measured in sticks. One stick is the equivalent of 8 tablespoons. One tablespoon of butter is therefore the equivalent of ½ ounce/15 grams.

SOLID MEASURES

U.S. and Imperial Measures		Metric Measures	
ounces	pounds	grams	kilos
1		28	
2		56	
3½		100	
4	¼	112	
5		140	
6		168	
8	½	225	
9		250	¼
12	¾	340	
16	1	450	
18		500	½
20	1¼	560	
24	1½	675	
27		750	¾
28	1¾	780	
32	2	900	
36	2¼	1000	1
40	2½	1100	
48	3	1350	
54		1500	1½
64	4	1800	
72	4½	2000	2
80	5	2250	2¼
90		2500	2½
100	6	2800	2¾

OVEN TEMPERATURE EQUIVALENTS

Fahrenheit	Celsius	Gas Mark	Description
225	110	¼	Cool
250	130	½	
275	140	1	Very Slow
300	150	2	
325	170	3	Slow
350	180	4	Moderate
375	190	5	
400	200	6	Moderately Hot
425	220	7	Fairly Hot
450	230	8	Hot
475	240	9	Very Hot
500	250	10	Extremely Hot

LIQUID MEASURES

Fluid ounces	U.S.	Imperial	Milliliters
	1 teaspoon	1 teaspoon	5
¼	2 teaspoons	1 dessertspoon	10
½	1 tablespoon	1 tablespoon	14
1	2 tablespoons	2 tablespoons	28
2	¼ cup	4 tablespoons	56
4	½ cup		110
5		¼ pint or 1 gill	140
6	¾ cup		170
8	1 cup		225
9			250
10	1¼ cups	½ pint	280
12	1½ cups		340
15		¾ pint	420
16	2 cups		450
18	2¼ cups		500
20	2½ cups	1 pint	560
24	3 cups		675
25		1¼ pints	700
27	3½ cups		750
30	3¾ cups	1½ pints	840
32	4 cups or 1 quart		900
35		1¾ pints	980
36	4½ cups		1000
40	5 cups	2 pints or 1 quart	1120
48	6 cups		1350
50		2½ pints	1400
60	7½ cups	3 pints	1680
64	8 cups or 2 quarts		1800
72	9 cups		2000

EQUIVALENTS FOR INGREDIENTS

all-purpose flour—plain flour
arugula—rocket
confectioners' sugar—icing sugar
cornstarch—cornflour
eggplant—aubergine

granulated sugar—castor sugar
half and half—12% fat milk
lima beans—broad beans
scallion—spring onion
shortening—white fat

unbleached flour—strong, white flour
vanilla bean—vanilla pod
zest—rind
zucchini—courgettes or marrow